THEORY

OF

THE

IMAGE

THEORY
OF THE
IMAGE

*Capitalism,
Contemporary Film,
and Women*

Ann Kibbey

INDIANA
University Press
Bloomington & Indianapolis

This book is a publication of

Indiana University Press
601 North Morton Street
Bloomington, IN 47404-3797 USA

http://iupress.indiana.edu

Telephone orders 800-842-6796
Fax orders 812-855-7931
Orders by e-mail iuporder@indiana.edu

The paper used in this publication meets the minimum
requirements of American National Standard for Information
Sciences—Permanence of Paper for Printed Library
Materials, ANSI Z39.48-1984.

Manufactured in the United States of America

Library of Congress Cataloging-in-Publication Data

Kibbey, Ann, date
    Theory of the image : capitalism, contemporary film, and women / Ann Kibbey.
        p. cm.
Includes bibliographical references and indexes.
    ISBN 0-253-34469-7 (alk. paper)—ISBN 0-253-21746-6 (pbk. : alk. paper)
    1. Women in motion pictures. 2. Image (Philosophy) 3. Capitalism—Philosophy.
4. Motion pictures—Philosophy. 5. Suitors (Motion picture) 6. Before the rain
(Motion picture) I. Title.
    PN1995.9.W6K53 2004
    791.43'6522—dc22

                                                                                        2004008467

        1 2 3 4 5 10 09 08 07 06 05

In memory of Beth Nelson

Contents

Essay Three
Relief from the Production of Certainties   133

Acknowledgments

Thanks to Tom Gunning for helping to arrange my interview with Ghasem Ebrahimian, to Bruce Kawin and Hamid Naficy for their encouragement and advice early on, also to Andy Horton for his interest and support, and for his urging me to apply for the Director's Guild workshop. Much thanks to the Director's Guild for providing funding for my sojourn in Los Angeles at the Director's Guild Film Educators' Workshop, and to the many directors, producers, actors, editors, agents, and writers who talked with us. It was a great learning experience and one I would recommend to any film scholar, regardless of their field. I am grateful to the University of Colorado for providing me with sabbatical time that enabled me to write this book.

This project would not have been possible without the generous cooperation of people connected with Ebra Films. First and foremost, I want to thank writer and director Ghasem Ebrahimian, who is extraordinarily articulate about his work, and whose insights about film have been invaluable in formulating the second essay in this book. Special thanks also to Pouran Esrafily, who graciously steered me through many perplexing aspects of Iranian culture and gave me a lively sense of film acting and production, and who also helped me contact other members of the cast. I am deeply grateful to Bani Babila, Leila Ebtehadj, Ali Azizian, and Shahab Navab for consenting to be interviewed and for sharing their knowledge of Iranian culture as well as film-making and acting. Although I haven't quoted from these interviews, this material laid the groundwork for the essay in many ways and made it possible to cross many cultural boundaries that would otherwise have been closed to me. Mariyam and Simin, who spoke their minds about political matters at a time when many others were reluctant to do so, changed many of my initial ideas and made it possible to develop a very different kind of analysis. They have not been identified by their real names, and neither have the many individual members of the audience whom I interviewed. However, fictitious initials have been consistently applied throughout so that readers may follow individual viewpoints if they wish to do so.

Carol Siegel read the crucial draft of the whole book and made important suggestions that enabled the final version to take shape. Many other people contributed to the progress of this manuscript, through reading portions of it and conversations about it. This is undoubtedly a better book for their comments, and they have made the process of authorship a more enjoyable adventure than it would be otherwise. Thanks to Marianna Amicarella, William Andrews, Carol Benjamin, Melody Brod, Alain J.-J. Cohen, Jill Cohen, Rosemary Crowley, Amy Dauer, John Deely, Margaret Eisenhart, Azadeh Farahmand, Abouali Farmanfarmaian, Neal Feigenson, Larry Frieder, Casey Gardner, Manucher Ghaffari, Jamie Gordon, Anne Hanks, Marina Heung, Susan Howe, Dina Iordanova, Marina Kosova, Sarah Kubley, Christine LeMieux, Jan Lemmon, Frank Lisa, Lauren Mayer, Merun Nasser, Karen Jacobs, Cathy Preston, Mike Preston, Elayne Rapping, Claudia Rose, Barnaby Ruhe, Kayann Short, Elisa Synder, Christina Spiesel, Chris Sharrett, Tasha Sparks, Michele Tarter, Pam Thoma, and Mark Winokur.

Thanks to the Video Station in Boulder, and especially to Scott Woodland, for recommending *The Suitors* one dark and stormy night. His knowledge of international cinema, the fantastic collection he assembled, and his willingness to buy yet more videotapes for this project were an invaluable aid in my research. The friendly advice, opinions, and recommendations of the front desk over the years, especially Leslie Swallow, Scott Poston, Zilph Feiser, and Jim Kosenski, have helped to bring this book to fruition.

Michael Lundell has been an insightful and helpful editor, and Richard Higgins has provided able and timely advice on assembling the final manuscript for production. Ghasem Ebrahimian and Ebra Films kindly provided the illustrations for the second essay. Thanks to Milcho Manchevski for providing the illustrations for the third essay, and for spiriting them from Macedonia to Colorado so quickly.

Last and very special, my heart goes out to my furry co-authors, Samantha and Tybear, who brought me many gifts of distraction, some of them quite astonishing. Their patience and impatience with the mysteries of writing have made these long days in my study a delightful time.

THEORY

OF

THE

IMAGE

Introduction

The theory of the image is an elusive topic, even though there is a rising awareness of the importance of the image in modern society. The image is a cultural construction of the most fundamental kind, yet social and political critiques continue to focus on the content of images without considering the importance of the image itself as an ideological construct. The widespread interest in the economic history of the film and television industries has developed as if it were far afield from theories of the image. However, it would be strange if the U.S. film industry, so highly capitalized in studio production and distribution, did not also have a capitalist theory of the image informing its films.

This book begins with a historical critique of the ideology of iconoclasm to locate the sources of the modern capitalist theory of the image, a path of inquiry suggested by Jean Baudrillard.[1] He proposed that the capitalist theory of the image could be traced to the dynamic interaction between Protestant iconoclasm and the concept of the commodity. However, Baudrillard himself made only a half-hearted attempt to follow this line of investigation. Unlike Baudrillard (and more recently W. J. T. Mitchell),[2] I have gone back directly to the Protestant sources on iconoclasm in early modern Europe to understand why early Protestants attacked images. What I have found is a paradigm far different from our common assumptions about the motives of the iconoclasts. The initiating premise of iconoclasm was a belief in *true* images rather than a hatred of false images. Because early Protestant iconoclasts believed there was such a thing as a true image, the significance of images as a source of power for them has been greatly underestimated. As I demonstrate in this book, these early sources show not only a belief in images, but specifically a theory of the image that binds a person to corporate identity through the consumption of commodities as true images. Protestants defined the crux of this social relation through the trope of metonymy—a concept qualitatively different from representational art or the idea of metaphor.

By taking a materialist approach to the Protestant semiotics of the image in Essay One, I show the congruence between the Protestant sacramental image and the commodity of Marx's theory. As well, I explain how corporate distribution and consumption add another layer of mystification beyond what Marx described in the fetishism of commodities. I also critique the image theories of French post-structuralists Barthes, Debord, and Baudrillard, and briefly consider the psychoanalytic theory of Lacan, to show how these widely regarded critical theories stayed within the parameters of the iconoclastic/capitalist theory of the image, describing its effects rather than offering an alternative. This limitation also informed the development of post-structuralist film theory from the 1960s to the 1980s. This era of film theory was fueled by an iconoclastic assault on the false images of Hollywood film, from the theorists of the cinematic apparatus to Laura Mulvey's famous essay on images of women in film.[3] Like the French post-structuralists, Mulvey elucidated the workings of the iconoclastic/capitalist image, but she did not critique it.

Because society has strongly linked women with image-ness and vice versa, a critique of images of women in film can be a point of leverage for a larger critique of a whole system of images in contemporary society. Recent feminist critiques in media studies have focused on the social content of images, but without attending to the ideological structure of the image itself. Consequently, this approach has veered away from the central theoretical problem, the conceptual symbiosis of woman and image. There is nothing inevitable about this symbiosis. It is important to understand how it is socially constructed, to break through it and thereby liberate 'woman' and 'image' from each other. To do this requires new theoretical models.

One place to find new theories of the image is contemporary film, and especially transnational films where cultures collide and where women are major characters in the narrative of that collision. Such films are well situated to create a more complex and variable relation between people and images. There are many contemporary films that might be considered here. However, rather than discuss many films in a cursory and superficial way, the second and third essays in this book explore in depth the significance of two very different transnational films. Each dismantles the symbiotic relation between woman and image, but they go about it quite differently, and with different consequences. My intent is not to find a single grand theory of the image—I doubt that any exists—but instead to articulate the specific theories of the image that inform these films.

Essay Two, "Liberating a Woman from Her Image," is about Ebrahimian's *The Suitors*,[4] an Iranian-American film that was made in New York but nonetheless draws on Persian artistic and narrative traditions. This film directly engages cultural differences between American and Middle Eastern women through its main character, Mariyam, a veiled Iranian woman who immigrates to New York and relinquishes the practice of veiling. Mulvey's iconoclastic theory considered the problem of woman and image from an exterior frame of reference, emphasizing the dependence of the image on Woman. This film shows that actual women experience this symbiosis in its reverse form, as the ideological threat that a woman ceases to exist without her image. For American women viewers, this film resonates deeply at a figurative level, especially in the black screen sequence, where Mariyam removes her symbolic cinematic image as well as her symbolic veil. To demonstrate the complex interaction between audience and screen image, my discussion of this film draws on individual interviews with more than thirty people who saw the film in the U.S.—some of them Iranian, most of them American. I quote extensively from individuals to demonstrate how the film's imagistic and narrative structure allows 'woman' and 'image' to move freely in variable ways—not only in the film, but in the minds of viewers as well.

Essay Three, "Relief from the Production of Certainties," develops a film theory that is adequate to the unusual features of Manchevski's *Before the Rain*,[5] one of the most acclaimed transnational films of the last decade. In its multi-sided narrative, the film goes back and forth between London and the ethnic conflicts of the Balkans in the 1990s. Linear narrative and nonlinear narrative face off, producing a conflict of meaning that brings the theory of the image forward as the film's subject—in relation to ethnic conflict, the realism of photography, the effects of globalization, and through all this, the pivotal role of women characters whose quest for social equality necessarily disrupts the theory of the image that structures linear narrative. This film not only arranges provocative collisions within itself. It also collides with one of the most basic Western ideas about photography, namely, that photography records rather than makes an image.

The cultural belief that photography and cinematography record images underlies the work of theorists as diverse as Peirce, Bazin, Barthes, Mulvey, Deleuze, Metz, and Wollen, to name just a few. Bourdieu asserted that belief in photography as a recorded image is a social construction of great significance for the middle class.[6] To understand the ideology underlying this belief, in both its social and its cinematic impact, the last essay begins with an analysis of the theory of the image in the works of C. S. Peirce, an American social conservative, and Sergei Eisenstein, an Eastern European leftist. Each brings out what is most distinctive about the other. As a careful consideration of Peirce shows, the concept of the natural or indexical sign, the belief in linear narrative, the semiotics of racial prejudice, and the theory of the photograph as a recorded image all share the same basic semiotic philosophy.

Before the Rain demands a different theoretical approach, and for that I turn to essays by Sergei Eisenstein. Eisenstein's essays on cinematography offer a theory of the photographic image based on a concept of the image as a dynamic relation, not an immobilized, fetishized thing. Eisenstein's theory of montage, understood in this way, serves as a point of departure for an analysis of *Before the Rain* in terms of Manchevski's own description of his work as cubist narrative. A film that is cubist looks nothing like a painting that is cubist. The apparent realism of Manchevski's film is quite convincing at the outset, indeed well into the film, but no viewer forgets the jolt of finding out that the film is actually constructed in a completely different way.

Although all three essays in this book involve capitalism, contemporary film, and women, each takes a different approach to the theory of the image and generates a different emphasis. The essays overlap in their themes, but since each has an independent point of departure, the essays can also be read separately. I hope they will demonstrate how important transnational cinema can be in the increasingly international culture in which we live our lives.

Essay One
The Capitalist Theory of the Image

As Jean Baudrillard observed in his influential and still widely read essay "The Precession of Simulacra," the beginnings of modern thinking about the image, including his own, can be found in the iconoclasm of the Protestant Reformation in early modern Europe. The iconoclasm to which he refers was the widespread destruction of images in churches across Europe that began in the early sixteenth century and lasted well into the seventeenth century. Taking a more historical and systematic approach in *The Mirror of Production,* Baudrillard situated the iconoclasm of the Reformation and its continuing popularity in relation to the history of capitalism. Evoking the well-known arguments of Karl Marx and Max Weber, who both saw Protestantism as the most fitting religion for capitalism, Baudrillard traced the origins of the modern simulacra of capitalism to the Protestants' iconoclastic repudiation of the value of artistic images. Iconoclasm, he argued, marked the demise of representational thinking, the end of the idea that images could represent things, reality. The concept of a representational image was discredited, and this was the crucial act of disbelief that informed the iconoclastic destruction of images. People simply no longer believed that images could be representations of anything real. What Baudrillard called the "simulacrum" took the place of the representational image. Among its vexing attributes, the simulacrum made it impossible to distinguish the real from the imagined, and blurred the distinction between subject and object.[1] While Baudrillard made some provocative speculations about how the simulacrum has functioned in contemporary culture, his idea of the simulacrum remains unclear. It also remains unclear why the simulacrum serves a capitalist economy, or why a representational system of thinking does not.

Baudrillard did not directly discuss the iconoclastic controversy itself, nor did he analyze the ideas of its most famous and systematic French proponent, Jean Calvin. Had he done so, he would have found a more complex and resilient theory of images than his essays describe. Calvin was arguably the first modern French theorist on the theory of images, widely read throughout Europe in his own time and immensely influential. Among the proponents of iconoclasm, he is the most significant for understanding how French post-structuralism in the twentieth century unwittingly drew on the core ideas of iconoclasm, giving them a more secular form that would shape much of contemporary critical thinking. Lacan's mirror stage, Debord's spectacular image of commodity capitalism, the colonized French soldier of Barthes' mythologies, Baudrillard's tantalizing simulacrum—these theories reflected the iconoclast's suspicion of images as false, deceitful, deluding, misleading, even treacherous. If psychoanalytic theory and theories of the commodity-image have seemed less than satisfying as social critiques of contemporary life, it is because they unwittingly revitalized the assumptions of Protestant iconoclasm, offering descriptive phenomena rather than critical leverage.

In the following sections of this essay, I will first discuss the theory of images that informed Calvinistic iconoclasm to understand what the components of this paradigm were. I am in search of something more than isolating a sign-object or image-object for analysis. The more comprehensive idea of a paradigm includes an understanding of the epistemological assumptions and social relations that constituted the image. I then consider some French post-structuralist versions of this theory to show how post-structuralism in the late twentieth century adapted the Calvinist iconoclastic paradigm to a more secular mentality congruent with the massive expansion of corporate capitalism of that era. My critique of Laura Mulvey follows upon this to show how she also participated in iconoclastic assumptions, codifying a secular and cinematic version of iconoclasm that has become the most widely accepted version of this paradigm.

The Iconoclastic Theory of the Image and the Corporation

Although Calvin was an avowed iconoclast, his value to the iconoclastic movement was not in his actions but in his intellectual justification of the general assault on images that characterized the rise of Protestantism. He spent most of his life in Switzerland, having fled his native France because his life was in danger. He was involved in establishing Protestant churches throughout Europe, and was frequently consulted by clerics. His work both reflected and shaped what would become the prevailing set of beliefs among Protestants. Historical studies generally acknowledge Calvin's importance and widespread influence, based on the circulation of his works throughout Europe. Even before his death in 1564, his primary work, *The Institutes of the Christian Religion* (composed in Latin), had been translated into French, English, Spanish, Italian, and German. Shortly after his death, it was also translated into Czech and Hungarian. Although his *Institutes* in effect served as the gold standard for Protestant religious beliefs, Calvin was not a theologian. He received an education in law and classical literatures.[2] His secular orientation is reflected in the importance he gave to rhetoric, in the lawyerly, disputatious manner in which he argued the case for Protestant beliefs against Catholics, and more generally in his synthesis of the secular and the sacred.

The anti-imagist beliefs of Calvinist iconoclasts were grounded in a much broader concept of the image than is now generally recognized. The iconoclasts interpreted "icon" quite broadly to include many kinds of three-dimensional forms as well as two-dimensional images such as paintings. Besides destroying paintings and stained glass windows, they also smashed statues, tombs, altars, baptismal fonts, reliquaries, rood screens, ritual vestments—any material form that contained or suggested representational figures. Roadside shrines as well as churches were targets of their violence against religious icons, so it was the icon itself, not its situation, that determined whether an image was fair game. Not all acts of iconoclasm were about smashing images. Sometimes it involved changing the use of a material form to destroy its symbolism. Altar stones became paving stones, bridges, fireplaces, or even kitchen sinks. Basins for holy water were used to salt beef, and a triptych was used for a pig trough. For some iconoclasts, the idea of offensive material forms extended to clothing and ritual activities as well. English Puritanism coalesced around the refusal to wear the traditional clerical vestments and a refusal to kneel at the sacraments. One cleric used his vestments as a seat cushion to protest both icons at once.[3]

The underlying concept of the image that ranges through all these acts of iconoclasm is the classical concept of *figura*, which simply meant dynamic material shape. In its earliest usage, *figura* referred to the shape of a woman's face. The idea of *figura* is still a commonplace in contemporary culture, as in "human figure" and, particularly among women, having a "good figure." As a concept of figuration, the idea of *figura* in Latin culture gradually came to include a wide range of material shapes, from architectural forms to representational images—all the kinds of things that became the targets of iconoclastic violence. But in its initial and most abiding meaning, this concept of figuration was qualitatively different from representation as such. A *figura* didn't necessarily represent anything, and its figuralness had nothing to do with a distinction between literal and figurative meaning. It was also unequivocally grounded in the material world, as a *material* shape, even though it later came to include the mental images of metaphor. Also important, *figura* could be used in reference to the human body or its movements. This is why kneeling could be considered a figure, an image, by iconoclasts, why vestments were an image, and why altar stones or stones with inscriptions that invited adoration of the material form were also an offending image. Iconoclasm, then, was conceptualized at its most comprehensive level in terms of *figura* rather than just visual images such as paintings. That said, there was no question that the scriptural commandment against graven images included any "visible image," any "likeness" such as paintings.[4]

The source of the iconoclasts' contempt for what they destroyed, and their satiric redeployment of material shapes, was based on their belief that there could be no viable representation of the deity. As Calvin stated, "It is unlawful to attribute a visible form to God, and generally whoever sets up idols revolts against the true God."[5] Calvin rejected all visual representations of the deity on the grounds that they were "forged by human ingenuity" (101). He advanced this argument in the context of an epistemological debate concerning what can be known of the deity. He asserted that visual art is epistemologically useless in revealing knowledge of the deity and therefore sinister in its presumption: "Whatever knowledge of God is sought from images is fallacious and counterfeit" (105). Calvin scoffed at the long-held Catholic justification of images in churches, that images were "the books of the uneducated" (105). For Calvin, such condescension to the populace was a violation of the church's responsibility for the edification of church members, a cynical manipulation of an illiterate populace.

Although Baudrillard did not cite his sources, it is likely that this well-known Protestant belief—opposing visual representations of the deity—was the basis of his interpretation of iconoclasm as a categorical rejection of representational thinking. If this was his source, his conclusion was mistaken. The supposed categorical rejection of images was a rejection only of visual representations of the deity. Calvin made clear that, as long as an artist did not attempt to represent the deity, and as long as visual art was displayed outside the church, visual images that were representations were acceptable, indeed that painting and sculpture were "gifts of god," and had a "legitimate use" (112). Painting and sculpture could legitimately represent secular subjects, that "which the eyes are capable of seeing" (112). As to what could be materially seen, he suggested historical events and representations of the body. Depictions of historical events could be instructive in a secular way. Representations of the human body were for pleasure.

We need to look elsewhere for the Protestant rejection of representational thinking that resulted in the simulacrum—a source Baudrillard failed to identify. The prototype of the simulacrum emerges in another kind of argument for iconoclasm, a perceptual one. The perceptual argument was diametrically opposed to the epistemological argument. It argued for the rejection of images precisely because they *were* compelling, because they had great power to influence (and thereby mislead) the mind of the viewer. Where the epistemological argument had cast images as insignificant and incapable of disclosing any knowledge of the deity, the perceptual argument for rejecting images was based on the idea that images were overwhelmingly powerful. Calvin insisted that the viewer of any religious image would involuntarily worship it, for an image had the power "to compel the mind" to fetishistic adoration. "Men's folly cannot restrain itself from falling headlong into superstitious rites" (113), and so the images had to be destroyed or at least put out of sight to prevent idol worship. Calvin made clear that he had a hatred of religious images in themselves, that he was not only against "the worship of idols," but against "idols themselves" (113). His hatred had nothing to do with whether or not the image was erotic. It was the image's appearance of being alive when in fact it was "dead matter" that made it pernicious and evil (103). Calvin explained, quoting Augustine, "For the shape of the idol's bodily members makes and in a sense compels the mind dwelling in a body to suppose that the idol's body too has feeling, because it looks very like its own body" (113). Although images "do not speak, or see, or hear, or walk," they seem able to do these things because "they have mouth, eyes, ears, feet" and therefore "seem to live and breathe" (113). The counterfeit quality of images that seem to be alive was the source of danger, indeed of "very much danger" (113). Iconoclasts feared that images were somehow alive, and their fear is reflected in their methods of violent destruction. As historian Phyllis Crew noted in her study of iconoclasm, iconoclasts employed an execution style. "They hammer away mainly at the faces," said one observer of iconoclasm in the Netherlands.[6] In the Lady Chapel of Ely Cathedral, encircled with over fifty statues at eye level, iconoclasts systematically smashed the heads of the statues but left the bodies intact.[7] In another case it was reported that iconoclasts "hung images of saints from the gibbets erected to execute iconoclasts."[8] Iconoclasts felt a need to 'kill' images in order to destroy their power. The so-called dead idols were not in fact dead until they had been smashed in an act of violence that irrevocably altered the material shape of the image. Only then did the image lose its power to enthrall the viewer.

In the fear of idols that seemed to be alive, there is a projection of the attribute of life. Insofar as the endangering liveliness seems to be coming from the image itself, and not from the beholder, there is also a projection of the act of projection itself. This second act of projection is fetishism, the belief that autonomous powers inhere in the image, especially the power to make the viewer perceive it in a certain way—making the image into an idol. In the iconoclasts' confrontations between people and images, one senses the underlying commonality of *figura* as it characterizes both the living human being and its representational image, that people and images were at some level equivalent, interchangeable, and indistinguishable. This implies that people were in some sense believed to be images themselves, living images who were out to destroy the threatening and dangerous representational images, the false images that mimicked their own living images. The implication was overtly stated by Protestant iconoclasts, as in this protest against the execution of iconoclasts in the Netherlands: "They [Catholics] have, against the express commandment of God, erected an infinity of beautiful images, paintings, and statues. . . . Finally, to sustain such an enormity by force, they have burned the true and living images of God, living men, in order to make sacrifices to their images and dead idols."[9] So, the history of iconoclasm shows not just a hatred of false images as that has been generally understood, and not just an oblique homage to the mesmerizing power of false images. It was predicated on the sanctity of "true and living images of God": the iconoclasts, themselves, were the true images. In this sense, iconoclasm was *in favor of* images. The anti-imagism now associated with iconoclasm, based on their destruction of artistic images in the church, was only the corollary, the consequence, of their belief in true and living images.

The idea of the living image emerged at the very heart, the very core, of Protestant sacramental theory, defining Protestantism as a religion that opposed false images, but not all images. Calvin describes the foundational idea of the living image at its engendering moment when he reaches the culmination of his argument against representational images in the church:

> When I ponder the intended use of churches, somehow or other it seems to me unworthy of their holiness for them to take on images [*imagines*] other than those that are living [*vivas*] and iconic [*iconicas*], which the Lord has consecrated by his Word. I mean Baptism and the Lord's Supper, together with other ceremonies by which our eyes must be too intensely gripped and too sharply affected to seek other images forged by human ingenuity. (113–14)[10]

He adds a sardonic taunt to the Catholics: "Behold! The incomparable boon of images, for which there is no substitute, if we are to believe the papists!" (114). With eyes riveted on the living images in the performance of sacramental ritual, no other images were needed. Unlike the humanly invented visual arts, living images were divinely created, and they were sanctioned as images in the performance of the central rite of

Protestantism, the Lord's Supper (essentially, the Protestant version of the Catholic Mass).

Calvin's description of the sacramental ritual emphasized the priorities of the iconoclastic mind. The rejection of images *of* people was only one aspect of iconoclasm, and a consequence of another, more fundamental concept: that the consecrated people and elements of the sacrament *are* images. The latter concept, that people are living images, was grounded in the ritual of consecration, presumed to be self-sufficient, without need of images made by people. But was it? To the extent that the very concept of an image was dependent on the humanly created images they claimed to despise, the living images seemed to appropriate this concept to use it as a metaphor for themselves—to describe their own imageness. Iconoclasm appears to pivot on this central contradiction. Although religion required that images be destroyed, rhetoric apparently required that they be kept around, as the literal material for metaphor. Where the epistemological argument was secure in its reasons for destruction, the fear that informed the perceptual argument expressed the hazards of metaphor, perceptually a love-hate relationship with the humanly created image.

Although this is where Calvin left the matter in his opening section of the *Institutes*, at the same time he directed the reader to his solution: the performance of the sacrament that frees the living image from the need for "other images." It was in his sacramental beliefs that he expounded the inner workings of the Protestant theory of the image. His interpretation of the sacrament suppressed metaphor in favor of metonymy to produce an iconoclastic theory of the image that was qualitatively different from the images of representational art or the images of metaphor. And as I will show, there is more—not only a privileging of metonymy, but, as well, a description of the social relations of the living image. Calvin's paradigmatic theory of the sacrament related the privileging of metonymy to a privileging of the performative utterance. It indirectly offered a concept of the commodity and the significance of use value. It was also a theory of what it means to consume commodities as images. Crucially, it was a theory of how images bind a person to that elusive social entity, the invisible corporate body.

The Protestant sacrament of the Lord's Supper, even in its name, was a largely secular event from a Catholic perspective. It was not done at an altar or in front of an altar, and there was no kneeling. People took communion standing up, or sitting around a wooden table as one would in eating supper. A minister pronounced the consecrating words—sometimes the congregation did too—and all the participants partook of both the bread and the wine. The elements of the sacrament, the bread and wine, were common food, the same food as people consumed in their daily lives.

The Supper was a local event, short, simple, and inexpensive to produce. For the early Protestants, this was a profound spiritual experience. It was culturally profound in its rejection of the traditions of the Catholic Mass, and of everything else that might ordinarily be considered religious. The Protestant sacrament did not even need to be held in a building. It could be done outside, and this was not unusual in the early years of the Reformation, when people gathered in fields to hear Protestant preachers because Catholics were still in control of church buildings. Protestants believed that the church was the congregation itself, not the building in which they met, or ecclesiastical institutional structures. Wherever the communicants met and took the sacrament, there was a church.[11] What made this otherwise secular event into a religious event? What made these *figurae* into living images? The words of consecration—"this is my body" in reference to the bread and "this is my blood" in reference to the wine— introduced the spiritual presence of Christ into the secular event.

In a ritual that had been stripped of any other religious significance, the words of consecration became the sole juncture between the secular and the sacred, and consequently their interpretation became a matter of heated debate in the sacramental controversy. Calvin understood the enigma of the sacrament as a rhetorical problem, one that could be solved by the right understanding of tropes. Specifically, the consecrating words were to be understood as a metonymy. Somewhat defensively, he explained: "Let our adversaries, therefore, cease to heap unsavory witticisms upon us by calling us 'tropists,' because we have explained the sacramental phraseology according to the common usage of Scripture. For as the sacraments agree in many respects, so in this metonymy they all have a certain common ground with one another" (1386). Metonymy characterized the deity's communications. They were the signature of spiritual discourse, as Calvin himself put it, "a figure of speech commonly used in Scripture when mysteries are under discussion" (1385). In the Lord's Supper, the metonymies were the substitution of "body" for "bread" and "blood" for "wine."

Metonymy is the trope of renaming, the substitution of one name for another. Long before it was the trope of desire for Lacan, it was in Latin rhetoric the trope of invention and possession, of ownership. Quintilian explains, metonymies "are employed to indicate an invention by substituting the name of the inventor, or a possession by substituting the name of the possessor."[12] To take some modern examples: To refer to an automobile as a "Ford" or to call a computer a "Dell" is to employ metonymy. Metonymy also lends itself to the expression of ownership as an expression of power and subordination, as it does in the renaming that characterizes colonialism. Calvin in his examples understood metonymy in hierarchical terms as the yoking of "something lower" and "something higher," as "when God was said to appear to Moses in the bush" or when the Holy Spirit was called a dove (1385). Here, something higher is the deity, and something lower is the burning bush or the dove, which is temporarily held hostage to a higher purpose. Quintilian notes, "if, however, the process [of metonymy] is reversed, the effect is harsh."[13] In Calvin's examples, the reverse results in fetishism, a failure to remember what is higher and what is lower, a granting of powers to the bush or the dove that makes them into the kinds of idols he despised. The privileging of metonymy is the reason why fetishism, the worship of idols or images, becomes the paradigmatic act of *dis*belief for Calvin.

One of the striking features of metonymy is this: It does not call forth a visual image, as metaphor does. Metonymy, though definitely figurative, is a non-imagistic trope. Renaming a loaf of bread as the body of Christ generates a visually unintelligible concept that defies metaphoric representation. It creates a mental blank. Where metaphor creates a mental image, and in that sense is an act of imagination, metonymy shuts down the metaphoric imagination and directs the visual attention to the physical thing renamed by it. This enhanced the importance of the concept of *figura*, for it was the material shapes of people and things in the sacrament that became the focus of visual attention for Calvin. Remember that the oldest meaning of *figura* was not based on the idea of resemblance or representation. It was unencumbered with this function. A shape inhered in something as a part of the properties of something, an attribute. It was not a concept of a likeness or representation of something else. It might become representational, but to see a material shape as an image of something, as a sign representing something else, required an additional logical step. In Calvin's sacramental theory, a different kind of logical step occurred with the imposition of metonymy. Through the words of consecration, these shapes became signifying shapes, *figurae* that were now physical images marking or exhibiting the spiritual presence of a deity that was by definition physically "invisible." They became "living images" (1376). Calvin did not deny that they could also be understood as symbolic representations, but this was not important to his sacramental theory of the real spiritual presence. It was the metonymic significance, not the representational significance, that was sacramental.

How does someone know when the figure of metonymy is being used if there is no metaphoric image to see? Consider the use of metonymy in Calvin's paradigm. The recognition of metonymy depended on a perceived discrepancy between the name and the thing, between the words and the "physical and visible objects" to which they referred. It was the perceived *lack* of resemblance between body and bread, the nominal *in*appropriateness

of the word "body" in reference to the thing "bread," that indicated the
figurativeness of the consecrating words. Metonymy violated the customary representational meaning, and that violation was potentially invisible.
The figurative nature of the metonymic language could be perceived only
when word and thing were juxtaposed. In this sense, the material object
was crucial to the paradigm, a mere thing but nonetheless an indispensa-
ble thing.

Sacramental metonymy functioned in a qualitatively different way
from ordinary representational or symbolic meaning. Calvin conceded that
bread and wine represented and even symbolized "spiritual food," but this
was not what made the sacrament a salutary experience, or made living
images something special. Instead, it was the metonymy as a performative
utterance—*the belief that the words enacted what they declared*.[14] The objects of
the sacrament and the human participants in the sacrament became, with
the performative utterance, the visible marks of the invisible presence of a
corporate body, the mystical body of Christ. They didn't just symbolize the
mystical body. They "participated" in it (1387), they had "the reality joined
with them" (1385). They did not become the mystical body itself. They
marked it. They were informed by it, infused with it. They "exhibited" it.
Nonetheless, their spiritual significance remained derivative, dependent
on its source, the mystical corporate body of Christ.

As one Protestant preacher put it, evoking St. Paul, "Not I but Christ
liveth in me, as if 'I' were too broad a word for a Christian man to say."[15]
Calvin explicitly contrasted secular representational meaning, "humanly
devised symbols," which were "images of things absent," with the living
images of the sacrament, which were the "marks of things present" (1385).[16]
Mere representation was not performative, did not enact what it declared.
Representational signs referred to objects, but did not transform these
objects. In a representational system of signification, the sign and its object
remained two distinct things. By contrast, the performative metonymy of
the sacrament joined the sign and its object together. That joining created
the marks, exhibits, of the deity's mystical presence, transforming the
object, and mystically joining the object to the spirituality it signified.
The description of what happened to the objects in the sacrament was the
model for what happened to the people who consumed them. Conversion
to Protestant Christianity worked the same way in people as it did in
objects. The implied interchangeability of people and objects was an important aspect of the idea. The reconfiguration of subjectivity, of identity was
another. The individual's identity was transformed into a member of the
mystical body of Christ. Conversion joined them to that body, informing
their material and social existence with the real spiritual presence of the
mystical, invisible Christ.

Although Calvin insisted that the bread and wine were really and spiritually transformed, he also insisted just as strongly that this conversion did not violate the materiality of the bread and wine. The elements of the sacrament, and the people who consumed them, ingesting (or internalizing) their power, remained materially what they were. Retaining materiality, they nonetheless lost that thing-in-itself quality through the renaming of metonymy. Secular representation became a debased system of meaning, for its referents—the bread, the wine, and converts themselves—became "empty tokens" in their own right (1385). The sacramental object "not only symbolizes the thing that it has been consecrated to represent as a bare and empty token, but also truly exhibits it" (1385). In "conversion," the sacramental object became "something which it was not before" (1375). To state this in terms of a modern analogy, when you get into your Lexus to take a drive, the corporation that sold it to you hopes that you will believe (and we *are* talking about an act of faith here) that you have become something that you were not before, even though you remain physically the same person. The paradigm not only offers a converting enhancement of the individual, making them something more desirable than they were before. It also converts the ordinary person or object into something that is retrospectively perceived as inadequate. Something's missing without the Lexus. And if you can't afford the Lexus, don't just have a beer. Have a Budweiser. If you're not old enough to have that, don't despair, and don't just have a soda. Have a Coke.

Through the performative utterance, Calvin made the spiritual, mystical body of Christ the central tenet of his belief system. The social identity of the Protestant was a corporate identity, and membership in this corporation, the church, was the definitive social identity. Although Catholics also believed the church was the mystical body of Christ, the idea stands out in stark relief in Protestantism, which had jettisoned so many Catholic religious practices that there was little left that could be called religion. It is difficult to overestimate the importance of this concept in Protestantism, and particularly in Anglo-American Puritanism.[17] Unlike Catholic transubstantiation, which made the incarnate and crucified Christ the axis of belief, the Calvinist doctrine of the real spiritual presence, as it came to be called, focused on the mystical body of Christ, a corporate identity. Belief in the salutary power of this mystical corporate body was the unifying idea of Protestant religious practice. To participate in the Protestant sacrament was to belong directly to a corporate body, the mystical body of Christ, and this belonging was salutary.

The living images of the Protestant sacrament articulated a corporate theory of the image, not just inadvertently but consciously and crucially. This theory of the image defined what happened in the most important

Protestant sacrament. Airy though it may seem, the mystical corporate body depended on a religion that was first of all a visual practice. In Calvin's summary of what it took to make a sacrament, the enabling device of metonymy yoked the physical and the spiritual in a visual experience that was salutary:

> The Supper consists in two things: physical signs, which, thrust before our eyes, represent to us, according to our feeble capacity, things invisible; and spiritual truth, which is at the same time represented and displayed through the symbols themselves. (1371)

Thomas Norton's 1561 English translation of the *Institutes*, reprinted many times, rendered Calvin's description of the lively and iconic images of the sacrament as "lively and natural images," images in the divinely created natural world, as opposed to the images of visual art forged by human ingenuity.[18] In the first century of Protestantism, this perceptual paradigm extended beyond the confines of the sacrament itself to the phenomena of everyday life, the providentially found imagery of experience in the world as opposed to the unnatural images of art. The sacrament became an instructive instance for how to understand this larger world:

> It commeth to passe, that the signes, as it were certaine visible words incurring into the external senses, do by a certaine proportionable resemblance draw a Christian minde to the consideration of the things signified, and to be applyed. This mutuall, and, as I may say, sacramentall relation, is the cause of so many figurative speeches and Metonymies which are used: as when one thing in the Sacrament is put for another.[19]

Calvin's iconoclastic successors in English Puritanism were not shy about their love of images. They turned the second commandment (against graven images) into its opposite, a mandate for images: "for the Law itselfe in condemning Images and the imaginations of mens devising, commandeth and establisheth the Images and imaginations ordained by God."[20] Protestantism has usually been characterized as a religion of the text, a religion without images. Nothing could be further from what the historical sources on Protestant iconoclasm demonstrate. At the heart of this religion was an imagistic belief system, a belief in the sacramental true images that marked the deity's presence in the world, and most of all marked it through the conversion of Protestants themselves into "lively and natural images" of the real spiritual presence. To be such a "true and living image" was to live a privileged—and imagistic—existence in the world.

CONGRUENCE WITH THE CAPITALIST ECONOMY

Calvin's imagistic theory of the sacrament provides a way of understanding the semiotic link between capitalism and Protestantism that yields a deeper understanding of the capitalist theory of the image. As Baudrillard argued in *The Mirror of Production*, Marx did not develop a model that could describe the semiotics of capitalism. Marx is well known for his remarks about the commodity as "a mysterious thing," something "transcendent," "enigmatical," a thing "abounding in metaphysical subtleties and theological niceties," but Marx did not make a compelling connection between religion and the mysterious properties of the commodity.[21] He simply proposed that, since exchange value is an abstract idea, it can be on friendly terms with Christianity, that "Christianity with its *cultus* of the abstract man, more especially in its bourgeois developments, Protestantism, Deism, etc., is the most fitting form of religion" for capitalism. This seems a weak argument at best—a cult of the abstract man might just as easily and more obviously be extracted from philosophy.

In fact Marx tried to derive the mystery of commodities, its fetishistic character, not from religion, but from the laborers, who, in Marx's model, do not understand that other people have made the commodities they buy. Because exchange is an abstract idea, he argues, "the relation of the producers [i.e., the laborers] to the sum total of their own labour is presented to them [in exchange] as a social relation, existing not between themselves, but between the products of their labor" (72). What Marx describes is at best a coerced forgetfulness. It is not that laborers don't know this, but that *it is of no consequence that they know it* because there is no place for this idea in the semiotics of exchange orchestrated by a capitalist market that assumes value is created in the market rather than created by labor. Marx's paradigm also does not follow through in conceptualizing the act of consumption beyond the act of exchange, and it is here that the semiotics of exchange in capitalism coincides with the semiotics of Calvin's sacramental theory. The taking of bread and wine was the prototype of the consumption of commodities. Protestantism enjoined a consumer practice as the means that mystically allowed the communicants to participate in the corporation, and in which the objects consumed were just as important as the people consuming them. That is, the sacramental object was the prototype of the commodity, and participants were the prototype of the modern consumer. They consumed the elements of the sacrament and believed they were transformed by this consumption. In that transformation, they were joined to the mystical body of Christ, and it was through this corporate identity that they experienced their relations to other people and to the commodity/objects of the sacrament.

The transposition of Calvinism and capitalism was possible because of the equivalence between the commodity and the sacramental object. Calvin emphasized the use value of the objects of the sacrament, and he meant that in the same way that Marx meant it. Without consecration, the bread and wine used in the sacrament were no different from "common foods intended solely to feed the stomach" (1375). Both Marx's commodity and Calvin's sacramental object depended, then, on the same concept of use value as one aspect of their signification. Also in both cases, this aspect was placed in binary opposition to another, contradictory value—for Marx, exchange value, and for Calvin, spiritual value. In both cases, the binary model of the object (and the person as object) was there, along with the principle of contradiction, of use value and something else, another value that contradicted it. The things Marx said about the commodity and exchange value could just as well be said about the sacramental object and its spiritual value. "So far as it is a value in use, there is nothing mysterious about it, whether we consider it from the point of view that by its properties it is capable of satisfying human wants, or from the point that those properties are the product of human labour" (71), said Marx of the commodity, and Calvin thought the same thing about the use value of bread in the sacrament. Marx wrote, "The mystical character of commodities does not originate, therefore, in their use-value" (71), and Calvin could not have agreed more that the unconsecrated elements of the sacrament could not be the origin of the mystery of the sacrament. Marx continued, "But so soon as it steps forth as a commodity, it is changed into something transcendent" (71), and Calvin thought likewise, that the bread became infused with the transcendent when it was consecrated. Spiritual value and exchange value were further commensurable, interchangeable, because they both carried the presumption of circulation. The spiritual value circulated among the sacrament's participants, making them equivalent objects and joining them in a system that piggy-backed on their use value, in the manner of metonymy. Marx even echoed the idea of the real spiritual presence. Speaking of the exchange value of commodities as it was rendered in money-form, he explained, "Although invisible, the value of iron, linen and corn [as commodities] has actual existence in these very articles" (95). This was the model of the commodity as it was perceived in exchange. Exchange value, though invisible, had an "actual existence," a real presence if you will, in the commodity.

I do not want to dispute which came first, the chicken of material history or the egg of religion, but only to propose that they operated together, affirming each other, in the development of the capitalist system. An important part of that affirmation was the way that religion functioned as a source for the idea of the corporation. Although we now think of the corporation as an economic entity, the history of Protestantism shows a conceptualization of the corporate body and corporate identity that was initially social rather than economic. Protestantism also provided the semiotic paradigm for the mystification inherent in capitalist distribution and consumption. Most leftist theorists, following Marx, delineate the relationship of labor to capital in production and consequently focus on the commodity as it is produced. While this is important, the sacramental model shows how corporate capital also intervenes in consciousness a second time, in its ideology of distribution and consumption. Indeed it would be surprising if it did not, since distribution, the circulation of commodities, is essential to realizing profit. That is, the full mystification of the commodity is completed in distribution and consumption because exchange value is exchanged, so to speak, for spiritual value. It is not just the images of advertising that partake of the sacramental model of the commodity. The products themselves are perceived as true images, and their consumption is analogous to the consumption of the elements of the sacrament. This is not to say that capitalist consumption makes everyone into good Protestants, only that capitalist consumption is a participation in the "religion" of corporate capitalism. Consumption is not simply a matter of use value. While Marx recognized the contradiction between use value and exchange value, there is more to the process of mystification than he described. The occlusion of production and the denigration of use value, the belief that objects can in fact mediate and control relations between human beings, is the result of Protestant semiotics. It is the concept of spiritual value that renders the material object an "empty token," that empties the material object of any social significance in its own right.

To put this another way, the social character of labor is obliterated by an alternative idea of a collective subjectivity, the Protestant idea of the corporate body. Sacramental semiotics cuts off the perception of production by labor because it finds its ultimate rationale in the corporate body, not in labor. This is where recourse to Calvin's model shows that the semiotic system of capitalist consumption was not launched into a void. Its initial rationale was the redemptive power of the mystical body of Christ. The sacrament made believers out of participants, and established primary allegiance to the corporate body rather than to any secular social identity. If we consider that Calvin developed his religious beliefs in the milieu of mercantile capitalism, it seems also that they did not reach fruition until the invention of the capitalist corporation.[22] When the capitalist corporation was finally recognized as a legal entity, one mystical body could be exchanged for another. Like its religious counterpart, the capitalist corporate body is itself invisible. It has logos, buildings, stock, employees, products, and so on, but none of these entities is the corporation itself, which exceeds them all and is marked by them but not contained in them. The corporate sign is what Baudrillard calls the simulacrum, and Calvin's model of the sacrament is its prototype. This is why it is possible to "sell your soul" to a corporation, in a synthesis of labor power understood as a commodity, and a commodity understood as a sacramental element. Today, what most people mean by "capitalism"—especially when they are decrying its pernicious influence— is corporate capitalism. With the flourishing of corporate capitalism in the latter part of the twentieth century, French post-structuralism flourished along with it, developing a semiotic vocabulary to describe its workings, apparently unaware of its massive indebtedness to that earlier French theorist of signs, Jean Calvin. The post-structuralist act of compulsion is not now belief in the deity, but allegiance to the semiotics of corporate capitalism as the only semiotics: true or not, there is no other way.

CRITIQUE OF BAUDRILLARD

Among its most eloquent and most anguished proponents, Baudrillard provides a capitalist version of sacramental theory, of what it looks like from the vantage point of a disbelief in the deity—but not disbelief altogether. Baudrillard relocates belief to the sign system itself (note his religious language at the outset): "It is the sanctification of the system as such, of the commodity as a system: it is thus contemporaneous with the generalization of exchange value and is propagated with it."[23] Baudrillard calls this fetishism, that is, an idolization of the sign system. This way of thinking invests the sign system itself with the power to reconstruct "the object eviscerated of its substance and history, and reduced to the state of marking a difference, epitomizing a whole system of differences" (93). This is like saying that the objects of the sacrament are marks of metonymy, rather than marks of the presence of the mystical Christ. Baudrillard's own act of belief locates omnipotence, if not omniscience, in the semiotic system itself. Epistemologically condemned, the semiotic system nevertheless holds sway as an omnipotent authority.

Baudrillard's fetishism veers away from concluding that objects are marks of the corporation, which would have related the system directly to economics, to the Marxian base. The semiotic system intercedes, blocking perception of the corporation and its processes of production, and making the semiotic code seem autonomous, empowered in itself and answerable only to itself—as if to say, it is not the corporation that produces these eviscerated objects for exchange, it is the semiotic code. Most people use *fetishism* as a term to deride other people's false beliefs, and while the term seems to carry that connotation here as well, it also describes Baudrillard's own discourse in *For a Critique of the Political Economy of the Sign*. He describes various ways that the sign system works, he occasionally hails "monopoly capitalism," but he does not articulate a vantage point of critique, another way to think. Late in the book, chapter 8, he is still moving "towards a critique." Nor does he recognize historical antecedents such as Calvin, or explain his use of religious terms such as "sanctification" other than to say that he is describing magical ways of thinking. He implies throughout that everyone is hopelessly engulfed in this semiotic system. The semiotic religion of the capitalist consumer is a religion of the damned because, while it excises belief in the deity, it retains the inner logic of Protestant semiotics, granting what had been the power of the deity to the sign system itself. The consumer is hopelessly bound to it because, as one can see in its Calvinist antecedent, consecration always precedes consumption.

In his most well known essay, Baudrillard describes this phenomenon as the "precession of simulacra."[24] The semiotic system always precedes and determines a person's experience of any object. More than that, it prevents any experience of the object in its own right. Or rather, it creates a wish to experience the object directly, without the intercession of the semiotics of capitalist distribution. Calvin, describing the performative utterance of metonymy, had said the consecrated objects of the sacrament became empty tokens in themselves as they exhibited the real spiritual presence of Christ. For Calvin, this was something good, an enhancement of the object. For Baudrillard in *The Critique of Political Economy*, it was an evisceration, a reduction, not good, a debasement. In Baudrillard's essay on the simulacrum, the same phenomenon is called "hyper-realism" (45), a more ambivalent term. Here, Baudrillard discourses on the power of the Protestant living image, though he does not realize that is what it is. In his truncated and confused discussion of iconoclasts, Baudrillard omits any discussion of the sacramental living images at the heart of Protestantism, and he seems completely unaware of this dimension of their beliefs. He understands them merely as the destroyers of images, and even here he ignores what they said about themselves and their actions. Instead, Baudrillard projects his own fetishism of the semiotic system—in this case the simulacrum—onto the early Protestant iconoclasts. He depicts them as having destroyed images out of "metaphysical despair" (8). While it would be appropriate to say the Protestants perceived the images of the Catholic church as simulacra, because of "this facility they have of effacing God from the consciousness of men," it is not accurate to say that Protestants therefore concluded "that ultimately there has never been any God, that only the simulacrum exists" (8). That is Baudrillard's view, but was certainly not Calvin's. There is no metaphysical despair in the *Institutes*, or any other kind of despair. There is the zeal, conviction, and elation of someone who believed that the

Protestant reformation would be triumphant because a very real deity was absolutely on their side. As I discussed earlier, the Protestant destruction of artistic images in the Catholic church was only the corollary, the consequence, of the Calvinists' belief in the true, living images of their own sacraments. They had no reservations about destroying the simulacra of the Catholic church because they already believed in something else, the living images of the Protestant sacrament.

Baudrillard's idea of the simulacrum does not come from the false images that were destroyed by iconoclasts, as he claims, but instead from a nonbeliever's stance toward the living images of Protestant sacramental theory—this is what the "hyper-real" evokes. Again, he absents the deity, but not belief altogether. By relocating power in the sign system itself, in this case the simulacrum, Baudrillard bows to a fetish he loathes, a fetish without truth but not without power. Baudrillard's discussion of his idolatry explores the fallout from privileging metonymy, as the Protestant sacrament did by interpreting the consecrating words as metonymic. That is, the simulacrum does what the metonymic sacramental object does. In the act of renaming, of substituting "body" for "bread," the metonymy replaces and thereby repudiates the representational sign (or name), creating a disjunction between signs and things, generating a disruption of representational meaning. The terminology of a "mark" rather than a "sign" is a shorthand way of referring to the denial of representational meaning, the disjunction between the representational sign and the thing it represents. Metonymic disruption, though figurative, does not generate a mental image, as metaphor does, but instead generates a mental blank—appropriate for the invisible quality of the mystical body of Christ. Confronted with invisibility, or flummoxed by it, the metonymy sends the communicant back to the consecrated *figura* of the bread, now seen as an image that is exploited to mark or exhibit or radiate the spiritual presence rather than its own qualities as bread. It enters the state of the hyper-real, and hyper-real also points to the performative nature of the consecration that enacts what it declares, altering the material object, making it a different kind of "real" than it was before. So it is not surprising that Baudrillard measures the apostasy of the modern perceiver by the increasing distance from a system of representational meaning:

This would be the successive phases of the image:

[1]—it is the reflection of a basic reality
[2]—it masks and perverts a basic reality
[3]—it masks the *absence* of a basic reality
[4]—it bears no relation to any reality whatever: it is its own pure simulacrum. (11)

The figure of metonymy, if one rejects it, could easily be seen as a mask or perversion, creating confusion where previously there was clarity—but even this view is a function of metonymy. It is the rename that *creates* a sense that the representational name replaced was the original, authentic, true, and literal name of something, now hidden beneath the overlay of metonymy. This is reflected in Baudrillard's gloss on his four categories: "In the first case, the image is a *good* appearance—the representation is of the order of sacrament" (11–12). Baudrillard locates his own sacrament in representational meaning, which is now something more than a conventional system of signification. It is sacramental, true—it tells us about the real. When it is fully suppressed, as in the fourth category of the simulacrum, there can be no relation to the real as Baudrillard has defined it. One would have thought he would have stopped at category three as the definition of the simulacrum—and this is the definition he uses in talking about the iconoclasts. But there is something more—stage four, that carries the perceiver over to the living image, a simulation purified of the embarrassment of absence, a simulation invested with an idea of a real presence, the rename inhering in the thing itself: absolute apostasy. Disneyland is his paradigm, "the perfect model," the experience of which is a "*religious* revelling in real America" (23).

As Baudrillard observes, the simulacrum is accompanied by nostalgia (12), and his own nostalgia revolves around the longing for some Golden Age of representational meaning, now short-circuited by the simulacrum (32, 48). But, though Baudrillard fails to acknowledge it, it is metonymy that makes representation look so good, so simple, so unadulterated, "the old polar schema which has always maintained a minimal distance between a cause and effect, between the subject and an object" (56). He contrasts this with the "implosion" of the simulacrum, "a collapsing of the two traditional poles into one another" (57). Baudrillard might simply have said that he preferred metaphor, defined in Latin rhetoric as the transfer of meaning from one place to another, a trope that asserts a conceptual distance between one locus of meaning and another. Metonymy, by contrast, yokes two places together, creating the implosion effect. Calvin liked metonymy for the same reason Baudrillard hated it. For Calvin, the consecrating words yoked the grubby sinner to the majestic deity, annihilating vast distances. For Baudrillard, relegated to the view from the parking lot at Disneyland (24), the shimmering hyper-real power of the simulacrum compelled the homage of a nonbeliever who was overwhelmed by the power of the image even if it was false. What Baudrillard described and demonstrated was a modern fetishism of the image, locating power in the simulacrum itself as if this sign were a living force capable of generating its own power to master the perceiver.

CRITIQUE OF BARTHES

Unlike Baudrillard, whose sacramental semiotics was filtered through an analysis of the commodity, Roland Barthes' semiotics drew more directly on the basic premises of the Calvinist sacrament in his *Mythologies*, the most widely read post-structuralist theory in the U.S. In a collection of meditations on mass culture and the media, Barthes critiqued the culture of the French bourgeoisie, which he saw as permeated with the culture of myth. In a long concluding theoretical essay, "Myth Today," Barthes spelled out what he meant by myth.[25] In doing so, he virtually duplicated Calvin's terms, but again, without recognizing that his critique was thoroughly indebted to the system he thought he was criticizing. What Barthes meant by "myth" was what Calvin meant by "consecration." Barthes described myth as a "second-order semiological system," built on the back of a first-order system of representation. What his famous diagram showed was the layering of names (or signs) that characterized metonymy (115). The myth fulfilled the function of the renaming of metonymy, actively infusing the first-order semiological system of representation that was drawn from ordinary non-mythologized society—an arena of material, social, and historical relations. In vocabulary reflective of the workings of metonymy, Barthes called the first order of signification a "language-object" that was robbed of its meaning in its appropriation by myth, its renaming. Like Calvin's empty token of the sacrament, "it empties itself, it becomes impoverished, history evaporates, only the letter remains" (117) and "its newly acquired penury calls for a signification to fill it" (118). That signification was myth, and, like the sacramental words of metonymy, it had a performative dimension to it: "myth has in fact a double function: it points out and it notifies, it makes us understand something and it imposes it on us" (117). Importantly, myth was not just observation and analysis. Barthes understood myth as a performative utterance. It was transforming and it actively commanded belief. Barthes described the bourgeois citizen as a "myth consumer," echoing the sacramental rite of consuming the elements of the sacrament and the manner in which Calvinist elements of the sacrament intersect with capitalist commodities at the point of distribution and consumption.

Because Barthes was not aiming to tie his idea of myth to the commodity per se, his examples show how the idea worked for media images and how it functioned in colonialist thinking. His primary example of myth in his theoretical essay was the magazine picture of the French soldier:

> I am at the barber's, and a copy of *Paris-Match* is offered to me. On the cover, a
> young Negro in a French uniform is saluting, with his eyes uplifted, probably

fixed on a fold of the tricolor [the French flag]. All this is the *meaning* of the picture. But, whether naively or not, I see very well what it signifies to me: that France is a great Empire, that all her sons, without any colour discrimination, faithfully serve under her flag, and that there is no better answer to the detractors of an alleged colonialism than the zeal shown by this Negro in serving his so-called oppressors. I am therefore again faced with a greater semiological system: there is a signifier, itself already formed with a previous system (*a black soldier is giving the French salute*); there is a signified (it is here a purposeful mixture of Frenchness and militariness); finally, there is a presence of the signified through the signifier. (116)

Like Calvin, Barthes discerned an active "presence." Myth was not simply a symbolic interpretation but an inhabiting of the first-order signification by a myth whose presence was comparable to Calvin's idea of the real spiritual presence in the sacrament. As Barthes explained it, for the myth-consumer, "the saluting Negro is no longer an example or a symbol, still less an alibi: he is the very *presence* of French imperiality" (128). Reeking of "presence," the myth created an absence of the soldier's social and material conditions of human existence. Analogously, colonization was an active inhabiting of another's territory, not mere interpretation but an act of aggression and conquest. Barthes' sense that the image of the Negro soldier was intended to convey a happy acquiescence to French Imperialism echoed the centuries-earlier pronouncement of Calvinist Puritans in their attitude toward Native Americans in New England: "As you reap their temporals, so feed them with your spirituals. Win them to the love of Christ, for whom Christ died."[26] The rationalization of colonialism was cast as a fair trade, but in fact it was a double exploitation. It reflected both the robbery inherent in myth, rendering material goods as available for plunder, and the cultural evisceration that myth imposed on its language-objects as a supposedly salutary benevolence. Barthes' analysis of myth reverberated with the classical idea of metonymy as expressive of domination and possession, of the renamer as the self-designated creator—here the creator of significance and the rightful possessor of the material, perceived as the "raw matter" used to create the myth (109).

Barthes' theory of myth is valuable in showing that the articulation of the negative subject (the Negro soldier) did not require a psychoanalytic model and that its semiotic characteristics were not necessarily gendered. Barthes' theory did not define any inherent gender identity for the language-object. Feminist psychoanalytic theory defined the negative subject as a universal truth (as psychoanalysis claims for all its premises), making sexuality the definitive difference, dismissively closing off other social differences as insignificant.[27] Barthes' theory was far more inclusive and did not privilege gender. Barthes represented the negative subject as socially constructed, the work of culture, and therefore culturally variable. For Barthes, the negative subject was a cultural practice, pervasive among the middle class, but not therefore inevitable or universal, and not true in the sense that psychoanalysis claimed it was true. Barthes' more expansive cultural approach to the semiotics of myth emphasized its capacity *to create* absence, lack, emptiness, in its language-objects. Feminist psychoanalytic theory, by accepting emptiness/lack as a given and further identifying this as a uniquely female phenomenon, lost its capacity for social critique. Feminist psychoanalytic theorists became, in effect, apologists for the power of myth, a power they saw as compelling, inevitable, universal, and true—the same attributes that myth-consumers assigned to myth.

Like Calvin, Barthes took pains to repudiate the natural world as a source of second-order meaning. Myth "cannot possibly evolve from the nature of things" (110), but Barthes said this for quite different reasons than Calvin said it. Where Calvin's interest was to assert the reality of divine intervention, Barthes took the materialist view that myth was a social construction, notwithstanding its tendency to "naturalize" its second order of signification. This is why Barthes was fundamentally at odds with psychoanalytic theory, whose underlying premises were naturalized. Although Barthes did not fully succeed in getting outside the Calvinist paradigm, he knew his way around within it extremely well and provided valuable insights into how it worked.

Barthes' meditations, together with his theoretical essay, were an indication of how extensively the metonymic second order of signification characterized both political and consumer culture and how metonymic thinking invoked a sense of ownership and possession, even for children with their toys. He conveyed the increasing social reach of corporate capitalism, and he also connected this phenomenon not only with political imperialism but also with the domestic life of the bourgeoisie. He observed that the bourgeoisie, the middle class, was the social class that did not want to be named, that did not want to be known as a social class (138–42)—an idea consistent with the social identity of the corporate body as nonmaterial, not involved in social relations or social conflict. Barthes associated this phenomenon of "denomination" with the middle class as the most ardent of myth-consumers.

Barthes located alienation in the transformation that the second order of signification worked on the first order of signification, of what happened in the performative metonymic renaming to the language-object, the sacramental object. He described more fully the quality of emptiness that ensued, an emptiness that was salutary for Calvin, but desecration for Barthes. What was lost in the imposition of myth was the recognition of the history, the material and social relations of the language-object in the first order of signification (118, 122, 125): "One must put the biography of the Negro in parenthesis if one wants to free the picture, and prepare it to receive its signified" (118). However, this did not constitute extinction or obliteration: "they are half-amputated, they are deprived of memory but not of existence." The concept of myth "literally deforms, but does not abolish the meaning; a word can perfectly render this contradiction: it alienates it" (123). Like Calvin's sacrament that required real bread, the bread ordinarily eaten in ordinary life, myth required real people like the soldier pictured in the magazine. Barthes describes the alienation from the point of view of the myth-consumer. Calling myth a *"metalanguage,* because it is a second language, *in which* one speaks about the first," Barthes described the semiologist of globalization as a myth-consumer:

> When he reflects on a metalanguage, the semiologist no longer needs to ask himself questions about the composition of the language-object, he no longer has to take into account the details of the linguistic schema; he will only need to know its total term, or global sign, and only inasmuch as this term lends itself to myth. (115)[28]

The distancing produced by myth provided an ignorant safety for the myth consumer, who need only deal with the existence of the soldier, not his history, social relations, or material conditions or his subjectivity. These were stripped away by the second order of signification that isolated the soldier, taking him out of this material social context and relating him exclusively to the meaning of the myth, French Imperialism, the political form of capitalist expansion.

As in Calvin's paradigm, the imposition of the imperialist myth in capitalist expansion is valued in the perspective of the corporation: alienation is good, not bad. Barthes also articulated the sense of possession, of ownership, in the metonymic workings of myth, speaking of myth's paradoxical action on the language-object: "it puts it at a distance, it holds it at one's disposal" (118). To put all this in terms of the performative, the language-object performed the myth, which was invariably a myth that legitimized reductiveness through images. Whatever its subject, myth "abolishes the complexity of human acts, it gives them the simplicity of essences, it does away with all dialectics, with any going back beyond what is immediately visible" (143). Myth produced a world free of social contradictions, making it impossible to conceptualize social conflict: "it organizes a world which is without contradictions because it is without depth, a world wide open and wallowing in the evident, it establishes a blissful clarity: things appear to mean something by themselves" (143). Just as the commodities of the marketplace obscured the means and social relations of production, myth presented an image of a fact, with no connection to anything or anyone else except through the structure of myth that produced and contained it. Barthes emphasized the vacuousness of myth in its capacity to take a subject and purify it, make it innocent, give it an eternal and natural justification, a "euphoric" clarity that was not the clarity of explanation but the euphoric determination of fact (143).

Finally, Barthes described the language-object as suffering from immobility. It was reified, turned into an immobile thing, by its interpellation, its appropriation into myth: "This interpellant speech [myth] is at the same time a frozen speech." He explained further:

> This is a kind of *arrest*, in both the physical and legal sense of the term: French imperiality condemns the saluting Negro to be nothing more than an instrumental signifier, the Negro suddenly hails me in the name of French imperiality; but at the same moment the Negro's salute thickens, becomes vitrified, freezes into an eternal reference meant to *establish* French imperiality. On the surface of language something has stopped moving. (125)

The result was like "a malaise producing immobility" (125). Fredric Jameson focused attention on instrumentality as the defining reductive characteristic of reification.[29] Barthes saw this degradation into instrumentality as the effect of immobility. The sign system stopped moving. To recognize the lack of movement in the language-object was to recognize the manner in which the dynamic meaning of social and material relations in the first order of signification was arrested by myth. In being arrested, it was made to seem not to exist. Liberation required *conceptual* motion, an active "transitive" semiotics that resisted myth by directly engaging the world (146). The "intransitive" semiotics of myth froze the language-object, excluding it even from narrative change except as an object to be acted upon.

Convinced of the social and political conservatism of myth, Barthes looked for an alternative but was hard pressed to find one. He sought a way to confront the stasis of myth, to attack myth's strategy of preserving and immobilizing things (or people) as images (146), but he was unable to conceptualize what this would be about. An important problem that stood in his way was his veering away from the image-ness of the image. His diagram of the first and second orders of signification, the crux of his analysis of myth, was an adaptation of linguistics. Barthes' "language-object" was in fact an image-object, as his paradigmatic example of the magazine picture of the French soldier suggested. (Though he also used a grammatical example from a textbook, this example did not carry the same weight in his argument, and almost all the examples from his meditations are images.) By borrowing from linguistics to describe the capitalist theory of the image informing myth, Barthes made the image curiously inaccessible. As to why he chose this approach, a remark early in the essay suggested the fundamental problem. Barthes wrote of images: "pictures, to be sure, are more imperative that writing, they impose meaning at one stroke, without analysing or diluting it" (110). In other words, the image was the ultimate performative. In this moment, Barthes was no different from Calvin standing before the image with overwhelming power, a power that made the interpreter not only weak in the knees but also weak in the head. That is, images as such could not be thought about. Barthes' solution was to suppress the image-ness of the image: "Pictures become a kind of writing as soon as they are meaningful" (110). Barthes interposed language between himself and the image to think about the image—hence the phrase "language-object." Barthes found a perch for his nonbelief in *Mythologies* by avoiding the image as image. His critique of myth was a defensive action, and his remarks about revolution are directed toward how to mobilize against the power of the image, the myth, not how to reconceptualize the image itself. The image as such remained indistinguishable from its deployment in myth.

In asserting that the corporate version of the sacramental image was humanly created, a social construction, Barthes often appealed to Marxist ideas to support this materialist perspective. However, he also unwittingly drew sustenance from the Calvinist tradition of rejecting humanly created images because they were false. His later work on images, *Camera Lucida*, suggests that the undertow of the old Calvinist conflict of true and false images proved to be more important than Marxism in determining the course of Barthes' thinking, for what appeared in his later work was a theory of true images. His credulity in this work is a stunning contrast to the author of *Mythologies*. Again, he confessed his powerlessness before the image, but where he had previously sought a remedy in language, he no longer believed a remedy was necessary. Barthes, we might say, had come to enjoy his Calvinist symptoms:

> If the photograph cannot be penetrated, it is because of its evidential power. In the image, as Sartre says, the object yields itself wholly and our vision of it is certain—contrary to the text or to other perceptions which give me the object in a vague, arguable manner, and therefore incite me to suspicions as to what I think I am seeing. This certitude is sovereign because I have the leisure to observe the photograph with intensity; but also, however long I extend this observation, it teaches me nothing. It is precisely in this *arrest* of interpretation that the Photograph's certainty resides: I exhaust myself realizing that *this-has-been;* for anyone who holds a photograph in his hand, here is a fundamental belief, an "ur-doxa," nothing can undo, unless you prove to me that this image *is not* a photograph. But also, unfortunately, it is in proportion to its certainty that I can say nothing about this photograph.[30]

He conceded the loss of interpretive power and consciousness that went with this yielding to the image: "it is in proportion to its certainty that I can say nothing." He found it gratifying because he believed he was overwhelmed by a true image, not a false one. Having made contact with the Real, he had no need to interpret anything to know it. In his contrast between the photograph and the text, he asserted the Real could be known directly through images, but not through languages.

Although this work reiterated many of his comments about the photograph in the essays collected in *Image/Music/Text,* it also took those ideas further, developing them as a kind of religious belief in the power of the photographic image. *Camera Lucida* reverberated with the Calvinist belief in sacramental true, living images, the lively and natural images that were distinctively true as they marked the real spiritual presence. Barthes described the photograph as a "living image" (79). The true image of the photograph was not the work of human invention: "The Photograph is indifferent to all intermediaries: it does not invent; it is authentication itself" (87). It was "a *magic,* not an art" (88). It was contact with the Real, and moreover, a Real with a spiritual presence (as the sacrament required). "Every photograph is a certificate of presence," he explained (87), in which "the power of authentication exceeds the power of representation" (88) and "on each occasion it fills the sight by force" (91)—no need for other images here! Barthes elaborated on the humbling spiritual dimension: "the air (I use this word, lacking anything better, for the expression of truth) is a kind of intractable supplement of identity, what is given as an act of grace, stripped of any 'importance': the air expresses the subject, insofar as that subject assigns itself no importance" (109). And in case there was any ambiguity, he added, "the air is that exhorbitant thing which induces from body to soul—*animula,* little individual soul, good in one person, bad in another" (109). Photographs had a salutary capacity to effect "the return of the dead" (90). He demonstrated their efficacy by talking about his own encounter with pictures of his recently deceased mother, how they produced "a sudden awakening" in him, a realization of her presence: "There she is!" His moment of "photographic ecstasy" revealed his mother to him, marked her presence *in* the photograph because "a photograph always carries its referent within itself" (5). Barthes achieved a secular-yet-still-spiritual equivalent of the Calvinist sacramental experience with a photograph. It is in this work that he confessed his own Protestant background (75). Now a believer, Barthes suppressed in *Camera Lucida* what had been so important in *Mythologies,* an awareness of the metonymic second order of meaning that created the aura of authenticity.

In his secularization of Calvinist beliefs, Barthes found his true living images in the photograph and not in the people-as-images of the sacrament.

He insisted that to find the person in the photographic image of them was to find the person's soul or essence. This was his version of spiritual revelation. The Calvinist sacramental idea that people *are* images was presupposed by the equivalence Barthes made between the photograph and the person. In fact, Barthes' equivalence captured the sense in which it was the image-ness of the person that consecration bestowed, the image-ness that was the distinguishing mark of the immortal divine spiritual presence, the spiritual essence of the true believer who consumed the consecrated objects of the sacrament. Barthes pushed sacramental beliefs to the next logical step: if people *are* images, then images sacramentally mark their presence. Photographic images were mystically infused with the real, just as believers who consumed the consecrated elements were mystically infused, taken over, by the real spiritual presence of the mystical body of Christ.

Barthes was able to eliminate the difference between the person and the photographic image because of his belief that the essence of the photographic image was its spirituality, an immaterial idea or essence. This was why he rejected its representational aspect as unimportant (the repudiation of representation that Baudrillard attributed to iconoclasm). This is also why he found it pointless to develop a semiotics of the photograph: "To ask whether a photograph is analogical or coded is not a good means of analysis" (88). Analyzing the formal composition or semiotic properties of a photograph was not significant because this was merely analyzing an empty shell. That is, Barthes didn't deny that the image had such properties, but for him, they didn't matter. Barthes treated photographic images as if they were objects of the sacrament, empty tokens filled with spiritual significance. In doing so, Barthes emptied the photograph of all its attributes as an artistic image, reducing it to a transparent instrumentality. Continuing to invert his argument in *Mythologies,* he also praised the photograph for its exemplary quality of stasis, immobility. Still photographs were a more viable instrument than cinematography, he believed, because they did not change what was being seen (89). In *Camera Lucida,* Barthes achieved a thorough reification of the image, praising what he had previously critiqued.

Barthes did not change his theory of the image from one book to the next. The reification of the image that was featured in *Camera Lucida* is harder to see in *Mythologies* because of Barthes' reliance on linguistics, his focus on an image reconceived as a language-object, but the idea is the same. He assigned it a different significance in each work, incredible in *Mythologies* (the earlier work), highly credible in *Camera Lucida.* Although Barthes made some effort to distinguish between the photography he praised and the photographic images of consumer capitalism, he did not pursue this argument. In fact he could not pursue it because he would have collided with the realization that he was using the same theory of the image, the same semiotic paradigm—loved and believed in *Camera Lucida*, hated and condemned in *Mythologies*. With regard to the theory of the image, Barthes upside down was the same as Barthes right side up. Barthes' work demonstrated how the iconoclastic pressure to perceive images as either true or false was itself part of the paradigm, and that the paradigm functioned just as well with the one as the other. Whether true or false, the reified image was consistently present as the conceptual precondition of both truth and falseness.

DEBORD AND THE SOCIAL PRODUCTION OF THE IMAGE

Guy Debord's *The Society of the Spectacle*, originally published about ten years after *Mythologies*, retraced much of the same ground as *Mythologies*. More sure of its Marxism, Debord's essay also focused more clearly on the reign of the visual in commodity capitalism. Debord did not, as Barthes had, avoid the image-ness of the image. Debord's book was about "image-objects" in contrast to Barthes' "language-object" in *Mythologies*.[31] And where Barthes had later capitulated to the photographic image as true once he recognized the image as an image, Debord did not, or at least not directly. Debord argued that the image was being used to stupefy and deaden the viewer/consumer in the social system of commodity capitalism. Its effects were simultaneously banal and subtle. The spectacle for Debord was paradoxically a "visible negation of life" (10) and consequently, "It is only inasmuch as individual reality is not that it is allowed to appear" (17). The result: "For one to whom the real world becomes real images, mere images are transformed into real beings—tangible figments which are the efficient motor of trancelike behavior" (18). Echoing the Calvinist belief in the living images of the sacrament, Debord described the workings of myth in the same manner: "The perceptible world is replaced by a set of images that are superior to that world yet at the same time impose themselves as eminently perceptible" (26). What Debord recognized and struggled to express was the consecrating power of the corporate capitalist theory of the image, at once eminently visible and eminently invisible.

Debord traced the spectacle to the doorstep of "our old enemy the commodity," for the spectacle is "the world of the commodity ruling over all lived experience" (35, 37). He argued that "spectacle is *capital* accumulated to the point where it becomes image," that capitalist semiotics in the late twentieth century conceptualized the reified commodity as an image (34). While Debord placed this phenomenon in a clearly Marxist framework, his Marxism could not account for why the image had become so paramount, or how exactly the transposition from industrial commodity to commodity-image occurred. Debord's critique of capitalism was noticeably missing one thing: He failed to articulate a theory of how the image was produced, even though he insisted that the society of the spectacle was socially produced. Without a concept of the social production of the image, he retreated to natural weakness as explanation, blaming the power of images on the sense of sight as "the most abstract of the senses, and the most easily deceived" (18). Tapping into Marx's arguments about abstraction, he simultaneously tapped into the Calvinist iconoclastic sense of the image as deceiving. That images induced trancelike behavior elaborated on the thoughtlessness inspired by the image, a thoughtlessness so profound that it expressed nothing more than society's "wish for sleep" (21). Debord vilified the commodity, but along with it he vilified the image. He reduced the image to a viable instrument for the deceptions of commodity capitalism, viable because images deceived as capitalism deceived.

Immobilized in its capitalist instrumentality, the reification of the image became the methodology of Debord's analysis. The conspiratorial tone of his chapter on the commodity as spectacle emphasized the effects of the reified image and the powerlessness of the individual who perceived it, implying that the overwhelming power of the image, while supported by capitalism, ultimately came from the image itself, which exploited the consumer's natural infirmity of sight. In other words, Debord succumbed to the fetishism of the image, now as commodity-image. Notwithstanding the great significance he gave to images in the capitalist system, it seems to have been inconceivable to Debord that a theory of the social production of the image as such could be the basis for a radical political critique.

French post-structuralists in their leftist arguments—such as those of Baudrillard, Barthes, and Debord—were intent on exposing the way reification turned people into things, and they concentrated on how that reification was achieved by means of images.[32] However, if one shifts the focus of attention to their theories of the image as such, what emerges is a consistent reification *of* the image, the image immobilized in its instrumentality for capitalism and the conceptual stasis that makes instrumentality possible. The reification enacted *by* the image drew its explanation from commodity capitalism, a semiotics that suppressed awareness of the social character of the commodity as it is produced by labor. The post-structuralist reification *of* the image drew its rationale from iconoclasm and the theory of sacramental objects, which—in the intermixing of exchange value and spiritual value—made the fusion of commodity and image possible.

SCREENING OUT: LACAN'S MIRROR STAGE AND
THE CINEMATIC APPARATUS

It is hard to imagine a more thoroughgoing iconoclasm than the reification of the image, but that is what Lacanian psychoanalytic theorists offered. They sought the extinction of the image altogether, and they sought it with the hammer of language. It is more than ironic that film theory in the late twentieth century was most beholden to the theory that was the most hostile to the image. As Jean-Joseph Goux explained in "Lacan Iconoclast," Freudian psychoanalysis was already potentially iconoclastic even before Lacan's more radical revision of it: "Freud staked out a deep unconscious, subject to the power of the image, predating language, eluding verbal signification; the goal of analysis was to link this unconscious to the verbal, bringing it to consciousness."[33] The power of the images of the unconscious was for Freud a potential danger that needed to be tamed. However, the extent of Freud's iconoclasm was ambiguous—Lacan frequently criticized Freud for straying from his iconoclastic premises, Goux points out (114–15). When translated into the practice of film theory and criticism, the Freudian approach drew out the more iconoclastic reading of Freud. Jameson provides an example in *Signatures of the Visible*. He introduced his study of film with an iconoclastic confession of mental helplessness before the image. "The visual," he said, produces "rapt, mindless fascination," and so "movies are a physical experience, and are remembered as such, stored up in bodily synapses that evade the thinking mind." Jameson described his own film criticism as a process comparable to Freudian analysis. For him, this meant that film criticism succeeded in proportion to its capacity to extinguish the visual: "when successful, it liquidates the experiences in question and dissolves them without a trace; I find I have no desire to see again a movie about which I have written well."[34] Jameson interposed the barrier of language not only with the actual writing, as he said, but also a second time with his belief that a film is like a novel. Like many studies of film, his analyses of films treated film narrative as indistinguishable from novelistic narrative. In this second presupposition, similar to Barthes' transformation of the image into a language-object, Jameson sought a kind of Freudian compromise in the mental images of writing that, while not acknowledging the film image, did not quite banish it either. Žižek effected an analogous compromise by exploiting film narratives as popular vehicles for illustrating principles of psychoanalysis.[35]

Goux has argued that Lacan's iconoclasm was more harsh, and more thoroughgoing, than Freud's, that Lacan thoroughly repudiated the image. In saying the unconscious was structured like a language, exterminating the image from the unconscious, Lacan had no tolerance for the difference,

the tension, between image and verbiage that characterized Freud's interpretation of dreams. For Lacan, "the verbal, the phonetic, the letter are at the
heart of the mechanism of the unconscious. Dreams themselves are inter-
pretable by the letter (visible or phonetic) and not by the image. There is no
such thing as irreducible figuration" (110). Lacan's theory of the unconscious was, Goux observed, "a phonetic interpretation that dissolves every
product of the imaginary in the sovereignty of the letter" (111). However,
given this unbridled hostility toward the image, it seems strange that Lacan
brought the idea of the mirror stage into psychoanalytic theory. One would
have thought he would construct great barriers against it. Goux's interpretation of Lacan's iconoclasm is a partial one, dealing only with the side of iconoclasm that was about the hatred and destruction of images. Lacan's theory
demonstrated not only the iconoclast's wish to destroy the material image. It
also demonstrated its simplistic homage to the image.

Lacan took the idea of the mirror stage from Henri Wallon, also using
additional work by Charlotte Bühler and Elsa Köhler.[36] With his introduction of the mirror stage into psychoanalytic theory, Lacan staged his own
iconoclastic crisis, one that had nothing to do with dream images, Mosaic
prohibitions about images, or Freudian psychoanalysis. Lacan's concept of
the mirror stage brought back the old iconoclastic problem of false images,
and massively. The long-held fears of the power of images to overwhelm
the viewer, to bypass the conscious mind, to render the viewer helpless and
unable to think—even to imagine, as Augustine and Calvin had, that the
image was somehow alive—these ideas informed the entire life of a human
being in Lacan's version of the power of images. Like Debord, when faced
with a need for a theory of the image, Lacan retreated to natural infirmity
as explanation, a modern equivalent of Calvin's idea of original sin. According
to Lacan, the eighteen-month-old infant, stymied by its own inherent
clumsiness, was mesmerized by the pseudo-recognition of itself in the mirror. The Lacanian infant perceived an idealized image in the mirror that was
fundamentally false, but nonetheless it was constitutive of the ego, the
identity of the self (the 'I'): "The important point is that this [mirror] form
situates the agency of the ego, before its social determination, in a fictional
direction, which will always remain irreducible to the individual."[37] The
mirror stage was about "fiction," an alienation from the truth. Lacan also
believed that the image was the form of power, conceiving the person-as-
image as the form of power, "the total form of the body by which the subject anticipates in a mirage the maturation of his power" (2). Lacan again
emphasized the mirror stage as "the correspondences that unite the 'I' with
the statue in which man projects himself, with the phantoms that dominate him" (2–3). As fiction, as mirage, as statue, as phantom—the mirror
image conjured up the false image of iconoclasts, the deceiving image

with its fearful power to dominate the perceiving self. Lacan spoke of the infant being "captated," taken or seized, captured by the image, held hostage, never to be released (4).[38] Lacan also connected images with violence, going on to argue for an intrinsic connection between the mirror stage and aggressive violence.[39] The mirror image was overwhelming, fundamentally false, and inspired acts of violence.

Once "captated" by the image, the individual was seized by the image for life. The victim was forever prevented by the false image from knowing itself, or anything else (the image was the cause of the inaccessibility of the Real). Lacan went on to speak of "the deflection of the specular 'I' into the social 'I'" as the mirror stage ended, inaugurating "the dialectic that will henceforth link the 'I' to socially elaborated situations" (5). He distinguished between "identity," which he attributed to the mirror stage, and "subjectivity," which occurred with the entry into language. Lacan sought to control the power of images by the containment of the mirror stage itself, its parturition from "subjectivity" proper. However, the passage into the symbolic order of the phallus merely hid in symbolic language the problematic of the image. Its influence did not disappear. The image was only made more inaccessible as the metonymic deployment of language sought to rename the image to the point of extinction—a polemic typified by Lacan's insistence that the phallus represented the letter of "the law" and was not a visual image. The quest of Lacanian analysis was to make the image so inaccessible that it seemed extinguished—or consumed. Nonetheless, Lacan declared this quest a certain failure even before it began. The narrowness and rigid structure of the mirror stage was like a suit of armor, impervious to the power plays of language. He described the *meconnaissance*, the misrecognition, of the mirror stage as "the assumption of the armour of an alienating identity, which will mark with its rigid structure the subject's entire mental development" (4). The mirror stage permanently immobilized the ego. It was not just a passing phase, but something that characterized the entire life of the individual.

The enshrinement of the power of the image was the foundation of Lacan's psychoanalytic system because the child's act of *meconnaissance*, the false perception inspired by the material mirror image, was both inevitable and permanent in its effects. Lacan called it "the threshold of the visible world" (3), but the visible world it portrayed best was the world of advertising. The child was socialized into the false truth of myth as the sole theory of the image, and further made to submit to its premises as the foundation of identity, for the Lacanian ego was forever condemned to the acceptance of the false image as somehow true. In closing his essay on the mirror stage, Lacan warned the reader "not to regard the ego as centered on the *perception-consciousness system,* or as organized by the 'reality principle.'" Rather, "we should start instead from the *function of meconnaissance* that characterizes the ego in all its structures" (6). Corporate capitalism could not have agreed more. Lacan's semiotics was a capitulation to the imagistic requirements of circulation and consumption in corporate capitalism. His theory was a model of socialization into the capitalist economy, a capitulation to its semiotics as inevitable.

Lacanian theory's claim to universal truth, and hence its denial of its own political-economic conditions, was a part of that acquiescence. Where Barthes' mythologies, Baudrillard's simulacrum, and Debord's society of the spectacle understood the iconoclastic theory of the image as historically contingent, as a capitalist theory of the image that developed with the historical development of capitalism, psychoanalytic semiotics appealed to the nature of things instead, and especially to the nature of the human psyche, as the ground of its theory. It naturalized itself, and it naturalized the iconoclastic theory of the image, eliminating historical, economic, cultural, and social contingency. Although the leftists did not offer an alternative theory of the image, they at least hypothesized one. Psychoanalytic semiotics, particularly in its Lacanian form, carried no such hypothesis. It was not that psychoanalysis simply failed to include a recognition of historical or cultural contingency. It actively rejected it.

French post-structuralist film theorists who developed a theory of the "cinematic apparatus," such as Jean-Louis Baudry in his essay "Ideological Effects of the Basic Cinematographic Apparatus," appropriated the Lacanian version of iconoclasm rather than the leftist versions, even though their intent was a leftist social and political critique of mainstream cinema.[40] They were drawn to Lacan by the possibility of parallels between the Lacanian mirror stage and the spectator's viewing of the film screen.[41] Consequently, the theory of the cinematic apparatus reiterated the themes of iconoclasm with an especially Lacanian flair. The target of the cinematic apparatus was the credibility of "classical cinema," or more precisely, the credulity of the viewer who watched it. "Classical cinema" meant conventional dramatic films that relied on a representational system of meaning. The images of representational cinema seemed to live and breathe as Calvin's statue had, and as in Calvin's theory, the viewer was characterized as helpless before the power of the image.

For the apparatus theorists, the viewer was condemned like the Lacanian child to believe in a false image, victimized by the concealed artifice of the cinematic apparatus. Following the iconoclastic paradigm, they discredited the representational images of film by using the idea of the cinematic apparatus to expose representational cinema as the work of artifice.

For iconoclasts, to prove that an image was humanly created, and therefore unlike the divinely created "lively and natural images" sanctified by the sacrament, was to prove that the image was false, a lie, epistemologically useless. Perceiving representational cinema as a false image, the iconoclasts of "the cinematic apparatus" theory used the language of psychoanalytic theory to attack the credibility of the representational image in cinema. What would take its place? Here was the Lacanian part: Nothing. Or rather, nothing except the linguistic construction of Lacanian film theory itself. The extremity of Lacanian iconoclasm was the pursuit of happiness through the extinction of the image. Because the cinematic apparatus was a universal theory of spectatorship, a theory of seeing the film image, it indirectly discredited all films, not just representational cinema. The editor of *Film Quarterly* worried, even as he was publishing Baudry's essay, that the theory of the cinematic apparatus seemed to be a film theory without films.[42] It was. Its topic was not films, but the consumption of films as generic images, the Lacanian spectator as image-consumer. Rather than producing a political critique of classical cinema, it erected a barrier of psychoanalytic terminology between itself and actual films.

Mulvey's Symbiosis of Woman and Image

This was the context of Laura Mulvey's famous 1975 essay, "Visual Pleasure and Narrative Cinema."[43] Mulvey attempted to draw both on the historical, leftist post-structuralist critique of capitalism and on the psychoanalytic theory of the cinematic apparatus. She openly shared the "iconoclastic spirit" of the theorists of the cinematic apparatus, and saw herself as like them in announcing her intention to "attack" and "destroy" representational cinema, especially its Hollywood studio version. She reiterated their theory of the apparatus this way:

> There are three different looks associated with cinema: [1] that of the camera as it records the profilmic event, [2] that of the audience as it watches the final product, and [3] that of the characters at each other within the screen illusion. The conventions of narrative film deny the first two and subordinate them to the third, the conscious aim being always to eliminate intrusive camera presence and prevent a distancing awareness in the audience. Without these two absences (the material existence of the recording process, the critical reading of the spectator), fictional drama cannot achieve reality, obviousness, and truth. (33)[44]

Although adopting their theoretical framework, Mulvey also criticized the theorists of the cinematic apparatus for not having paid sufficient attention to women, for having "not sufficiently brought out the importance of the representation of the female form" (22). Within the logic of this theory, the omission occurred because the theorists of the cinematic apparatus had simply followed Lacan's placement of the mirror stage at a pre-sexual point of development. Consequently, the theorists of the apparatus had not relied on sexuality, either female or male, as a source of explanation. Within the development of film theory, it was the distinction of Mulvey's essay to gender the gaze male and the image female.[45] In the process of gendering the cinematic apparatus, she did exactly what she said she was against. She eliminated the spectator's critical (and hence variable) reading by invoking universal psychoanalytic categories as the only way to read a film. Then, after briefly discussing Von Sternberg's fetishistic use of cinematography, she also eliminated the material existence of the camera in the most influential part of her essay. She based her analysis on Hitchcock's characters and what they do within the screen illusion. She used the story lines of films such as *Vertigo* and *Rear Window* to explain and prove her analysis, in effect *accepting* Hollywood's representations as "reality, obviousness, and truth." She did not offer a critique of Hollywood cinema, as she had set out to do. Instead, she affirmed its ideology by making its illusions the crucial source for her analysis, achieving the opposite of her professed aim.

Mulvey's political turnabout rescued the film image from its total repudiation in the Lacanian apparatus theory of French post-structuralists such as Baudry.[46] This rescue was effected by addressing a problem that photography and cinema raised for iconoclasm: True and false images seemed to be occurring in the same place. Cinema intensified this problem of false and true images occupying the same space by presenting moving images of living images, that is, by recording images of live people moving, breathing, and talking. Calvin's statue really did seem to come alive in cinema. The artistic image and the living image seemed to merge. Barthes managed this contradiction in *Camera Lucida* by canceling out one of the images in question. He interpreted the photographic image as transparent, as not really an image. It was like a windowpane that one looked through to see the living image. As articulated by André Bazin, a key element to this theory of the photograph was to understand the camera as a mechanical device that simply recorded images without human intervention. In other words, the camera did not create images. It merely recorded them. This eliminated the problem of relying on humanly created images as true. Paradoxically, the technology of the camera was interpreted as a human invention that eliminated human intervention. (I take up this theory of the camera much more extensively in Essay Three.)

As her summary of the apparatus theory shows, Mulvey also believed in the idea of the photograph as a recorded image. If the camera only recorded, received an image, then what was photographed was the source of the image. Since cinema recorded live people, living images, Mulvey's theory ironically rationalized cinema as uniquely revelatory. Cinema could claim to record the image-ness of the living image, its salutary sparkle. In effect, Mulvey made this claim with her idea of "the woman as icon," the crux of the essay (29).[47] "An idea of woman stands as linchpin to the system," she said, meaning both the psychoanalytic system and the Hollywood narrative system (22). Like the French soldier who was, who meant, French Imperialism, in Barthes' theory, Mulvey's filmic woman was, and meant, Cinematic Image. This was much more than an association between woman and image, much more than an analogy. The core idea might be expressed in this way: The substance of woman is image. Mulvey accepted the misogynist precepts of psychoanalysis about the nonexistence of women. The empty token, the bread of the sacrament, morphed into the "structuring lack" of female sexuality, to be filled by a new kind of spiritual presence, image-ness itself. The compensation for the extinction of women—women as empty tokens—was the survival of Woman/Cinematic Image. What the camera recorded was the image-ness of women.

As a true living image, the woman as image was the "bearer of meaning, not maker of meaning" (23). As the bearer of the look, she exhibited the power of the male gaze that conferred the meaning and significance she displayed. The male gaze carried the power of consecration. That it was a metonymic power was articulated in the notion of the male gaze as a visual-less figure, as metonymy was a visual-less figure. The male body was invisible, in contrast to the marked visibility of the female body. The deflecting quality of metonymy cast visual attention away from the male body, made ideologically image-less by its metonymic power, and fastened on the female body as the vehicle of exhibition. This is not to say that male bodies could not be seen on screen. They could, but they could not be seen as sacramental empty tokens. In this theory, the male physical image could not display or be the idea of the image that was the structuring lack marking spiritual presence. Mulvey's adaptation of sacramental iconoclasm maintained the idea of the performative utterance as the consecrating words became the consecrating gaze, with all the power of the performative utterance to enact what it declared. The gaze was understood as a controlling gaze, as performative, not just visual observation. Mulvey aligned the work of the camera with the invisible male's gaze, a transmutation made compelling by the recorded-image theory of the invisibility of the camera.

Because Mulvey's paradigm depended on the iconoclastic theory of the camera as recording an image, in which the object of the camera's gaze was the source of the image that was recorded, the woman as object paradoxically had the power to ideologically displace the material means of the production of images to herself as object. The camera merely recorded the images she produced. Film images lent themselves to this idea because the position of a camera can be roughly inferred from an image. The viewer can read back from the film image to the idea of a camera, creating the sensation of the image-object as causative.[48] Women potentially had a controlling power as the source of images, for he/the camera could see only the images that emanated from her physical body. Within the iconoclastic paradigm of the sacrament, an image-generating object was a fetish, and belief in it an act of apostasy. However, within the equally iconoclastic paradigm of the theory of the camera as a recorder of the object's image, the image-object was a true image. Simultaneously true and false, the Woman/Cinematic Image was a contradiction that located visible true and false images in the same place, the body of Woman.

Although Mulvey interpreted the woman as fetish as a threat to "the spell of illusion" in narrative film (33), the woman as fetish was nothing of the kind. Far from threatening it, she affirmed it. If the male character feared the power of this image, that, too, was well within the bounds of the iconoclastic paradigm and no threat to it either. In general, Mulvey's ideas about what was threatening existed totally within the iconoclastic paradigm, never disrupting its boundaries. The male might move about, rattle his cage, and feel renewed fears about the overwhelming power of the image, but neither he nor the fetish object of his gaze threatened the corporate theory of the image. Hollywood narrative played with these threats as threats *to the characters,* not to the structure of Hollywood film itself, because these threats were the dramatic material of iconoclasm— myth talking about itself, as Barthes would say. The Hollywood narrative was frequently a drama of sorting out the true image from the false one, as Mulvey herself indicated in her description of Hitchcock's films. That a woman character could be either or both made for interesting drama, not a threat to the paradigm but a further indulgence in it.

The significance attributed to Mulvey's essay, as much outside film studies as within it, was indicative of the way it drew on an array of cultural ideas about women, and particularly ideas about Woman as material vessel and Woman as Nature. Mulvey's essay crystallized the way those ideas functioned in corporate capitalism's theory of the film image, but the essay has also served as a description of woman's place in corporate capital's imagery generally—in advertising, in the media, and so on. As Barthes pointed out, the bourgeoisie has typically rationalized its own cultural beliefs as natural, as eternal truths, inhering in the very nature of things. Ideas about women have often been cast in this light, and Mulvey herself did so when she grounded her theory of the cinematic image in psychoanalytic myth. Barthes rejected the assumption that ideas of long standing have some validity as myth:

> Are there objects which are *inevitably* a source of suggestiveness, as Baudelaire suggested about Woman? Certainly not: one can conceive of very ancient myths, but there are no eternal ones; for it is human history which converts reality into speech, and it alone rules the life and the death of mythical language. Ancient or not, mythology can only have an historical foundation, for myth is a type of speech chosen by history; it cannot possibly evolve from the nature of things. (110)

Even myths about Woman are the product of history.

Psychoanalysis itself, particularly in its Lacanian version, was caught up in the much larger sweep of corporate capitalism's theory of the image. From the perspective of the centuries-long tradition of iconoclasm and its convergence with the logic of capital, the developments of post-structuralist thought from the 1950s to the 1980s revived with great intensity the preoccupations with the power of the image that it saw everywhere in the burgeoning economy of the society of the spectacle. This was the historical context of Lacan's essays and seminars, and the historical context of Mulvey's essay as well. In this larger context it becomes apparent that iconoclasm as a paradigm was not necessarily inflected with sexuality. Calvin's iconoclasm had been formulated without recourse to sexuality; this was also the case in Lacan's theory of the mirror stage, which preceded the sexualization of the subject in the symbolic, language phase. Barthes' examples in *Mythologies* involved images of men as well as images of women. Baudrillard's theory of the simulacrum was not particularly a sexual idea. Theories of the cinematic apparatus preceding Mulvey's were not sexualized either. In the larger context of post-structuralist thought, Mulvey's essay was quite striking in its insistence on a sexually coded iconoclastic theory of the image, and, moreover, an insistently heterosexual one.

Why make heterosexuality even more compulsory than it already was? It may be that the appeal was not heterosexuality as such, but a particular interpretation of heterosexuality that involved metonymy, and thus coincided with the iconoclastic paradigm. Metonymy was not only the privileged trope of the sacramental paradigm. It was also the trope of traditional marriage—when a woman married and was renamed with her husband's name. The metonymy of marriage articulated a social relation that put a woman in a place analogous to that of the sacramental object, sexually coding the hierarchy expressed by metonymy. The iconoclastic paradigm and the marriage paradigm reinforced each other. The viability of Hollywood film, and the viability of Mulvey's essay, drew on this traditional metonymic structure of heterosexuality, deriving its credibility more from cultural tradition than from its viability as a theory of the cinematic image as such. Although Mulvey's theory reified the gender categories of heterosexuality, the iconoclasm that supported this reification was not gendered. The iconoclastic paradigm of capitalism can accommodate other sexualities, since the iconoclastic paradigm of capitalist consumerism is not inherently sexual. The bread and the wine were not gendered. Metonymy and its hierarchy were not gendered, and the corporate mystical body of Christ was, to borrow a Deleuzian phrase, a body without organs. Barthes' example of the French soldier, and much recent advertising, suggests that the corporate society of the spectacle is happy to colonize any consumer.

Mulvey's theory inflected iconoclasm with sexuality, but the reverse could also be said, that it reinforced the interpretation of sexuality through iconoclastic beliefs. By proposing that the substance of woman is image, it limited what could be said about women to what an iconoclast could say about images. Women are true and privileged images, good women; or women are false images, deceitful and treacherous, noirish women; or women are overwhelming, reducing otherwise rational men to helplessness in their presence. The heterosexual coding of iconoclastic principles also evoked the iconoclastic belief in the culturally legitimated use of violence to destroy false images. When heterosexually coded, this assumed that men were inherently violent, iconoclasts at heart, driven by a destructiveness that was naturalized as inevitable rather than perceived as the product of cultural mandates. In this paradigm women were destined to be the objects of violence, and men were equally destined to be its perpetrators. By grounding its approach in supposedly universal truths, Mulvey's approach unwittingly added sanction to cultural rationalizations of men's violence against women, just as it added sanction to misogynist beliefs in psychoanalytic ideology. Although Mulvey voiced objection to prejudices against women in film, she also made its existence appear inevitable, conveying a political message of acquiescence that limited women to a world circumscribed and infused with iconoclastic assumptions about gender. Mulvey's codification of cultural beliefs shows that what holds this ideology intact is the iconoclastic theory of the cinematic/photographic image that binds 'woman' and 'image' together. The problem of reification in the symbiosis of woman and image is that neither moves in relation to the other. They are glued together, and thereby mutually immobilized. What is needed is a different theory of the image, or better still, theories of images, that allow a complex and variable relation between 'woman' and 'image.'

Mulvey was surprised at the effect of her essay when it was published.[49] It drew a great deal of analytical attention to the Hollywood studio cinema she thought she had repudiated. It is not difficult to understand her surprise if one considers her stated intentions in the essay—an often overlooked part of what she said. She had begun and concluded her analysis with paragraphs about the technological possibilities emerging in film-making, especially 16 mm film, which made it possible to create feature films without extensive capital resources. In fact Mulvey underestimated the possibilities. The development of a technique for blowing up 16 mm to 35 mm made it possible for film-makers without extensive capital to enter the arena of mass-market distribution in regular theatrical release. Her intent in writing the essay was to support these new developments in film-making, to critique Hollywood film on their behalf. This was the leftist, historical, and cultural part of her essay, which was cognizant of the conservative influences of the increasing capitalization of film production, epitomized by the Hollywood studios Mulvey thought she had attacked. Mulvey's suggestion is just as valuable now as when she made it, all the more so with the extensive development of international cinema. The second essay in this book is about the kind of film that Mulvey urged her readers to explore. The film I discuss at length develops a new theory of the film image that breaks the symbiosis of woman and image. As Mulvey implied, and rightly so, important new theories can come from films and film-makers outside the studio system. After all, Mulvey herself was a little-known film-maker when she wrote and published her famous essay.

Essay Two
Liberating a Woman from Her Image

WITHIN THE LEGACY OF ICONOCLASM, FILM IMAGES OF WOMEN FUNCTION PRIMARILY to provide a vocabulary for iconoclasm, the medium through which iconoclastic struggles are reiterated. Continually reasserting an intrinsic and unquestioned relation between the film image and the visible shape of a woman, this semiotic structure asserts that women are inseparable from iconicity, as if the concept of the image could not exist without women. The substance of the image, its essence, is Woman.[1] However, actual women experience this ideology in its reverse form—as a belief that a woman's image is essential to her being. Without her image, a woman faces extinction, she ceases to exist. This is a considerable threat, to say the least.

THE SUITORS

Some recent films critique the assumptions of American iconoclasm and offer significantly different ways to think about the image of a woman. One of the most important and effective of these films is *The Suitors*. Produced in New York, it was the only American film (among fifty entries) that was selected for screening at the Cannes Film Festival in 1988.[2] It was released theatrically in the U.S. and Europe in 1989, to favorable reviews.[3] (It is currently available on VHS.) U.S. reviewers praised it as "a riveting, deliciously macabre tale of cultural alienation," "remarkably accomplished in its shifts of tone," with "striking photography" and a "subtle wit and complexity" that distinguished the film as "a rarity" among contemporary films.[4] Described as "a fascinating study of a beautiful young woman determined to be free of the bonds of social custom,"[5] the film also challenges the bonds of the image itself. *The Suitors* makes the semiotic crisis of a woman and her image the plot of the film, breaking the iconoclastic symbiosis of a woman and her image. In its final scenes, *The Suitors* dares the

Mariyam at customs with her new husband, Haji.

separation of a woman from her image, but not for the purpose of killing off the heroine. Instead, *The Suitors* faces the threatening loss of image for the purpose of liberating its heroine from the oppressiveness of a gendered ideology of the image. This radical move, the culmination of the story, occurs not just at the level of the plot, but also in the imagistic and narrative structure of the film, at the semiotic level. This allows the viewer to experience an alternative iconology, to actively think in a different way. As one viewer described it, "You don't just watch the movie. You experience it. Most movies, you just sit there, but with this movie, you experience it."[6] As the reader will see, my analysis of *The Suitors* in the following pages draws substantially on thirty individual interviews with people about their experience of seeing the film.[7] I also rely on my lengthy interview with the writer and director of the film, Ghasem Ebrahimian.[8]

What's the plot? Stated in conventional terms, it goes like this: The story is about an Iranian woman, Mariyam (Pouran Esrafily), who immigrates from Iran to New York in the late 1980s as the new wife of an Iranian arms merchant. Her husband Haji (Assurbanipal Babila), already established in New York, has recently gone back to Iran to get married, and brings Mariyam back to the U.S. with him. The viewer first sees her when she arrives in New York wearing a chador, the enveloping Islamic black veil that is obligatory for women in Iran. To honor their arrival, Haji's friends sacrifice a sheep in their New York apartment. A Christian

Haji's friends meet him at the airport.

fundamentalist in the apartment below sees blood dripping through the ceiling and alerts the police. Believing the Iranians are terrorists, a SWAT team attacks the apartment and Haji is killed in the melee. Now alone, Mariyam decides to stay in New York and begins to explore living in the city on her own, even going out without a veil. However, Haji's friends quickly become suitors to Mariyam. One of them, Ali (Ali Azizian), enlists the support of Haji's business partner, Mr. Amin (Bahman Maghsoudlou), who takes charge of Mariyam's life, virtually kidnapping her and taking her to his house in the country. Mariyam refuses to acquiesce to the proposed marriage. She tears up her wedding dress and stabs the prospective bridegroom the night before the wedding, escaping the house with the help of another suitor, Reza (Shahab Navab), who doesn't know what she has done. She decides to go to Europe with Reza, but she can't board the plane because she no longer has her passport. She decides to hide in a suitcase and be shipped to Europe as baggage. Reza succeeds in checking her through as baggage, but at the last moment, nearing the plane's hold, Mariyam gets out of the suitcase. Sneaking back through the terminal, she hails a taxi and leaves the airport, finally on her own.

A conventional plot summary does little to convey the most distinctive qualities of this film in terms of what viewers experienced in watching it. While some may think plot summaries reveal what a film is about, they don't necessarily accomplish this. Conventions of plot summary tend to assume the film narrative is basically linear, and the diegesis (the plot) can be separated from how the story is told. This assumes that the form and imagery of the narrative have no real impact on what the story is. For an innovative film such as *The Suitors*, conventional plot summary is inadequate, even misleading, in conveying what the film is about. A consideration of viewers' responses to the film bears this out. For example, KL liked *The Suitors* exactly because its story is greatly complicated by the way it is told. As she put it, the film's narrative is more like a fable, with reversals and transformations that create shifting and multiple meanings:

> I was really impressed by the design of the film, and not just the cinematography. The way it works and moves and reflects back on itself. I thought it was a wonderful, very strong and simple design, and very ancient. There are patterned plots. In terms of fable, one act is balanced with another. There are all sorts of reversals and transformations and they're there, staring at each other.

LC described the main character, Mariyam, in a similar way: "The way she went about things was not linear. There were all these convolutions." To closely follow the story of Mariyam is to be pulled out of the complacency of linear narrative into a more complex world of reversals, transformations, and convolutions, as the significance of the plot is transformed from scene to scene.

Plot summary also tends to emphasize events that are easily recognized as significant genre characteristics within patriarchal conventions. *The Suitors* has these, but viewers treated them as secondary to the main story. They fastened instead on other events that show a fundamentally different kind of narrative is at work. Together, the viewers' comments reveal that, in their experience of viewing the film, the images of greatest dramatic intensity involved (1) Mariyam with her veil, (2) the capture and sacrifice of the sheep, and (3) Mariyam's journey in the symbolic suitcase as represented by a black screen. For example, CK, summarizing the film, described it this way: "The sheep and the chador and her zipping herself into that case were the most riveting images." For CK, the chador (the veil) was the most prominent:

> The way she takes off that veil when the husband dies and tries to cram it into her purse—she's always wrinkling the veil into a little package or trying to put it in something, and then pulling it back on and taking it off. That's the big thing in the movie.

For VL, the sheep was the most important. When asked at what point did the film emotionally engage you, VL responded, "when they lifted the sheep into the back of the American car." As for the dramatic climax of the film, NC had no hesitation in saying "The big moment came when she emerged from the suitcase." While viewers acknowledged scenes that an American plot summary would emphasize, such as the SWAT team raid and Mariyam stabbing Ali, these scenes were not as important as those in which Mariyam puts on or takes off the veil, or scenes involving the sheep or the suitcase. As LC explained it, "The issues were different from American films. Like, there wasn't much tension after she killed Ali. There would be in American film." As with other viewers, LC was far more fascinated by Mariyam's emergence from the symbolic suitcase: "That was beautiful! Uncanny!" Scenes involving Mariyam and whether or not she's wearing her veil were valued as dramatic and emotional high points of the story, even when their overt content seemed unimportant to forwarding the plot. BW remarked on the scene "when her chador was off and most of her clothes were off, and she's lying back in bed reading *Elle* magazine. . . . I thought that was really powerful, those images of her relaxing at home." HT said, "The image I liked best was her in the hotel, pacing around in her slip— an animal in a cage. You feel the claustrophobia, her frustration." Viewers' comments imply that Mariyam is ultimately defined by her relationship to the veil itself, rather than through her relationships to men. That is to say, this is a story about a woman's relation to her image. As she explores that relation, the film traces her increasing divergence from the patriarchal plot that runs alongside her own story and contests it. Her uncertainty about her veil, putting it on and taking it off, becomes an intense drama because, as RT described it, "she's taking off who she is." There is much more at stake than discarding a material practice. The symbolism of the veil resonates at a more profound level of ontology and identity.

It might justly be asked if the viewers, and particularly American-born women viewers, were reading into the film of another culture a story that wasn't there. My interview with the director suggests not. There was strong agreement between Ebrahimian and the audience regarding what was most important in the film. That is, the viewers' sense of what was important about the film's drama matches up with the writer/director's own priorities. During the interview, Ebrahimian volunteered that the story of the veil and the story of the sheep were "the motivating factors for making the film." Other parts of the plot, including the stabbing of Ali, gain their value as they relate to the story of the veil or the sheep. At this level—the story of the veil and the story of the sheep—the film's plot is ultimately a semiotic one because it is the figurative meanings, not simply the literal events in themselves, that generate the emotional intensity viewers experienced in watching the film. At the dramatic climax of the film, I will show, the story of Mariyam's veil and the story of the sheep semiotically converge with the image of the black screen, a very complex, highly original cinematic event that is the longest black screen sequence in dramatic film. Not a disruption of the story, the black screen is part of the narrative, a dramatic representation of Mariyam and her perspective from within the symbolic suitcase. As we hear her gasping for breath, the culmination of the film's suspense circulates around whether Mariyam can survive this semiotic convergence. I will return to this scene at the conclusion of this essay. To appreciate what it accomplishes, it is necessary to consider first how the stories of the veil and the sheep develop semiotically, how they build to the film's climactic scene.

Persian Narrative Structure and Activating the Audience

Reflective of the writer-director's Iranian background, *The Suitors* derives its basic narrative structure from the conventions of Persian literature, drawing on the Persian literary tradition exemplified in such works as the popular *1001 Tales of the Arabian Nights*.[9] NJ, who was familiar with this work, said watching the film was like "walking right into *The Arabian Nights*." The Persian-based narrative of Mariyam yields a concept of character that is different from what American viewers are accustomed to seeing in film. As Ebrahimian himself explained it, a major difference is the concept of character in relation to events. From Ebrahimian's perspective, in conventional American media characters tend to have "their own set place." They don't change. "They only say who they are, what they are, and what they represent." By contrast, in Persian narrative "characters go through changes and that's the subject of the story, the object of the storytelling." In American series television and genre films, for example, characters "fill out this role they have been given. They are the husband, or the wife, or the kid. They fulfill that need for the audience, so when the audience watches a film, they watch a story, but it mainly turns out that all the characters are pretty much set in their ways and minds."[10] Persian narrative tradition conceptualizes character in a different way:

> The characters go through a lot of changes. Not that they want to, but events dictate certain things. It's more playful in terms of how things happen. The motivation for action is when something happens around the character, and that shifts them.

In Persian narrative, "the shift of events creates shift of character." Persian stories do not ask *whether* people will change, as American stories about change tend to do. The Persian cultural expectation is that characters will change. The interest of the Persian story is in *how* characters change when events shift, "what that resonates, what that does to them." Persian narrative is about "the metamorphosis of characters," and this concept was reflected in comments by viewers. GB said of Mariyam that "she transformed from what my original view was." TG concurred: "You feel there's a very different person at the end."

Ebrahimian summarized the relation between character and plot in Persian narrative tradition this way:

> It's about discovery and the emotions these characters have that are corresponding to events. So the character is not in the center always. The character is important, but it's not important at the same time, because the mechanics of the storytelling are important. It's really both.

Mariyam can be the focus of the narrative even when she is not an action character (so to speak), because the heart of the story is how she reacts to events such as the killing of her husband. Action sequences and reflective, psychological sequences are continuously interwoven in the film, but the one predictable element of the narrative structure is that the story will always take the viewer back to Mariyam to find out how each event resonates with her and especially what she does with her veil in response. The focus on Mariyam's responses to events makes her the primary character in the narrative. The men in her life were considered elements of the plot rather than characters in the same sense she was. As JD put it, "I really focused on her. The men were more what's happening to her."

The narrative structure of *The Suitors* presupposes an active viewer, someone who becomes involved in working out its narrative logic. Far from attempting to control how the viewer sees the film, the director thought of the audience as participants in the act of storytelling:

> To activate the audience is important. They really have to decide and think. They become involved in the whole process. . . . What I believe, personally, is, when you show an image or a series of images, those images have reverberations. There is an inner logic to that that they [the viewers] would follow. And to find that logic, that inner storytelling is playful, is interesting, discovering those moments. Because you're not walking in a territory you already know.

Instead of suppressing the consciousness of the viewer, the film evokes conscious viewing.

The viewer's experience of the film mirrors the primary character's experience. When confronted with the unexpected, when something shifts, viewers must, following the character, examine their own emotions and changes in perception. A single, unified understanding of the main character is fleeting at best, for as the director said, "from moment to moment, things shift, and every moment is different." GA explained it this way: "It was a surprise movie for me. I don't know what I was expecting to see, but it wasn't what I saw. I didn't have an expectation of what I saw. But I did have an experience of what I saw." This experience was marked by a sense of "not-knowingness." GA was aware of the first time she sensed this, in the early sequence of Mariyam's arrival at the airport with her husband:

> The first time it comes up in the movie is when she doesn't get on the elevator or misses the elevator and he gets in and she runs away and you don't know if she's running to try to catch up with him or running to escape. And then he's looking all over for her and she's nowhere to be found for awhile. There's a not-knowingness. Did she do this intentionally? Or did this just happen, was it a fluke? You don't know if she's escaping or running to try to find him or what. There's this feeling of ambiguity. Where's she going? What's she doing? Is she running to him or away from him?

CK, though less elaborate in her commentary, responded to this scene with similar questions: "Is she trying to run away and get free at that point? Or is she just completely lost and scared?" CM also selected a scene in this sequence as the moment she became aware the main character would not be a predictable construct in the story. While Mariyam is running through the airport, the veil suddenly slides from her shoulders. Said CM, "You're just holding your breath and hoping she'll grab it quick. But then you wonder, was it really an accident? How could she just let go of it like that?" Ironically, it is in these first moments when we see Mariyam without her veil and without her husband that questions about her are generated, rather than dispelled. This is a touchstone of the way the audience activation generated an attitude toward the film that was not based on patriarchal censorship or its revocation.[11] Although viewers did see Mariyam as someone who was censored by Iranian fundamentalism, the removal of the veil is not revealing of the censored woman underneath. Mariyam becomes harder, not easier, to read when the veil falls away and she is separated from her husband.

In American mainstream films, there is often an unexpected, unpredictable moment near the beginning of the film that sets the plot in motion, that provides a dilemma that it takes the rest of the film to resolve. As that dilemma is increasingly confronted, the viewer's expectations of genre and character are increasingly fulfilled and affirmed. Particular turns of plot may be surprising, but the basic narrative structure and its outcome are predictable. In *The Suitors*, unpredictability characterizes the whole narrative right to the last scene. LC commented, contrasting *The Suitors* with American films, "You really don't feel like you know what's going to happen. It's not the director saying, I know what you're expecting and I'm going to give it to you." DS relished her involvement in the narrative logic of the film, especially the sense of never being able to anticipate what would happen next:

> It held me to the very end. I never suspected the ending. I never guessed things ahead of time. I didn't guess she would scissor-death the guy in the mansion and hide the body, and that she would have all these incredible survival skills. I was absolutely blown away by the end! I thought it was incredible—the whole scene of her in the suitcase and traveling through the guts of the airport and the breathing routine in there. And I was trying to decide if she was panicking and would flip and kill herself, or if she was really going to do this trans-Atlantic flight in the bowels of the plane and I never, never, never thought she would exit the suitcase into her life! I mean, I didn't pick up on that until she did just that.

As this viewer describes her experience of seeing the film, she relates not only what was happening on screen, but also what was simultaneously happening in her own mind. She was involved in the narrative logic, not just in general but in quite specific ways: "I was trying to decide if she was panicking . . . or if she was really going to do this trans-Atlantic flight." Continually, the film provided her with a narrative development she hadn't thought of, showed her a different way the narrative logic could develop than what she had herself imagined, a process that is most acute at the very end of the film. No viewer anticipated that Mariyam would get out of the suitcase. As to why they did not, I will explore that further when I discuss the meaning of the black screen.

The quotations above are indicative of the frame of mind that occurs in "audience activation" as Ebrahimian conceived it. Again, the viewers and the director match up in their sense of the relation between the film and the audience, a further testimony to Ebrahimian's intercultural eloquence. While viewers were aware that the Persian narrative structure and concept of character were different from their previous film experiences, they were not confused or distracted by it. Part of the clarity of their orientation toward the film depended on the kinds of expectations that were made of them. Viewers of *The Suitors* did not feel they were being asked to forget themselves in "experiencing" the film. When viewers talked about the film, they referred to both Mariyam and themselves in the same sentence. Speaking metaphorically, GB said, "I felt like I was in her cage with her." HT said, "I felt her claustrophobia and frustration and impotence." First-person references do not disappear from viewer's comments. They feel "with" Mariyam, but they do not become her. Their own consciousness, their own thoughts and feelings as such, are evoked and changed by the scenes of the films, but they remain recognizably the viewer's. The viewer sympathizes

The new bride in America. Photo: Patrick Gries.

with Mariyam, sometimes very strongly, but the viewer does not become confused about who is the viewer and who is the character.[12] Their comments deftly interweave self-references with references to Mariyam, as in this comment by GA as she elaborated on what it meant for her to "experience" the film:

> I experienced the contrast of her outside the veil and within the veil, and I can't say there was an objective experience. I felt like there was some sort of a bond, some kind of a bond I was experiencing there, that I couldn't live with that, that I wouldn't want to live with that. Watching her do her veil, it embraced an emotion—you could feel what it felt like.

It's not an objective experience—as in FH's version of this idea, you don't just watch the film—but it's not an engulfing experience. There is a sense of balance, of equivalence, of sympathy or even empathy, but not self-negation or negation of Mariyam. No matter how intense the film became, viewers did not describe themselves as overwhelmed or swallowed up by it at any point. Instead viewers maintained a self-awareness, and they did so without difficulty. They remained aware of their own consciousness and their own emotions, aware of how the film was affecting them and altering their perceptions. This is the "audience activation" that Ebrahimian's adaptation of Persian narrative structure evokes. It is by no means an abdication of the writer-director's role in making the film. It is a carefully designed film, and the manner in which the narrative logic is opened up to the audience is carefully constructed.

In relation to the audience, Ebrahimian's choice of narrative structure—where one has no idea what happens next—was especially apt for the subject matter of the film because Mariyam herself is entering a culture about which she knows very little. She has come to the U.S. because of a marriage arranged by her family. Mariyam is an ordinary, average woman, not unusually adept or insightful about negotiating a transition between two different cultures half a world apart. She knows very little English and, in the course of the story, the film impresses us with her excruciating lack of cultural knowledge. She doesn't know how to leave the country house of her kidnappers except to start walking down the highway. She doesn't realize she needs a passport to fly to Europe. Yet the film also shows us that Mariyam is not particularly at a disadvantage for being so culturally ignorant. In the lived juxtaposition of two cultures, what constitutes meaning, what constitutes knowledge or knowingness, becomes uncertain. Similarly, the viewer is not at a disadvantage for not knowing about Persian narrative structure. What constitutes an appropriate narrative structure for a woman main character is an open question. By building the narrative along the fault-line between two cultures, a Persian narrative for an American audience, the director opens up the film itself to the full uncertainty of Mariyam's character. To experience that uncertainty in watching the film was an important dimension of what viewers thought the film was about.

The Story of the Veil

Historically, the story of the Iranian veil is a story about state terrorism, but this is not readily apparent in the film. Viewers did agree that the film's story as a whole opposes the practice of veiling, that it portrays veiling as a coercive and abusive practice that should not be forced upon women. Nonetheless, the element of terrorism is an elusive one because Mariyam is a young woman who has grown up in post-revolutionary Iran, someone for whom the practice of veiling is normal. Few American-born viewers knew about the fundamentalist revolution in Iran in 1979, assuming that historically, Iranian women had always worn veils. In fact, the practice of veiling had been discontinued in Iran by the Shah (that is, by state decree) in the 1940s. Not wearing a veil became widely accepted, especially in urban areas of Iran. Women wore Western clothes, and teenage girls of the '60s and '70s often adopted popular American standards of dress such as blue jeans and mini-skirts. After the Islamic fundamentalist revolution in Iran in 1979, the practice of veiling was reinstituted by the new government.[13]

When the revolution broke out, Ebrahimian was in Iran on contract to make a documentary about the constitutional movement in Iran. During the time he was there, he saw firsthand how the practice of veiling was enacted through terrorism. He witnessed the fundamentalists' violent imposition of veiling, how women were beaten, had acid thrown in their faces, were imprisoned and even executed if they did not veil themselves. It was a practice that many Iranians described as "state terrorism" against women. Ebrahimian's documentary was confiscated by the new Iranian government and he had to return to the U.S. without it. A few years later he began work on *The Suitors*. Although *The Suitors* is about an Iranian woman who veils herself, this dramatic film does not try to reproduce the subject matter of the confiscated documentary or the revolution that disrupted its making. Indeed, the film takes place entirely in the U.S. While Ebrahimian was knowledgeable about the overt state terrorism that enforced the practice of veiling in Iran, and could have made a film about it, he chose to conceptualize this fictional film differently. American viewers who perceived Mariyam's veiling as a normal practice saw what the director intended for them to see: veiling as a cultural norm.

In making *The Suitors*, Ebrahimian's primary interest was to explore what happens after state terrorism becomes "normalized," when the knowledge of coercion, discrimination, and oppression have become submerged in cultural norms, when the perspective of alternative experience has been thoroughly suppressed and, as he expressed it, "terror seeps into the law and becomes the law." At that point, he explained, "the threats against you become hard to articulate," and that's why, and how, people are "molded into conformity to terror." Mariyam is culturally situated as a post-revolutionary young woman who has never known anything but the practice of veiling. She is someone who has been molded into conformity to terror, who accepts veiling as a normal practice. In Mariyam's first scene in the film, it is clear that she fully accepts wearing the veil, even covering her face further than she needs to, up to her eyes, as a symbol of her willing acquiescence and obedience to the practice of veiling in general and to her conservative husband's wishes in particular.

The normalization of terror is an important, even defining, premise of this film, as I found when I interviewed two Iranian women, now U.S. citizens, who had had some experience with wearing the veil. I had thought Iranian women in the U.S. or Europe might be the core audience for the film, its most sympathetic and interested viewers. This was not so. While they understood and appreciated that the film opposed the practice of veiling—as they themselves did—Mariyam's story did not resonate with them. That they were Iranian women did not matter nearly so much as the fact that they had experienced veiling as a bizarre and arbitrary, deviant imposition, *not* a normative practice from their own perspective. LF had been a student at Tehran University when the revolution began. The state-run university was closed for over a year, and when it reopened, she had to wear a veil to be admitted again. In her mid-twenties, she had never worn a veil, but now she covered up in the manner she was ordered to do at her interview for readmittance. She conformed only because of the threats against her, and especially the threat against her life if she refused to veil herself: "They take you to jail. They have the authority to kill you. Two of my classmates were killed. They were executed." As to what it was like to conform to the practice, LF explained, "It's difficult if you don't believe it. That's why I left the country." The alien power of state terrorism was obvious to her, and her only means of refusing the practice was to leave the country, to put herself outside the range of Iranian state power.

LF had no doubts that it was the power of the state that had taken away her freedom, and would not hesitate to take her life if she disobeyed its laws about veiling. She also had no doubts about her own feelings of revulsion for the practice as unfair to women, as contrary to the societal norms she had known in pre-revolutionary Iran. Commenting on the ideology that the veil represents value, she also associated this with state terrorism. At her interview for readmittance to the university, when she was ordered to wear the veil, LF had been told: "This is your value. It gives you value. If you don't have it, you lose your value. You should be proud of the veil. This is your value. I couldn't accept it. I don't believe it would make me more valuable." She resented the government's attempts to persuade her to value the veil as well as wear it. Acknowledging that some fundamentalist women might want to wear it, she continued, "If you decide to accept it for your own satisfaction, that is acceptable to me. You decide for yourself. Let them have it if they want it, but don't force people. Don't try to brainwash me that this is good for me." She left Iran alone, secretly planning her journey for fear the Iranian government would prevent her from leaving.[14] Although she said she was now safely beyond their reach, she also acknowledged that the threat of reprisal from the Iranian government still lingered in her mind.

SR's experience with veiling was brief and temporary, but left an impact on her nonetheless. She had left Iran with her family soon after the revolution. Still a girl, about ten years old at the time, she then had no experience with the practice of veiling. Her family moved permanently to the U.S. and they became U.S. citizens. When I interviewed her, she had recently gotten her first job, as an account executive at a large advertising firm. She told me about a recent visit she had made to Iran to visit her grandmother in Tehran for a couple of weeks. During that visit she wore a veil (provided by her grandmother). She described the veil as "hot," "oppressive," and "like a uniform."[15] Like LF, SR experienced the practice as non-normative, and as imposed by the state. SR recounted how a restaurant owner had reprimanded her for having some hair showing while she was dining with her grandmother. His explanation: he didn't want to lose his operating license from the state. During her visit, SR looked up a childhood friend, who had also recently gotten her first job. The friend told her that when she had taken off her veil at work, she had been reported by someone. It was a small office, and she thought she could trust her co-workers, but she could not. She was arrested and spent the night in jail, where she was beaten. SR described herself as a strong person, saying, "If you're strong, you do what you want." Yet she added, citing her friend's experience, that "you wear the veil whether you want to or not, because there are some things you don't mess with." State terrorism is one of those things.[16]

For both LF and SR, *The Suitors* was a film that inspired them to talk about their own experiences rather than Mariyam's. They had little engagement with the film's story, and only at a literal level. LF did not detect any ambivalence or "not-knowingness" in the main character. Her description of Mariyam was simple and categorical, more reflective of her own frame of mind than the film's drama: "She hated the veil. She wanted to get rid of it, to be free and change her life." She was impatient with Mariyam's apparent lack of a plan: "Why didn't she try to escape and hide herself for awhile if she wanted to get out?" LF cautioned me that her views of the film might not be representative because "I've never enjoyed fiction. I like biographies." However, SR, who did like dramatic films, and especially independent films, responded in essentially the same way. The symbolic meanings of *The Suitors* were not meaningful to her either. Unlike LF, she could tell that "there's something going on besides the straight narration of the story," but she said she couldn't figure out what it was. Notwithstanding their Iranian cultural background, both women saw the practice of veiling as non-normative. Nor did they find their objections to veiling hard to articulate. They knew exactly what they feared when they put on a veil, exactly why they hated it, and they had no hesitation about taking it off as soon as they were safe from threats. For both, that ultimately meant being U.S. citizens, out of the range of Iranian state power. A typical American viewer had described her experience of watching the film in this way: "I watched to find the woman under the veil" (DS). LF and SR did not find this an interesting pursuit. They felt they already knew who was under the veil. They had no difficulty separating themselves from the image of the veil, or understanding their own value apart from it, because they perceived it as an alien practice that was externally imposed on them, that was never a part of who they were, even in Iran.

Women viewers who liked *The Suitors*—who were the most engrossed in the story, the most moved by it—were American women who had never experienced the practice of veiling.[17] The film allowed the American woman viewer access to what she perceived as an unfamiliar symbolic language, the non-Western idiom of the veil. As a dramatic and cinematic subject, the story of a woman and her veil was perceived by the American woman viewer figuratively as a parable about the ideology of a woman and her image. For these viewers, the film resonated strongly at an imaginative and symbolic level, as it did not for Iranian-born women. For American women who knew nothing about the Iranian revolution or Iranian culture, Mariyam's veiling was perceived as a normative practice—alien to themselves as viewers, but not alien to Mariyam. They understood Mariyam's reluctance to go without a veil as the reluctance of someone who was giving up a cultural practice she was long accustomed to. GA remarked on a scene in the middle of the film, when Mariyam tries going out in New York alone without her veil, that she sensed "the nervous anxiety with which she traveled the streets without her veil. You felt her vulnerability, because you knew she was used to being in a veil. Yet she wanted *not* to be in it. I felt the trepidation—she's not safe, she's out there, she's vulnerable." GA's feeling of trepidation was a common one among viewers, though viewers selected different scenes about veiling where they thought it was prominent. CM felt this early in the film, at the point where Mariyam becomes separated from her husband at the airport and the veil drops from her shoulders:

> I was so frightened for her! All of a sudden it just slides off her shoulders and floats to the floor. And there it is in a heap on the floor and there she is so exposed without it, and with all those people around and what will they think? What will they do to her? You're just holding your breath and hoping she'll grab it quick.

The sense of threat was palpable for this viewer, and it stands out as a response that derives its force from some other source than the representational level. For one thing, Mariyam is in the midst of people at an American airport. "What will they do to her?" Nothing. As for her being "so exposed without it," by American standards Mariyam even without her veil is much more covered up than most American young women. In this scene she is wearing a conservative, loose-fitting, long-sleeve black

Mariyam retrieves her veil.

dress and black stockings. Nothing happens to Mariyam. She stops, picks up the veil, and puts it back on. On the periphery of the frame some people stop and stare momentarily, but no one moves toward her. No one arrests her, no one beats her, no one throws acid in her face. There is nothing on the screen that would suggest Mariyam is literally in danger from anyone.

The film's story evokes in the American viewer a feeling of danger about a woman and her image. This feeling of danger comes less from Mariyam's represented experience and more from the American viewer's *own* concept of what it means to violate a normative ideology about a woman and her image. In this sense, the American viewer engages with the film at a symbolic and figurative level more deeply than a representational one. Nothing happens at the airport or on the New York streets to endanger Mariyam. She is not physically harmed at any time in the entire film. There are no incidents of violence like those that LF and SR described as their experiences in Iran. Such experiences do, however, surface in the viewers' figurative language. CK summed up her general impression of the story of the veil: the film was about "the use of the veil as a prison." PN and NC repeatedly talked about the feeling of "entrapment" and HT and KL talked about the feeling of "claustrophobia." Although American viewers saw veiling as an alien practice, Mariyam's story readily evoked feelings of fear, hostility, entrapment, and imprisonment that showed they were quite knowledgeable, themselves, about the

Mariyam reading an American magazine.

experience of normalized terror, though none of them put it precisely in those terms. However, as Ebrahimian insightfully observed, with the normalization of terror, the threats against you become hard to articulate— hence the value of the film for American women.

Internalization of social intolerance was indirectly evident in the exacting demands viewers made on the main character. Although viewers thought of themselves as liberal and tolerant people, and reasonably well informed, for many that tolerance did not conceptually extend to veiled women until they had seen Mariyam not only without her veil, but also without some of her clothes. Initially, Mariyam seemed to be all veil and no woman. For some viewers, it was only when they saw Mariyam in a state of semi-undress that they were able to perceive her as a woman. BW referred to the scene "when her chador was off and most of her clothes were off, and she's lying back in bed reading *Elle* magazine" as an important and surprising scene because "you see them in their chadors and you assume that they're not even whole people. They're not even women, not even people we can relate to, and then you see, wow! she's fully a woman just trying to be at ease in her bedroom." Only at this point did BW identify Mariyam as a woman like herself, the point at which Mariyam looks to her like an American woman, lounging in bed and as scantily dressed as the images of women in the magazine she's looking at. The magazine images emphasize the image-ness of a woman's body, the prerequisite for BW's

acceptance of Mariyam as a woman. Only in her conformity to the normative image of a woman as capitalist advertising presents it does Mariyam
gain acceptance from this American viewer. For BW, to be veiled is to be
unseen, and the image of a woman needs to be seen. For women to be concealed is to be "not even women, not even people we can relate to."

For JH, the same attitude was evoked by another, similar scene, in
which Mariyam is in bed asleep when Mr. Amin comes to tell her of her
husband's death. When Mariyam hears the doorbell, she gets out of bed
and the viewer sees she is wearing only a black slip. She puts a veil on over
her slip and answers the door. Mr. Amin's presence makes the viewer
more aware that the viewer, unlike Mr. Amin, knows how little Mariyam
is wearing under the veil. JH described her response to this scene:

> I thought it was great when she had on the nightgown. When they came to
> tell her Haji is dead, she's in her nightgown. She's sexualized in a way that,
> honestly, I was surprised at. It's embarrassing that I would be so naïve as to
> think she isn't sexual. But once I see her in a Western negligee I see her as
> more sexualized, even though I recognize it [the veil] is connected to the
> sensual part of her as a woman, I still don't see her as sexualized until I see
> that, and it was surprising. . . . I didn't see her as sexual until I saw her in
> the Western slip like anyone in the U.S. might be wearing, or in the West.
> And that's connected with the desire to see what's underneath, what she's
> wearing underneath the veil. I was surprised when I saw what was under-
> neath—or when I *knew* what was underneath—because they seemed
> incongruous and that reveals my naïveté—not naïveté, but stereotyping
> along cultural borders of sexuality or physicalness.

Striving for accuracy as she groped for words to express these feelings and
ideas, JH concluded by referring to herself as prejudiced rather than
naïve, acculturated into a particular way of thinking rather than simply
ignorant. Her way of thinking not only required Mariyam to appear in the
customary imagery of women in U.S. magazines and movies. It also
extended to the veil itself, which JH understood conceptually in terms of
the symbiosis of a woman and her image:

> The reason I was surprised is because I have this understanding of the veil as
> being permeating beyond the physical self, as having a lot more connotations
> and extending beyond just the physical kind of wrapping of the woman, and
> that's why maybe I was surprised to see the sexual being underneath, or to
> see it covered by—, as if those were somehow incongruous, that the veil
> would somehow seep into the essence of, whatever that is, the woman so
> thoroughly that she wouldn't have an expression of sexuality like that.

JH read the symbolic image of the veil in American terms. Like the bodily
images of American women, the veil "would somehow seep into the

essence of, whatever that is, the woman." The symbiosis of woman and image characterizes her understanding of the veil and shows, again, that there is a way, an important way, that a woman does not exist without her image. JH's inarticulateness is also a touchstone of Ebrahimian's observation that the implicit threat is hard to articulate. JH, usually a very articulate speaker, not only gropes for vocabulary. She also struggles with grammar to describe her insights, as if her realization is antithetical to the norms of language as well as the norms of culture.

Other viewers did not experience an opposition between the normative images of the veil and the flesh. They perceived the polarization as two versions of the same idea, emphasizing the parallels between the veiled Muslim woman and the Western scarcely dressed look. LF, refusing the idea of the veil as expressive of value, then added, "On the other hand, I don't like bikinis in public." For CM, the magazine-reading scene was not liberating, but cause for wariness instead, another instance of entrapment:

> The pictures are of women with a lot of skin showing. That's freedom for Mariyam, but for American women that's entrapment, having to show that much skin. Women work to achieve that veil of skin and they're able to conceal everything else with that.

The veil of skin may seem to be strikingly different, but ideologically it is not. It, too, is a form of concealment of the person, a tyranny of the image. CM interpreted herself as subject ultimately to the same demand for concealment of herself, paradoxically accomplished by the exposure of flesh. As GA put it, an American woman is expected to "keep herself under wraps," to wear an "invisible veil" wherever she goes. These observations bring out the sense in which both Iranian and American women face a similar contradiction. The woman who is veiled, either literally or figuratively, is both highly visible and highly invisible. NJ saw Mariyam similarly as "translating from one form to another," trying to choose between apparent alternatives that were really equally entrapping:

> She's caught between two different ideologies, and neither one of them is going to work. She doesn't want to be a [veiled] Muslim woman, but what she's looking at in the apartment are all these magazines—*Elle* and *Vogue* and that kind of thing—that whole dichotomy between veiling and nudity. She's got the veil on a hook and she's in her underwear looking at other women in their underwear. It seems to be a trap between one pose and another.

Mariyam seems unable to get rid of the veil. She takes off her Muslim veil, but she puts on the veil of flesh. Both are an entrapment. At this relatively early stage in the film, NJ saw little hope of liberation: "It's enclosing a female character one way or the other. I mean, what's the difference?"

Interpretations of the magazine-reading scene demonstrate the enigma of the woman's image and the difficulty of ideologically contesting it. Simply to remove the Muslim veil reveals, at best, that Mariyam can be as subject to the American version of the veil as she has been to the Iranian version. With this scene, the film articulates the depth of the problem. To represent Mariyam without a veil removes some prejudices, but it does not remove the ideological belief that a woman is her image, does not show us a fundamentally different relation between a woman and her image. The symbiotic entrapment of a woman in her image, and the fear that goes with it, are not dislodged by this means. This is also why escaping from men would not resolve the dilemma she faces. The crisis that Mariyam must resolve is her own normative relation of a woman to her image as she experiences it.

Although American viewers did not express a concept of terrorism explicitly, their comments evoke an idea of the ideology of the female image as entrapment, as a means of controlling women by force, of socialization as being lured into a cage. Given the underlying source of the tyrannizing image in the sacramental commodity and its distribution, "capitalist terrorism" might be a more apt phrase than "state terrorism" for the American veil of flesh. GA, commenting on the significance of the veil, conceptualized the American version of the veil as an "invisible veil," one as confining and demeaning as Mariyam's Islamic veil:

> I think it extends beyond the concept of Muslim people. It's very much happening here. It might be a useful film in the sense of awakenings. I think [American] women are living under a veil, the invisible veil I talked about, and that they might, in seeing the visible, recognize the unseen, that on a subconscious level they might get it, that it's their veil, too.

She also articulates the sense of threat that accompanies an understanding of this commonality:

> I think it takes a little bit of time to allow what's subconscious or subliminal to float over into your awareness, to allow it passage in a safe way. And that would be my hope for the movie, that maybe subliminally people could start to get it without feeling threatened by it because it's about another culture—so they could depersonalize the message—yet at the same time it's really not. So maybe they could get that we are living under that same veil.

GA emphasizes the fearfulness of understanding the normalization of terror, the danger that is comprehension. For GA, as for CM, the use of "veil" as a metaphor for the fleshly image of the American woman is a way of "getting it," expressing what otherwise remains at a level of inarticulateness. GA sees cultural difference as a way to "depersonalize" the message so that it can be understood, allowed safe passage into consciousness, to be indirectly claimed by the viewer as their own through the bridge of metaphor. There is, however, another route to consciousness in the film, one that becomes increasingly important as the distance between Mariyam and the viewer closes. There are no subliminal cuts in the film, but there is something else interspersed through the viewer's perceptions, a depersonalization of the message in the story of the sheep.

THE STORY OF THE SHEEP

Although state terrorism is a common idea among people in countries in the Middle East and Central Asia, in the U.S. terrorism is perceived as an act committed by isolated fanatics, domestic or foreign, who are male and who *oppose* the state—such as Timothy McVeigh or, more recently, Al Qaeda. That the government *itself* might engage in systematic acts of terror against its own citizens is, for most Americans, unthinkable. "Police brutality," "excessive force," "violation of civil rights"—these are the names given to acts of violence committed by the state in U.S. culture. No matter how often they occur, they are generally seen as exceptional acts, committed by isolated individuals or groups, not characteristic of government acts or intentions as a whole. The SWAT team raid in *The Suitors* was perceived by viewers in this light. Ironically, those who were close to seeing it as an act of state terrorism also thought it was "unrealistic," an "exaggeration," something that occurred in countries they had come from, but not in the U.S. (Iran was specifically mentioned by Iranians, and Italy was mentioned by someone who had lived for a decade in Italy.)[18]

American-born viewers who had personal relationships with Iranians—as spouses, lovers, or roommates—were knowledgeable about Iran. Those without such relationships, the majority of people I interviewed, had only a very hazy idea of Iran, or no idea at all.[19] They did not perceive the veiling of women as something imposed by the state or enforced by the state, partly because they had no concept of state terrorism, partly because they saw it as a practice involving women rather than men, and partly because—with regard to the Middle East as a region—they had no concept of a Muslim state.[20] They could not distinguish between Iran and Iraq, interchanging them, and they had never heard of countries like the United Arab Emirates, Qatar, or Yemen. On their own, they perceived Mariyam as being simply from the Middle East—her nationality was not important. Rather than perceiving her practice of veiling as a political expression of Iranian nationalism, instituted and enforced by the state, American women perceived the practice as normative Middle Eastern Muslim behavior, determined by religion, and supported by the family and members of the community. This American concept of the cultural pressures on Mariyam echoes the religious origins of iconoclasm that underlie the problematic of a woman and her image in American society, and its enforcement through family, community, and the "religion" of capitalism rather than the state.

For the American viewer lacking basic political knowledge, it is the story of the sheep that provides the paradigm for a socialized act of normative violence. Because it culminates in a sacrificial execution, it visually renders the unspoken threat of normalized terror as an overt part of the plot. The blood of its death is the cause of the SWAT team raid, the cause of the building superintendent's fear that he is harboring terrorists in the apartment. Beyond its immediate consequences in the plot, the death of the innocent sheep has great resonance in its own right. The morality of the story is vested not in any human character, but in the story of the sheep, whose death is by far the most important killing in the story. It is the death that matters in the film, that is disturbing and even repugnant to watch, and that influences viewers' symbolic perceptions throughout the film.[21]

While the narrative of the sheep may be a Shakespearean subplot in its structure, the character of the sheep, especially the idea of an anthropomorphic sheep, is indebted to Persian literature. Again, the *1001 Tales* is an instructive example. There are many animals in the tales, almost all of them created by magic spells that transform a human being into an animal. One person casts a spell on another person, making them into a bull, or a deer, or a dog, or an ape, forcing them to live as a human being in a form not their own. When a spell is cast on someone, they lose particular capacities, but not all of them. The calligrapher who is turned into an ape can still do calligraphy, and play a good game of chess, but he is unable to speak and say who he 'really' is. The son who is turned into a bull still knows he is a human son, and who his father is, even though his father does not recognize him and thinks the bull is merely an animal to be slaughtered. These animal-humans who are victims of magic spells cannot break the spell themselves. Another character must figure it out, usually a person who also has the power to undo spells that someone else has cast, transforming the animal back into a human form. There are always those who don't recognize that the bull or the deer or the ape or the dog is really a human being. Only characters with special insight perceive this, characters who have greater wisdom, and act on that wisdom to break the spell and deliver the human victim from its imprisonment in animal form. Their wisdom lies in their understanding that the material shape of the body

Capturing the sheep, the men argue about what to do with it.

does not disclose the essence of the creature. People keep their human identity even though they inhabit another physical body with another, alien shape. As well, this wisdom is something akin to a subliminal knowledge, an awareness that differs from rationalist concepts of consciousness. It might be described as a wisdom that grants a higher degree of awareness to subconscious knowledge than most rationalists are prepared to admit.

In *The Suitors*, the story of the sheep is told in a way that reflects the animal-human characters of Persian literature. The sheep begins as merely a sheep, one of a flock, and becomes increasingly anthropomorphic as its story develops. The sheep's story begins the film. In the opening scenes, before the viewer sees or even knows of Mariyam, a group of four men take a ride in the country to see farmland that one of them has just bought. Standing on the neighboring farm, a sheep farm, looking at his new land, one of the men decides to take one of the sheep and bring it back to his apartment in the city. He and another friend chase the sheep around the field in a comical and chaotic scene—the sheep is harder to catch than they expected. Finally they separate one sheep from the flock and lead it back to their car. It takes all four of them to hoist it into the back of the station wagon. They grab its wool at the four corners of its back and lift it in unison—an act that seems evocative of ritual. VL said that this is the moment when the film emotionally engaged her. It is the moment when the sheep becomes "a prisoner in the car," as NC put it. The camera focuses on the imprisoned sheep looking out the window as the suitors pile into the car and head back to Manhattan, still quarreling about whether it's appropriate to take someone else's livestock. We know from what they have said that they intend to sacrifice the sheep in honor of Haji's return, and then make a meal of it—"Wait 'til you taste the kabobs I make out of her!" brags Muhammed. However, the sheep's fate is much postponed in the narrative that follows, giving the viewer a chance to know this sheep, often in amusing and endearing ways. As the viewer becomes acquainted with this creature, there is also time to wonder whether the men will really go through with it, since a couple of them were opposed to taking it in the first place.

The sheep is the subject of several close-ups in the film, the first of which occurs during the ride back to the city. As they cross a bridge going into Manhattan, the camera is inside the car with the sheep, as if both were sitting in the car together. The sheep looks out the window, then directly at the camera, not just once but several times. Consequently, viewers make eye contact with the sheep as if they were looking at themselves in a mirror. Such an image, the cinematic equivalent of direct address, is rare in film. Actors do not look directly at the camera as the sheep does here. This eye contact invites an equivalence, a humorous identification, between the viewer and the sheep. It is the film's moment of the Lacanian mirror stage, but its import is quite different. This is no perfected image of a human body. Its physical shape is not even human. The sheep is both a comic and a tragic figure, ignorant as well as innocent, symbolizing the dumb creature in all of us that is imprisoned, wasted, and cannibalized by cultural practices. The sequence of images involving the sheep are the most realistic images in the film, extraordinary animal cinematography that captures every movement of the sheep's face. Yet, because of the direct address of eye contact with the viewer, the sheep evokes an act of imagination that is profoundly figurative rather than literal, rendering in cinema an anthropomorphic sheep that is very similar to the animal-humans in the *1001 Nights*. "You're very interested in how the sheep is feeling. There's no words. It's very powerful," KL remarked about the effects of these and other close-ups of the sheep. A close-up shot is traditionally used to emphasize the emotions of a character. Paradoxically, the realistic cinematography provokes a strong act of imagination. Viewers saw the sheep as fully a character in the film—"she had such a sweet face!" (GB). JD imagined (out of what depths, one wonders) that "the hair on the top of its head was combed and arranged like a hairdo. I thought that was a strong female cue." For CK, also describing its wool as "hair," the sheep was the quintessential wild thing:

> The sheep at the beginning I thought was just beautiful! All the hair around the sheep's face, and then the sheep in the car, his eyes or her eyes—I can't remember if it was a her or a he—but the sheep anyway looking out of the car with those big wide eyes, and the wild thing captured and was going to

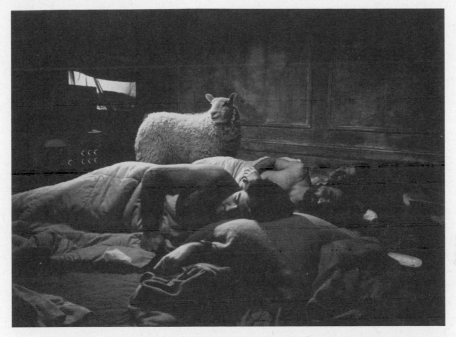

The sheep in the apartment. The men are asleep. Photo: Patrick Gries.

be sacrificed, I thought that image, particularly because the sheep had all that long curling hair around it, was stunning!

This understanding of the sheep is also encouraged by the way the men, themselves, treat it. Back at the apartment, as they open the door, the frisky sheep plunges headlong into the room, and they run after it again. They give it a collar, feed it and get water for it, generally fussing over it and exclaiming upon "her beautiful eyes." PN observed, "You get the feeling that they like the sheep. It's not just an object they're going to slaughter. It's precious to them." KL noted that "they talk about the sheep as if it were a very attractive woman." The more the sheep is the focus of human attention, the more anthropomorphic it becomes.

After the sheep arrives at the apartment, Mariyam's husband, Haji, calls from the airport, and the men go to pick up their friend and his new wife, Mariyam. On the return from the airport, the cinematography draws a formal parallel between Mariyam and the sheep by photographing Mariyam riding in a car from the same angle as the sheep was photographed, also crossing a similar bridge into Manhattan. The formal likeness is prominent, and viewers readily saw an equivalence between the woman with the veil and the sheep, drawing imaginative parallels despite the obvious physical differences between a woman and a sheep. NC was struck by "an extra-ordinary likeness of the face of the sheep and the heroine, the girl, which was very poignant, especially the sheep in the car, the prisoner in the car, and that the girl herself then was a prisoner in the car, in another car, but the same face looked out—of confusion." Because Mariyam and the sheep never representationally appear together in the same scene, because parallels are drawn only by parallel composition of the frame, the similarity between the two is generated only at the imaginative and interpretive level. The idea of similarity is the effect of montage. And beyond the similarity between Mariyam and the sheep is the unstated similarity—indirectly expressed in the numerous comments about the eyes of the sheep—that the mutual gaze between animal and viewer is itself a bond of importance.

The story of the sheep in *The Suitors* also involves another cultural tradition that plays upon the interchangeability of animals and humans: that of the religious patriarch Abraham, who intends to sacrifice his son Isaac to honor God, then decides instead to sacrifice a sheep in Isaac's place (a story that belongs alike to Muslim, Christian, and Jewish religious heritage). Islam is a religion that, in some areas, still includes animal sacrifice among its practices. In modern Iranian Muslim culture, the sacrifice of a sheep is a way of honoring a guest, "the most respect they can show you" (LF). A professional with a special knife for quickly cutting the jugular is hired to come to the house, and the sheep is sacrificed in front of the home at the arrival of the guest. The honored guest then steps over it to enter the home. The slaughtered sheep is cooked and either eaten at dinner at the home or given away as food for the poor (LF, BH). Although the slaughtered sheep is eaten for food, it isn't killed for reasons of hunger. It is a ritual killing, an Islamic ceremony to show respect and honor, and giving the food away to the poor emphasizes that the family who performs this ceremony is not in need of food when they do it. Some Iranians I interviewed were quick to point out that this ritual is not universally practiced by Muslims. They said their own Muslim families in Tehran never performed it, nor did their neighbors, but they did acknowledge that it was an accepted ceremony in "some other neighborhoods" in Tehran. Someone who had grown up with this practice explained that, when you are accustomed to it, you don't notice it. For another Iranian Muslim who had not grown up with it, but found himself thus honored on one occasion, "it was horrible" (BH).[22]

In *The Suitors* the men intend a ritual sacrifice to honor Haji on his return. ("Haji" is a name given to anyone who has made the pilgrimage to Mecca.) However, the sheep remains a strongly anthropomorphic creature even in its last moments. The four men take it into the bathroom, which becomes quite crowded. With the camera placed at a sheep's-eye level, representing the sheep's point of view, there is another close-up of the sheep's

The sheep-killers.

face as one of the men hands it a bowl of water. The viewer looks up at the men as they hover over the sheep. The sheep is friendly with its captors and innocent of their preparations. The sound of the knife being sharpened means nothing to it, and it licks the water falling off the blade as they clean the knife under the bathtub faucet. There is confusion and disagreement among the men about how the sacrifice should be done. They want to face Mecca but aren't sure which way it is. They get a compass and they take the sheep part way out of the bathtub to turn it in the proper direction. Through all this the sheep remains unsuspecting and continues its antic ways. It is not until Ali has the knife at its throat and is feeling hurriedly for the bone that the sheep realizes in fright what is happening and tries to resist. The camera cuts away to the men, but we still hear the sounds of the sheep's struggle as its feet kick the side of the bathtub in a frenzy. Then the live soundtrack is taken off as blood spurts up at the men and soaks their white shirts.[23]

In all, the ritual is rather shabbily carried out, and even viewers unfamiliar with the ritual perceived this. WL, though recognizing it was "a sacrificial lamb," nonetheless found it "really shocking" and "emotionally tough to watch." So did GA, who commented, "It's supposed to be some kind of ritual, but that doesn't help much." KL summarized the thoughts of many viewers:

They don't have the sacrifice right. Where's Mecca? They're lost, they don't really know where they are. The sacrificial act of killing the sheep, it's not a sacrifice. They're trying to pretend it's a ritual, but it's not. The ritual has broken down. It's not a sacrifice. It's just a killing, a senseless, gratuitous killing.

Although viewers experienced different degrees of anguish, they found the killing repulsive, not only a sacrifice gone wrong, but an act that was morally wrong in itself. Not a sacrifice, just a murder. ME said, "It seems like an outrage to murder something that doesn't have any way to protect itself, and has done nothing wrong." Rather than an efficacious religious ritual, it is a gratuitous killing that is immoral and inherently repellent. As KL acutely observed, "It's a criticism of sacrifice as a rotten basis for action." GB recapitulated her thoughts on the scene through the prism of Mariyam's later means of escape. The sheep, unlike Mariyam, is hopelessly trapped:

> She was so defenseless. You knew that it was just a done deal, and she couldn't reach out and stab them, you know. They had really ganged up on her, too. It was a gang violence type of thing, really. I mean even though they did it in the religious, sacred way of the killing, I just felt really bad for her. She was caged. She wasn't in a suitcase, but she was in this bathtub, she couldn't move. And sheep are notoriously dumb anyway. The only way any sort of sheep will be happy will be with a flock and they took her away from her flock. She really was alone. It was just really an unkind thing to do to her. They do give her stuff to eat, but the terror of it!

In the terror of it, it is indistinguishable from an execution. Haji, the honored guest, seems thoroughly repugnant when, after the slaughter, he lounges in the apartment waiting for the meal and remarks on how much he looks forward to eating "lamb's head soup."

The story of the sheep dismantles the normalization of terror that covers over the violence of terrorism. The veneer of sacrifice gives way and appears as just that—a veneer to conceal a violence that cannot be justified or contained within the symbolic structure of sacrifice. Viewers abandoned the interpretation of a legitimate or efficacious sacrifice as the depersonalized message turns out to be, through the anthropomorphic sheep, quite personal after all. Rejecting the interpretation of sanctioned sacrifice, they searched for their own alternative understanding—a murder, a senseless killing, gang violence. While alternative interpretations varied, they had in common the idea that the killing was wrong, that the story shows a violation of an innocent life that cannot be justified.

What they also shared was a sense of the victim's isolation, the sheep taken from the flock and made a prisoner in the car. Or, as NJ put it, "the

The SWAT team breaks in. Photo: Patrick Gries.

sheep's out of its element in the apartment." This interpretation is suggestive of what happens to the sacramental person or object in its conversion
and subjection to spiritual power. It, too, is taken out of its element of ordinary life, as the ordinary bread is transformed in the sacrament. These
interpretations also take a materialist perspective on the ritual: the victim-
object loses rather than gains something in this joining to a spiritual purpose. It is not redeemed, but irrevocably lost, as the sheep is not redeemed
but simply killed. Viewers were acutely aware that isolation is the threshold event that initiates the sheep into sanctioned victimage. For KL, who
did see the SWAT team raid as a terrorist act, isolation—in the sense of
being taken out of the ordinary—was also key. She explained, "you could
feel the isolation of the Iranians," and explained further why:

> The combination of crowds of New Yorkers, interspersed with the police.
> The police seemed like demons, from another planet. They're avengers. But
> it's of course random, gratuitous. It also suggests they're rather evil. You go
> back and forth between ordinary humanity and something that's not ordi-
> nary at all. The comedy reinforces the threat by sheer contrast. It's interest-
> ing they take time to vacate the building. It's just about as long as it would
> take to empty that building. You think that must be it, and then yet more
> people come down. There's a kind of concern for individual life as long as
> you belong. But if you don't belong, wham! They'll shoot you down.

Ordinary New Yorkers take their ordinariness out of the building with them, leaving the unsuspecting Iranians in their apartment a target for sacrifice.

Unlike the SWAT team raid, which many viewers saw as an "exaggeration," the story of the sheep was interpreted as realistic but not acceptable. The sheep's direct address alters the relation of the film's narrative to the viewer, breaking through the fictional separateness of the film. In Dayan's structuralist terms, it initiates what he thought of as impossible, a recognition of the viewer as the absent one. Here the viewer is drawn out of a profound absence, not only the absence Dayan describes, but the absence of a victim of normalized terror, whose own fears and angers toward that terror have received no voice, no consciousness.[24] Viewers did not accept this act of terror as normal, but instead rejected its social viability and legitimacy, opposing it, however fearfully, as a morally unacceptable act. Some said they cringed and covered their eyes when the sheep is about to be killed—a reaction that did not even occur to them in watching Mariyam with her veil, or the images of nearly nude American women, or even the deaths of Haji and Ali that follow in the course of the narrative. In this sense the story of the sheep plays a unique role in viewers' relation to the film, exposing to visual and emotional consciousness the frightening workings of the normalization of terror. It is the story of the sheep that allows viewers to think about, conceptualize, and oppose normalized violence in practices that are considered legitimate, sanctioned by custom and religion. The sheep, in its direct address to the viewer, evokes the viewer's identification with it. And the last moments of the sheep's existence demonstrate that even a dumb, ignorant, and unthinking sheep will resist.

How Images Move the Story Around

The story of the veil and the story of the sheep move in complicated ways in relation to each other. How they move and where they move has to do with the theory of the image that informs this film. In composing the film, the value assigned to film images in relation to the script was much greater than in the typical American film. In fact, the original script for the film was not words at all, but images, a sequence of drawings. American scripts are typically made up of novelistic scene descriptions and dialogue. Actual images become involved only at the stage of production to get an idea of "the look" of the film or to give the cinematographer some idea of how to shoot a particular scene. *The Suitors* was conceptualized in an altogether different way, beginning with the images that had narrative and dramatic substance, that would carry the weight of the story. The dialogue was added later, as something that facilitated the story but did not itself tell the story.[25]

Ebrahimian described his idea of a script as something that resembled a musical score rather than a book or short story. In working out the plan for the film, the writer/director orchestrates different kinds of images into a piece of music, so to speak, where there are always several things happening at the same time. This differs from the concept of a linear narrative as the organization of a film's story. It presumes, for example, that there are multiple meanings occurring simultaneously, not necessarily conflicting meanings but simply different things happening—something is going on with the violins, something else with the woodwinds, something else with the tympani, and so on. All must be orchestrated into a coherent work of art. As Ebrahimian explained it, there are three kinds of images in a dramatic film:

[1] images of the story that are intrinsic to the story
[2] images added to the story that comment on the story
[3] images that are not shown on the screen but are part of the story and are created by juxtapositions. The last kind of images, the unrepresented images, involve the thematic meanings of the story. These are the ones that make you aware of all your senses, and in this awareness, the meaning of the story comes back to you.

The first kind of images, the images that are intrinsic to the story, serve as the focal points for the story and resonate with emotional and semiotic significance. They are not necessarily images with a lot of action. The first intrinsic image of Mariyam's story is of her fully veiled, saying nothing, standing in front of a U.S. customs desk with her husband. Described in this way, it may seem like an uninteresting image, but it had great dramatic and emotional emphasis for viewers. As CM said, "When you see that, you know what the film is about. And you know that you know." Although the killing of the sheep and Haji's death are intrinsic images, so are images of Mariyam reading magazines or writing a letter to her mother. Mariyam wearing a veil over a negligee makes a scene intrinsic to the story, even if a conventional plot summary would merely describe the scene as the moment when she learns of Haji's death.

It might seem that composing a narrative in images rather than words would leave the audience in doubt as to what is happening, what the events are, but interviews with the audience did not reflect that. In general, viewers agreed on the objective story being told, although they sometimes disagreed about the relative importance of particular scenes. For example, some thought the stabbing of Ali was more important than others did, but all agreed that Mariyam stabbed him. Unlike a film such as Bergman's

Persona, a story of two women that depends strongly on its images and where the audience is uncertain at many points about what has or has not happened, *The Suitors* is very straightforward about events, about what is occurring. It is a simple and easy film to watch, and the basic story is easy to follow, even though there is no important plot point in the story that is carried by the dialogue *rather than* the image. The image is always paramount.

The second kind of images, those added to comment on the story, are not intrinsic to the plot. They serve as moments that crystallize important concepts in the story. The one mentioned most often in viewers' comments was the Persian cat in a travel carrier at the airport near the end of the film. While Mariyam sits and waits for Reza, who is at the ticket counter, a woman with a white cat in a carrier comes in and gets in line behind Reza, setting the carrier down on the floor. When Mariyam sees the woman with the cat, the camera moves in for a close-up of the cat, who peers out through the bars. Next to it the viewer can also see the woman's feet. Wearing black high heels, she taps a foot impatiently. In a typical gloss of this image, BH said of Mariyam, "She's like a Persian cat in a cage who wants to be free." KL interpreted it a bit differently, but with the same general idea in mind: "You see that cat and you immediately think back to the sheep. The cat's trapped in the carrier. The sheep is trapped in the car." LC, who disliked this image (but remembered it), said, "Don't smack my face with symbolism!" HT felt very differently. She said she especially liked "simple metaphors" like this one. Whatever their views, they all agreed on what they literally saw, and their interpretations indicate that they read the image as a symbolic comment on the main story rather than an intrinsic image that furthers the plot. We don't know who the woman is who brings the cat, she and the cat do not appear again in the film, and they have no part in the basic story of the film, which would not be changed if they were not in the film.

Other images that comment on the story are not as clearly demarcated as the cat in the cage, and their effect is more indirect. For example, after Haji and Mariyam get through customs at the airport near the beginning of the film, we see them walking through the airport. Haji is carrying several suitcases and an overflowing shopping bag, cumbersome baggage that he struggles with as Mariyam follows a customary several paces behind him. He seems more concerned with the baggage than with her. Indeed, she seems practically like a suitcase herself, baggage that moves along without having to be carried. The scene comments on the relationship between them, a relationship already established in the intrinsic image at the customs desk, where Haji does all the talking and treats his wife like a valued object he has to declare at customs. There isn't any particular reason to have them walk through the airport together.

Viewers can infer that they do without literally seeing it. The scene introduces the image of the suitcase, here as a commentary, as extra baggage, so to speak, but later on it will become a crucial intrinsic image when Mariyam conceals herself in a suitcase to board the plane to Europe.

The dialogue in the film functions in a way similar to the second kind of images, something added to tell the story. "It's not a loquacious film," HT remarked, adding, "There's whole other levels of communication." Many important scenes, including the last five minutes of the film, have no dialogue at all. In scenes where there is dialogue, it is interwoven with these other levels of communication rather than dominating a scene or the viewer's understanding of a character. Many important ideas in the film do not ever receive verbal expression. For instance, Mariyam never actually says she doesn't want to wear the veil, or that she is ambivalent about getting rid of it, or that she refuses to wear it any longer. CM pointed out, regarding Mariyam's character:

> The motion is what we have to go by—the movements of her face, her facial expressions, and how she moves and where she moves. When she darts into the alley and is looking around very self-consciously and stuffs the veil in her bag—I mean, you know how she's feeling by watching those actions. And it's very effective. She doesn't need to say anything. The motion takes the place of speech.

The audience understands what is happening to Mariyam by watching her actions, her gestures, and her expressions. When she does speak, her lines are usually brief. There are no long meditations from her about the frustrations of immigration or transnational complexities, or even about her own state of mind or emotions.

The viewers' observations reflect Ebrahimian's concept of a character's dialogue in cinema:

> The verbalization of those emotions are anti-cinema, anti-filmmaking. I mean when somebody tells you what they're thinking, you're not really— you pretend that you're at their center but there is really no center anyway. Because from moment to moment things shift, and every moment is different in its essence. So, to say that the character has an interior—you know, when some characters have interior monologue, and they explain what they have gone through or what they're going through, there is a falsehood to that because from moment to moment things shift. So, when you have this judgment of a character from an interior thing, it's a pretending. It's not really the character's interior. We don't get any closer. We're pretending that we're getting closer. I think when we get close is when we find moments where the character is reacting to what she is offered or he is offered. And what that resonates, what that does to them. We see if they step this way or that way, if they move this way or that way. . . . Because

again, when a character just tells you what they're thinking or what they're going through, it's forcing you to accept that this is it, this is what exactly happened. But the fact of the matter is that you want to say, this happens but there is more, there are other things that are involved.

When characters have dialogue, this is part of the story, but it doesn't tell us exactly what is happening. Ali, the prospective bridegroom, presumptuously tries to speak this way, laying out for Mariyam on the eve of their wedding what their marriage will be like, speaking his mind. She not only refuses what he says. She stabs him in the back mid-sentence. As GB described it:

> He just kept talking nonstop, and he wasn't even looking at her. He was just spouting off his plans for the two of them, that he had made for the two of them. He was just talking away. Nothing existed in the world but what he had in his mind.

GB thought of the stabbing as "the only thing that could stop him talking." As Ali speaks his state of mind, trying to force Mariyam to accept what he says simply because he says it, he seems pathetically unaware that there are other things, and other people, involved.

The third kind of images are the images in the film that are not shown on screen, but are created by juxtapositions. They differ from the first two kinds of images because they are "unrepresented" in the material film. Ebrahimian creates a tension between representation and the thematic meanings of the narrative by attributing thematic significance to this last kind of images. These images are *related* to the images shown on screen and are generated by them, but they are not identical with them. Sometimes this is called the rhythm of the film, which exists at the conceptual level of viewing, and is something different from the mechanical speed at which the film is shown. It refers instead to the progression of ideas, to the momentum that builds as the viewer takes in the ideas of the film, understanding connections between images, reading juxtapositions in a meaningful way. Sometimes in multiple meaningful ways, as the viewers' comments reflected when they spoke about reversals, transformations, and convolutions. Part of the action of this film is at this level of juxtapositions, where there is a lively interaction of images, where images sometimes reverberate like concentric circles in a pond. The splash of the stone, the shot, is only part of what you see, generating much more beyond itself. It is the lively action created by juxtapositions that make the chronicle of events only one dimension of what is happening in the telling of this story.

The influence of Persian narrative tradition is evident in the activity of juxtapositions in this film. As the director explained it, "in Persian fiction, you make up this world. Realism is not the intention. In this make-believe world there is more truth hidden than if you tried to be realistic or applied realism to the characters." This is the quality that KL thought of as "like a fable." LC commented on the editing style of the film: "There's no transitions. You don't see people moving from place to place. Like, she's on the beach, and then she's on the road. It lifts it out of the normal." In the way it cuts from scene to scene, the fictional narrative presents a fictional idea of space as well. These juxtapositions free the image from any single concept of a unified space in which the action occurs, inviting more playful combinations of images than is possible in a realist film. Even the elements of the film that do seem realist are drawn into it. As LC observed, "even something mundane—like the scene at the gas station—it looks different. There's something unfamiliar. It didn't feel familiar. I felt transported into something. It was a different way of looking at it." JD, also commenting on the style of juxtapositions, described it as a "sense" that there is more happening than what is literally seen. The juxtapositions invite the viewer to consider the space and events beyond what is represented, to enter the realm of the unrepresented as a real part of the story: "It always changed scenes abruptly. The editing was very noticeable. I liked that. It gave a sense that, these are the important scenes, but there are other things happening, other things are going on." The unrepresented images do not conflict with what is represented. This is not a deconstructive subtext. Like the editing itself, which is noticeable *while* the viewer follows the narrative, the off-screen space is noticeable while the viewer is watching what is on screen. There is a juxtaposition, as it were, between on-screen space and off-screen space. In this regard, the entire film is an open form at its most basic level of conception. This openness allows the viewer plenty of access to the realm of the third kind of images.

It does, however, take time to get there. As Ebrahimian explained of this kind of film, "When the film ends, a thinking process starts. There are afterthoughts. American film doesn't have that." With *The Suitors*, viewers needed time after the film to think about the film. I generally interviewed people several days after they had seen the film, and always waited at least one day. Some viewers who were impatient to be taped commented on the wisdom of waiting. For example, LC described her slow crescendo of response:

> It's not the kind of movie that, as you're watching it, you really are following it, because it seems like a real simple movie. But afterwards I laid on the couch and thought about it, and then this morning when I woke up I thought about the movie, and it did unfold as I thought about it more. I saw more connections. It definitely became more eloquent in my mind than when I was watching it. The visuals lasted in my mind longer than the dialogue.

TG had a similar impression. The apparent simplicity of the film, which makes the film easy to watch, also in time provides access to more complex interpretations:

> I was quite interested in my own response because, immediately after seeing it I had one set of interpretations, and then as I woke up this morning, I had a whole different series of interpretations. When I left last night, I thought it was a wonderful and powerful statement about the oppression of women and I thought that was quite wonderful but not very subtle. Then this morning when I had my second set of reactions, the film seemed far better to me because it seemed much richer when I thought more about it.

The experience of viewing lasts longer than the physical time it takes to see the film. Seeing the material film is a satisfying experience in its own right, with its own kind of closure, but seeing goes on after that, too, as the unrepresented images gradually cohere and take on a deeper meaning. This experience is something more than the resonance of a good film that lingers in the mind. Viewers did not feel they had fully seen the story, understood the story, until they had had time to think about its paradoxes and reversals.[26] For TG above, it wasn't until the next day that she realized it was the men who died in the film, not the women, and that the story of the sheep had altered her understanding of the entire film.

Viewers create complex juxtapositions in interpreting the film, particularly regarding a primary theme such as the story of the sheep. The sheep's death is an unrepresented image. It is not actually shown or heard in the film's representation. As well, the live soundtrack is taken off and music is heard in its place. Simultaneously the camera shifts away from the animal, yet still maintains a sheep's eye perspective, validating that perspective strongly as the camera tilts up at the men killing the sheep, whose shirts are being covered with spurting blood. Though the viewer sees the effects of the killing on the bloody shirts, the killing itself occurs off-screen. Because its death is not literally represented, the story of the sheep ends with a blank, with no representational image of its main character. Its loss of image is also its moment of death. This symbolically enacts the threat of the Western ideology of the image—that without her image a woman is nothing, she ceases to exist. However, off-screen is not 'nothing' in this film because the sheep's death is a crucial moment in the narrative. In effect, it defines off-screen space, the area of the unrepresented image, and makes the viewer aware that that space exists and that it is important. Because the validity of the sheep's perspective in the moment of its death is asserted by the camera angle, the perspective outlives the sheep. Since the sheep's death cannot be dismissed or forgotten, cannot go unnoticed, its off-screen death opens up a continuous thematic space/perspective outside the on-screen represented narrative.

In its image-less condition, the sheep as innocent victim continues to wander through the viewer's interpretations of the film's narrative. As CM said of her experience of the film in general, "You have a sense that there are violations taking place that you can't see." The film takes on a more serious and sinister aspect, as the symbolism of the image-less sheep and its violent death attaches itself to other scenes, expressing the otherwise unexpressed terror that underlies normality. For example, when Mariyam is taken out to Mr. Amin's country house, his wife and Ali's sister Zari (Leila Ebtehadj) try to persuade Mariyam to consent to the arranged marriage. They set about making an elaborate beaded wedding gown for her. The viewer sees them chatting and sewing in the living room, and on another occasion holding the dress up to Mariyam to see how it will fit. What is represented on screen is the conviviality and solicitousness of Mrs. Amin and Zari, but that is not what viewers saw conceptually. For PN, the trim on the wedding dress evoked the sheep: "One thing that struck me, the wedding dress, when Zari the sister was showing the bodice part of it to Mariyam, that looked to me like the sheep. That's the same as the sheep's wool hanging down in this tattered way." PN's parallel transformed the beaded gown into something foreboding, the "tattered" look of sheep's wool, an adornment for an execution victim. KL described the dress-making scenes, and especially Zari holding up the dress to Mariyam, as especially grim:

> The women in the film, the women making the wedding dress, they're actually quite sinister underneath that sweetness. "This dress will fit your body so well"—the claustrophobia really hit me, this idea of having someone force this clothing on you to meet a certain ideal. The women are the agents of this.

NJ described the dress-making scenes as a figurative act of violence:

> They were weaving it around her in the same way this man [Ali the bridegroom] was weaving his lifestyle around her. Trying to mold her and trying to fit her into the clothing to fit the part, that was just as much an act of violence as stabbing Ali.

Viewers expressed a sense that there are violations taking place that you can't see, an underlying terror, by reading these scenes of "sweetness" as a sinister and violent sacrifice of Mariyam.

The importance of unrepresented images is also reflected in the way that gender as a physical characteristic ceases to be definitive of characters. Viewers easily attributed the symbolic role of sheep-killer to women, even though in the literal sheep-killing scene, it is men who kill the sheep.

BT interpreted Mariyam as both sheep and sheep-killer in her apparent passivity toward the impending arranged marriage:

> Her and the sheep, they're similar as being an object of pleasure, you know. The suitors ate the sheep and enjoyed it! They're both objects, part of a ceremony. In the same way a sheep is being sacrificed during that ritual or that sacred ceremony, in the same way the woman is sacrificing her integrity and herself when she gets married because there's no room for any integrity, no recognition of who you are.

Drawing an analogy between the ritual of marriage and the ritual of animal sacrifice, BT saw Mariyam not only as the object of a sacred ceremony, but also as a "woman who is sacrificing her integrity and herself" by allowing herself to be roped into another arranged marriage. TG also saw a parallel that reversed the gender roles of the sheep's sacrifice, describing Mariyam's stabbing of Ali as a repetition of the first death, and Mariyam as the sheep-killer:

> It's a repetition of the first act. She stabs him in the neck or upper back. The men are also being brought up to be slaughtered. . . . The men talk about the sheep in very feminine terms, but both the men and the women are sacrificed or destroyed. Men are sacrificed to this patriarchal system. The men are destroyed literally. This kind of system is killing for both men and women.

That men have an inviolable power of sacrifice and that women are its predestined victims—this is the delusion of men like Ali who themselves becomes victims, in part because the role reversal is inconceivable to them. They are as unsuspecting as the sheep.

Paradoxically, the likeness between Mariyam and the sheep, an unrepresented image, is also the means of undoing the reification of the screen image. Initially, it seems dependent on reification. As HT described it, "The vision of the sheep in the car, and then her in the car, the feeling of a sheep taken to slaughter. That's why I thought she was doomed. I thought she was just going to be a sheep, and she wasn't." HT thought so because Mariyam's journey appears to materially repeat the sheep's. Each is shown in the back seat of a car crossing a large bridge, facing the same direction in the frame, and in the same afternoon light, with the camera at about the same distance and at nearly the same angle in the way each is photographed. However, the parallel between them is drawn without cross-cutting. There is five minutes of film time between the two scenes. This parallelism is not that of parallel action, the typical device used to state binary oppositions in American film. It is a conceptual juxtaposition, not a literal one. Since the scene sequences are separated, it requires a conceptual leap across intervening scenes for the viewer to make the connection.

This perceptual experience initiates the viewer into reading the sheep through conceptual juxtaposition, and juxtaposition in the minds of viewers will become the sheep's means of passage through the film. Very important, this early parallel also establishes a likeness across great physical dis-similarity. The subject of each sequence is thus paradoxically liberated from reification. Its visible physical features, in themselves, are not the basis of comparison. Rather, it is what is being done *to* them—in the narrative, and by the camera in the composition of the scenes—that makes them similar. Viewers, in reading this juxtaposition, learned to make others, to read similarity across gender difference, for example, and in general to stop interpreting people according to what they look like. This was true even for viewers who continued to parallel Mariyam and the sheep through later scenes in the film. GB, commenting on the "women" in the film, which included the sheep, made this observation about them:

> Being in such a strange land, in such a strange place, that was a similarity, too, between the two women of the film. I see much more similarity between the ewe and the heroine than between the heroine and the other Iranian women in the film—very little similarity there, other than the visual.

Mariyam looked like other Iranian women, but she had little in common with them other than her physical appearance, which had come to *not* signify Mariyam's identity for this viewer. The anthropomorphic sheep becomes valuable as the touchstone of refusing reification.

NJ described in detail the progression of changing interpretations associated with the sheep. Her interpretations were characteristic of many viewers' comments, which suggest that the movements of the sheep as an unrepresented image were not random or idiosyncratic, but, as the director says, a part of the film's story. The way NJ described this movement shows more clearly how the montage of unrepresented images works:

> When they were hauling the sheep into the car and taking it over to the apartment, it almost seemed like he was deliberately hitting you over the head with sheep/woman, sheep/woman. You were identifying the sheep over the woman up to a certain point because they slit the sheep's throat and there's blood all over them, and they were talking about, oh look at her eyelashes, so it's almost like you're led down the garden path: Oh, gosh, those sexist Iranian rustics desecrating this innocent kind of animal. And then the minute Haji is shot, then that whole thing spins around, and he's lying there in exactly the sheep's position with his blood dripping in the same way onto his own shirt. I mean that's when he pulls the rug out from under you. If it's signifying anything, this is what it's probably signifying.

Since the sheep's death is not literally shown in the film, when NJ says Haji is "lying there in exactly the sheep's position," she is superimposing the unrepresented image of the sheep, the mental concept in her own mind, on the represented image of Haji lying dead. That is, the parallel is a conceptual one. When she makes this parallel, she also has a sense of the montage suddenly changing in nature—it "spins around on you"—and a different metaphor comes into play—the film-maker "pulls the rug out from under you." The explosion of space implied by these metaphors suggests that off-screen space is conceptualized differently, functions differently in a film, inverts 'over' and 'under' and sets a viewer's mind spinning because it disrupts the space and time of traditional Western linear perspective.

Montage moves the story around, even up-ends the story, keeping interpretation in a constant movement, involved in a process that may seem like subliminal effects. Ebrahimian agrees that the film creates a sense of "subliminal effects," but the important word here is "effects." There are no subliminal cuts in the film. Instead, these intercuts occur figuratively in the minds of the audience as a way of interpreting scenes by creating juxtapositions that are not literally represented on screen. Because unrepresented images can skip over intervening sequences, they break the understanding of the linear sequence as definitive. The linear narrative is still there, but it is only one of multiple ways of reading the story. There is also a continuous dynamic and imaginative relating of different scenes to each other. The representational scenes seem stationary, but they are not. The unrepresented images of montage enable a symbolic and figurative, nonlinear understanding of scenes in addition to (not in place of) the literally represented story.

NJ did not remain long in her conviction that Haji was the definitive sacrificed one. Her interpretation changed again when Mariyam stabs the bridegroom Ali:

> When she was washing the blood off her, that was quite startling! It seems there's such an inherent—I wouldn't say purity, but cleanness of form. To have it mucked up with blood, that was really disturbing. Because it was being multiplied by everything. In the same way, it was multiplied in the bathroom, it was just splattering everywhere, she had it on her face and then she wiped her face, and it was on her neck and it's all over her dress and everything else. It was like she was the sheep-killer at that point.

Mariyam the victim has become Mariyam the sheep-killer. And Ali the bridegroom, the man who had held the knife to the sheep's throat, has himself become the unsuspecting victim. Now the montage functions as exponential expansion. The victim's blood "is being multiplied by everything"—language that is reminiscent of Eisenstein's idea of montage: images don't simply add together. They multiply.[27] Like the blood that NJ describes here, the unrepresented image can move in more than one direction, even splattering onto Mariyam as killer. That the unrepresented image of the sheep is again evoked beyond Haji's death, shows its refusal to come to rest, to become stationary. And, in its refusal to adhere to gender roles (to be stationary in this way), it is a symbol characterized by motion, by the continuous movement of the juxtapositions of montage that move the story around.

As the unrepresented image of the sheep accompanies different characters at different times, it provides a moral commentary on events that frees the interpretation of character from rigid binaries of good or evil. Characters do not have to symbolize a moral position to give the narrative an ethical dimension, because the ubiquitous story of the sheep supplies it. Its unrepresented image moves around according to what is happening, but it never exonerates a character, nor does it exact revenge. When Haji dies, a symbolic object of a summary execution by the SWAT team, he is innocent in the moment, but his other actions are not erased. He is still the man who treated his wife like baggage at the airport, still the man who forced an embrace she did not want, and whose business was being an arms merchant. Through the movement of its unrepresented images, the film condemns any act of violence against another being. Part of the wrong is the idea that a living creature is perceived as an image, as a living symbol whose symbolism is more important than who they are, more important than their very lives. This is wrong. So says the story of the sheep.

CHARACTER AND THE MUTABLE IMAGE OF THE VEIL

Without my asking, quite a few viewers volunteered comments about such things as the placement of the camera, the nature of the screen image, the way the film cuts from scene to scene—all comments about what apparatus theory called the "level of enunciation" as distinct from the "diegesis" of the film. JD, explaining why he liked the film, said of the director, "He put a lot of thought into the form of the movie. The cinematography and the editing—that's what makes it effective. It says a lot about the characters and what's happening." For JD, as for other viewers, the cinematic structure was not distinct from the story. The form of the film was a major part of understanding the characters and events of the film. *The Suitors* draws viewers into an awareness of the film's form to understand more deeply what story is being told. To grasp the film in this way is also a route to comprehending more fully what the director meant when he said of characters, "There is really no center anyway." Although this comment echoes deconstructionist theory, Ebrahimian's concept of character is quite different from a "de-centering" process. This section is about the character of Mariyam as a network of relations, a moving focal point where dynamic relations intersect. It depends strongly on the images and their sequence. Every shot in the film was carefully planned ahead of time by the director, whose knowledge of cinematography is comparable to that of directors such as Polanski and Bergman.

Ebrahimian, who is an admirer of Roberto Rossellini's films, especially *Open City* (1945), adapted many of the features of Rossellini's Italian neo-realism—the use of actual locations, nonprofessional actors, and a cinematography without glamour.[28] Source lighting was employed throughout *The Suitors*, and no filters were used. (That is, the film's lighting consisted solely of available lighting at the location—a lamp in a room, the light coming in a window, the actual daylight outdoors, etc.) These formal values coincide with the quality of realism in the *1001 Nights*, in which the style of narration employs "precise and concrete detail" and "a matter-of-fact way in description, narration, and conversation."[29] As well, the main characters of the tales are often quite ordinary people, without title, money, or renown.

Viewers' descriptions of *The Suitors* reflect these cinematic values, chiefly as an absence of the kinds of artificiality and manipulation that they associated with dramatic films. As KL put it:

> I didn't think it was a documentary, but he had this tremendous feeling for what the streets of New York really look like. It's quite bleak, and that's how those streets feel. I felt it was very honest and accurate. If you've ever been in New York, you knew where you were right away. He has a sense of ordinary architecture. He doesn't make a fuss about these things. He doesn't put anything in unless it's really essential. And it was really nice to see a film in which there's no mannerisms, no self-consciousness of, say, "oh look what I'm doing." It's such a perfect act of looking. Every minute of it works.

KL contrasted the cinematography with the attitude of the film's Iranian community that tries to coerce Mariyam—"What they're out for is Mariyam's soul. If they control her body, they control her soul"—an attitude very similar to the capitalist exploitation of women. By contrast, the cinematography of the film does not seek to control Mariyam: "The way the director photographed her, you get the sense that—the body, it's hers." CM agreed. Even as she was expounding on "the veil of flesh" in the magazine-reading scene, CM commented that the film's own visual portrayal of Mariyam was "not exploitative."

Viewers who focused on the acting contrasted this film with mainstream cinema along the same lines. JD remarked of Mariyam, "She was acting with her whole body, not just her face, the way Hollywood actors do. She was expressive with her whole body." BH, himself an Iranian and with an extensive knowledge of Iranian film, praised *The Suitors* for its realistic portrayals, as "a true representation of Iranian issues and conflicts, and in the types of characters." Commenting on the Farsi dialogue as well as the English, he added, "I liked the way they talk. They really talked naturally. Not like it was scripted."[30] And, he went on, not like literary characters, explaining that Persian literary traditions have influenced other Iranian film-makers to make artistic films that have literary dialogue rather than following the conventions of spoken Farsi. Along these same lines, he thought the cinematography, like the dialogue, distinguished *The Suitors*: "I liked the photography a lot. It was very beautifully photographed. I liked the realism. A lot of intellectual film-makers in Iran, they really get away from realism and introduce too much symbolism." That is, Iranian film-makers have often relied on the represented image to express symbolic ideas—as if one could simply photograph a literary symbol and have it function as a symbol.[31] While Iranian viewers may recognize these images as culturally significant literary symbols, BH's point is that they don't have the same force in cinema and can even interfere with or disrupt the telling of the story. They tend to function like Ebrahimian's second kind of images, images that comment on the story but are not essential to it. The major symbolism of *The Suitors* is instead composed by the montage, the third kind of images that are unrepresented images created by juxtaposition. For BH, the characters, too, were free of the weight of symbolism, which made the film more realist: "The actors played the roles quite well. They didn't exaggerate. All the characters were very true to themselves. There is a human element in all of them. They were not portrayed as good or evil. They just played their roles and you can like them or not. Iranian films have trouble with that." The characters are ordinary people, not larger than life, not wielding the power of good or evil.

What viewers called the realism of the film—the unadorned, documentary-like quality of the cinematography and acting—might seem to preclude any artistic sense of the film, the way in which the image in the frame is a created thing. Realism is generally considered to be incompatible with formal dynamics in the frame and typically works to suppress a recognition of significant form. Images are to be seen through, not seen. Cameras are mechanical devices that allow the audience to look through them to what is supposedly real. To see the image as image is to *not* see the film. Even in Godard's experimental film, *Two or Three Things I Know about Her*, the famous cup of coffee depends on an alternation between realism and form in different frames. The camera shows us first the cup of coffee in a café scene. Then, as the camera moves in very close, the screen is filled with form and color, with swirling shapes that suggest the infinity of a galaxy. However, this emphasis on form takes the viewer out of the realist plot (such as it is), and into another realm of thinking. First content, then form, then back to content as the viewer is returned to the mundane café scene. Viewing the images that compose *The Suitors* is a very different experience from this Godard scene because the realism of *The Suitors* works in conjunction with, not in contradiction to, the formal dynamics of the frame.

Viewers' comments about the realism of *The Suitors* were made in concert with observations about the construction of the image in the frame. They show a clear awareness of the cinematic apparatus and the design of the screen image in conjunction with the story. KL, whom I quoted above, also volunteered that "the interior scenes are all designed to intensify claustrophobia—the colors, the camera angles." BT also described the film as "realistic—they are just relating the story as objectively as possible." When I asked her if she could explain that further, she pointed out camera placement as an illustration of what she meant by a factual, documentary style:

> The whole movie was very factual. It was very documentary-like. The story is like a documentary. The filming was very factual. It didn't lose any filming on aesthetic stuff, you know, pretty pictures. And aesthetic stuff like the camera moving with a person—it would have interfered with the actual stuff. You don't want it moving down the stairs with her. When she comes down the stairs, the camera is at the bottom of the stairs. The camera was very direct, so things would be clear, as is. It is very straightforward. I liked it. You don't want it to be slippery.

What is realistic about the cinematography is its straightforward acknowledgment *that there is a camera*, and that it is depicting a human perspective rather than an omniscient one. The camera is placed at the bottom of the stairs and is stationary—as a person might be who is waiting at the bottom of the stairs for someone to come down. DS made a similar observation about the human perspective of the camera and described its effect. Because of "the camera," she explained, "you weren't just watching. It felt like you were part of the person looking at her." Often the camera in *The Suitors* is like a bystander on a street, or someone sitting in a room, evoking a particular human perspective within the material world, a limited rather than omniscient perspective. The same technique is used by another director that Ebrahimian admires, Chantal Akerman, in *News from Home*.[32]

The use of a stationary camera has multiple effects that radiate within the shot as well as between shots. Whereas in tracking shots the camera seems to adhere to the subject, maintaining an omnipresent surveillance of its subject that negates the movement of the subject, Ebrahimian's stationary camera values Mariyam's movement and gives it more significance in relation to the camera.[33] Within the frame, because Mariyam is photographed in motion, the angle of the shot vis-à-vis Mariyam is always changing, in effect a succession of diagonals (the strongest line of action in the frame) through a single take. This not only emphasizes the significance of Mariyam's movements, encouraging a semiotic reading of them. It also emphasizes her difference from the camera itself. She is another human being, different from the person whose perspective is represented by the camera. The camera asserts a relation between itself and Mariyam, including the analogy of human perspective, but it also asserts a divergence between Mariyam and the camera rather than an identity. It gives the impression that Mariyam has free will in relation to the camera, particularly for the American viewer who is accustomed to traveling shots in outdoor scenes. At the same time, the camera does not deny its own reality. This is cinematography with no center, and no de-centering, because it asserts relationality instead. Neither Mariyam nor the camera is in control to the point of excluding the other (or Other). This use of the camera gives dramatic form to Ebrahimian's idea that "the character is not in the center always. The character is important, but it's not important at the same time, because the mechanics of the storytelling are important. It's really both." His use of the stationary camera to tell the story of a moving figure allows it to be both. The camera work also gives the viewer a heightened awareness of the editing, which is visible rather than invisible in this film, and hence readily available to the viewer's interpretation. The viewer can see the cuts because the viewer can see when the stationary camera has changed its position—no two shots are alike. This breaks the illusion of linear narrative as a seamless totality. The viewer instead sees Mariyam in a succession of moments that are conceptually distinguishable.

In his thinking about the plane of the frame, Ebrahimian contrasts it with the three dimensional space of the set or location. The film image is a two-dimensional surface, "a created thing, made to order—it's make-believe." Rather than suppressing these qualities of the film image, Ebrahimian engages them, plays them up. Not, as viewers noted, with aesthetic indulgence, but instead with regard to the ways they contribute to the meaning of the story and the viewer's understanding of it. Each screen image is made up of both semi-abstract and representational elements. Nothing seems extraneous in the frame because everything fits into a designed image. When someone does something such as answer a door—a plot element potentially as mundane as a cup of coffee—the camera purposefully includes the angles and framing of the doorframe as an important element of the screen design. This is not just a backdrop for the character. It is a way of disclosing how the character is feeling in

Muhammed approaches the door.

that moment. For example, when Muhammed, gun in hand, guardedly approaches the door of his apartment after Haji's death, the starkness of the white door and its rigid angles fill the screen image around him. Surrounded by abstract lines, stark white surfaces, shapes without depth, his shadowy body seems immersed in disorientation, his depth of perception reduced to a peephole—and yet there is no element of the scene that is not at the same time "realistic." The viewer senses his anxious uncertainty about his surroundings, not only from his performance but even more strongly from the design of the screen image as a whole. Instead of splitting content and form, the film uses form to establish content.

The idea that no configuration of the image is purely representational has affinities with one of Iran's oldest and most distinguished visual art forms, carpet design. In several scenes of *The Suitors*, Persian rugs suggestively appear on the floor or walls, or both. The principles informing the screen image itself are similar to these textile designs. Also a two-dimensional art form, many rug designs combine representational images (such as birds, scorpions, leaves, flowers, and fountains) with more abstract geometric designs that contextualize representations in formal patterns of lines, colors, and shapes to make one unitary design. In viewing a rug, one can see representation and abstraction simultaneously. To say that one is a background for the other is much too simple to describe the lively interaction among the elements of the design.

Persian carpets hang on the wall behind a suitor.

A rug design does not foreground representation over other kinds of visual impressions, and discernibly representational elements are always formally linked by shape, color, and placement to other aspects of the design. At the same time, it is possible to keep representational images in focus while considering other aspects of the design. They do not disappear into abstraction when the viewer considers their formal relationships. Instead, these interactions encourage the continuous movement of the eye. Although boundaries are clearly drawn, they are simultaneously made fluid and flexible by analogies of design. A Persian carpet is the textile equivalent of a very complex intra-shot montage.

Viewers of *The Suitors* read the shapes and colors of Persian screen images with an awareness that these were a meaningful and integral part of the film's themes. For example, KL, who praised the film for its realism, was also fascinated by its formal design, describing two scenes late in the film that she related thematically by analogies of shape and color. In the first, she is referring to the sequence where Mariyam escapes from the country house with Reza in the middle of the night. As Reza drives down the highway, the screen shows the darkened view in front of their car:

Going to the motel, just after she's killed Ali, the darkness and the music come at you and it's really enveloping. But also, I remember from the video, yellow is the color of danger. I mean that bright, official yellow you see on warning signs here. You know, "Warning! Dangerous Turn Ahead." I felt the film was saying, okay, she's made this choice. Well, she hasn't made this choice. She's done this decisive thing and from now on, she's going down a road that's completely—you know, there's no sense of direction. That black. It's as if the veil is over everything. Oh yes!—including what's going to happen. At that moment in the film, the yellow posts seem to say, "You're moving in this direction and you can't go back. And you're going ahead and you don't have control over what's going to happen to you." Those yellow posts are also there when she's in the suitcase. It's a recapitulation of that drive.[34]

The dark highway is marked with yellow curve signs that loom out of the night and seem to float in black space. The yellow posts appear in the second analogous scene, where there are thick concrete yellow posts beside the conveyor belt that the suitcase passes as it makes its way to the plane—posts that are especially prominent when the conveyor belt, and the suitcase on it, make a sharp turn. The shots with yellow posts alternate with a completely black screen. While each sequence of KL's analogy has a very different realist content, the formal analogies of color, line, and shape bring out a thematic relation between the two scenes. This form-based montage does not ignore the realist content of either scene or its place in the sequence of screen images. It enhances the emotional intensity and symbolic meaning of both scenes as they are part of the plot.

There are many elements of shot composition that lend themselves to a semi-abstract design in the screen image. For instance, the realism of the source lighting creates many opportunities to design a screen image that is semi-abstract. Source lighting creates shadows, unlike artificial studio lighting (which is usually intended to get rid of them). Significant shadows are associated with older, black-and-white noir films, but the use of shadows can be effective in color, too.[35] In *The Suitors*, as in noir films, people emerge from shadowy corners, or a pattern of shadows plays across part of a face, or a character is silhouetted against a bright window. The pattern of light from a lamp in a room illuminates the edges of someone's body, but leaves the rest of the body in darkness. Every shot that is naturally lit offers some quality of light that can function at a semi-abstract level in screen image design. This is also true for outdoor scenes, where shadows of street buildings play across a city street and reflected images can make car windows opaque.

Aspects of a landscape can be used for their formal tones and shapes as well. When Mariyam sits with Zari on the beach, the two women are photographed against sunlit sand. As Mariyam listens to Zari's harangue about why she should marry again, the camera shows us their view of Long Island Sound: blue water, fuzzy gray horizon across the middle of

Mariyam, carrying her veil, emerges from the marsh grass.

the frame, lighter blue sky in the top half of the frame. It looks like a Rothko painting. After Zari leaves, angered by Mariyam's hostility, Mariyam looks for an escape from the country house through the marsh grass. The screen is filled with the golden stalks of high marsh grass, with Mariyam in a black dress moving through it, searching for a way through. CK was especially struck by this scene, which she read figuratively:

> She goes out to this house in the country, and she's sort of guarded and taken out there by those various women and men, and she's trapped. She's out on Long Island in the marsh grass but they made the marsh grass seem like a prison, too, which seemed like bars, she seemed to be trapped in the marsh grass.

The forms of golden stalks, appearing like a six-foot-high barrier, merge with the form of prison bars as this realist setting becomes a figure for Mariyam's imprisonment in the country house. The symbolism is created from this realist on-location set because of the way it is photographed, and particularly the lighting, the focus, and the way the shots are framed so the stalks fill the screen and surround the black space of Mariyam. When Mariyam finally emerges from the marsh grass, the view of the beach and Long Island sound continues the figurative dimension, too, symbolizing the possibility of freedom.

The one character who most enlivens the screen image with the dynamics of geometric form is Mariyam with her veil. When the viewer first sees Mariyam, she is standing veiled next to her husband at a customs desk at the airport. Mariyam is in the center of the frame, and she is riveting because she is a striking black shape—angular, geometric, and absolutely black. Only the upper part of her face shows. The shape of her body, because it is veiled, is only vaguely suggested by the veil. Because she is still and does not move, and because the black seems almost a flat space without depth, absorbing light rather than deflecting it, she is distinguished from everyone and everything else in the frame. Because she is also standing under bright fluorescent light, the image emphasizes that she is not a silhouette and not a shadow. She presents a striking visual contradiction: Although she is fully lit, the viewer can't see her human figure. What the viewer does see is a character known initially only by her semi-abstract form. This is the only point in the film where Mariyam stands absolutely still. Then she moves, slowly unveiling her face at the customs agent's demand. Her attitude of indifference bordering on contempt is evident in her gestures and facial expressions, and especially in her refusal to look at him. Without saying a word, she rejects his gaze as presumptuous and frivolous, his passport snapshot realism as ridiculous. This initial scene provides a visual vocabulary for interpreting the main character. As she moves from a static image to a figure in motion, Mariyam initiates the character she will be throughout the film, a continuously moving semi-abstract shape.

All viewers thought that scenes of Mariyam in her veil were important to what the film is. LC described her character as "a fluid black space" moving across the screen and talked about the experience of "seeing that black move with whatever was in the background." Mariyam's screen image keeps the viewer continuously engaged with the formal elements of the way the story is told—not just her image within the frame, but the image as a whole. LC explained her own experience of this:

> The background never seemed still either. So somehow they could keep it, the background and the person, so if the two were in motion, somehow the background never seemed really stable. The time when I think of that black fluid space is when she's walking in the city, she's walking to that alley where she's going to shove her veil in her bag. It doesn't feel like those buildings behind her are really still. And yet you get a really clear picture that she's the one, you know, she's moving.

Even the buildings, the most concrete and immovable of images, are not fixed in the viewer's imagination. LC felt that something was being clarified in this unsettling process, that it did not make the film confusing but instead gave it a special clarity. Things come *into* conceptual focus, not out of focus, when everything conceptually moves—"you get a really clear picture." With every move, the image of Mariyam challenges the fixedness of images and their meaning, their static reified state in the media of capitalism. Because this main character engages with the screen image as image, with forms, lines, colors, and shapes in dynamic interaction, viewers look *at* the image instead of looking through it.

Although Mariyam achieves her strongest engagement with the form of the image when she wears a veil, the same idea is kept up in the film even when she doesn't wear it. LC mentioned another instance of the fluid black space when Mariyam is walking down the side of the highway, trying to leave the country and return to her apartment in the city. In this scene (and several others), she wears a long-sleeved, loose-fitting black dress with a long and full skirt, a dress that achieves an effect very similar to the veil. In other scenes she wears a black-and-white print dress—the print is geometric—and this also engages the formal elements of the frame. Throughout the film, Mariyam is partly or fully dressed in black, and "that black" is enough to continue to evoke the viewer's awareness of the image's design. As she moves across the screen, her image interacts with the other elements of design in the frame, setting everything in motion as she herself moves. This does not mean that Mariyam blends into the frame. She is a striking figure in every scene in which she appears. LC pointed out that the sense of Mariyam as a black space is *not* a concept of negative space or "un-space." If anything, it marks her presence, not her absence. The viewer looks *at* her, not through her.

The context of LC's initial recollection of Mariyam as a fluid black space is a scene that many other viewers thought was important, too. As an event in the plot, it is utterly simple: After Haji's funeral, Mariyam goes to the park alone and writes a letter home to her mother—a scene that is quite prosaic, what any new immigrant is likely to do. The distinctiveness lies in the way the story is told here. It defines and articulates Mariyam as a polyphonic character. The letter-writing scene portrays Mariyam as a character who is constituted by a network of relations, whose subjectivity is the intersection of multiple meanings. Viewers described her as free for the first time. As LC said: "She's outside, completely out of the company of—out of that male-dominated culture. She's out in the street without her veil on, writing to her mother. It's the first time you ever see her in an actual sense of liberty." HT expressed a similar view: "When she goes into the park—that's when she stops being a sheep." She is free, not just because she is alone, and not because she's writing to her mother, but because of the *way* this is presented. It is the way the story is told that prompts viewers to say that she is outside "that male-dominated culture."

The shot sequence of this complex scene interweaves several different situations. (1) Mariyam cautiously leaves her apartment building and walks out into the street, with the sound changing from Iranian music to New York street sounds. She's wearing a black-and-white print dress and a black blazer. As she walks, she pulls off her headscarf and settles it on her shoulders. (2) The scene cuts back to her apartment door, where Ali is knocking. Realizing she's not inside, he sits down on the stairway to wait. (3) Mariyam walks into the park and sits down on a bench. She starts writing a letter to her mother in Iran. (4) In a whispered voice-over, Mariyam speaks the words that she is writing. The audience also hears her writing—the sounds of the pen scratches on paper. After a few sentences, the scene cuts away to (5) Mariyam on an earlier day, veiled and walking briskly down a crowded city street, the wind blowing the veil against her body. The live soundtrack of the crowded street is taken away and the audience hears only the whispered voice-over of the letter's contents and the pen scratches. The letter is about Haji—the audience finds out he was an arms merchant— and about Mariyam's life in New York, how she has decided to stay. In the accompanying street scene, she walks faster and then suddenly stops when she passes an alley. She ducks into the alley and, standing against the wall, looking cautiously about her, she takes off the veil and stuffs it in her purse. She then moves out of the alley and continues down the street, now at a calmer pace. (6) The scene cuts back to Mariyam on the park bench, finishing the letter, then cuts to (7) Mariyam crossing another street after leaving the park. As the voice-over signs off the letter, street sounds re-enter on the soundtrack, and Mariyam approaches two American men to ask them where the post office is. They are rude and taunt her instead of helping her. She hurries away, (8) returning to her apartment where she finds Ali outside the door. She is surprised to find him and treats him curtly. He chastises her for going out alone without her veil.

The structure of the sequence achieves complexity slowly, layer by layer, as each narrative element is introduced into this telling of several stories at once. It ends in a similar way, with a gradual release of each of its narrative threads. The scene sequence gives the viewer three interwoven versions of Mariyam, each with its own equilibrium of images, words, and sounds: Mariyam unveiled, going to the park and writing the letter, then returning to her apartment; Mariyam veiled, walking down the street and then taking her veil off; Mariyam in a whispered voice-over writing to her mother back in Iran. The montage is complicated because the voice-over is not an authoritative, transcendent voice, or even a unified voice. The viewer realizes from the juxtapositions of words and images that the voice-over is not a privileged authority in this mix of narratives.[36] The words she speaks in voice-over are an interior monologue with its own imaginative space and tempo, its own soundtrack, related to the woman in the park through the sounds of the pen scratches and a close-up of her letterbook—the viewer sees her writing—but the interior monologue is not identical with the woman Mariyam seated on a bench in the park. There is an absence of synchronous sounds from the park or the street. Moreover, the content of the letter, while it gives the audience some information about recent events, also excludes some information. The voice-over whispers about Haji's death, "I don't know why I could not bring myself to cry." Then she mutters, "No, that's not good" and the audience can hear her pen crossing out the words. The letter is censored. As we see Mariyam go into the alley and take off her veil, we hear ironically in the voice-over, "I can manage my own daily routines." Mariyam wants her mother to think she is still being a good Muslim woman, but the viewer sees something else on screen—a new daily routine of going without her veil. The varying juxtapositions of word and image do not invalidate the letter because it still represents one aspect of Mariyam's character, a partial view of her, one way of knowing her among several. It is another narrative thread that tells us something, but not everything, about Mariyam. In its relation to the other scenes of Mariyam in this sequence, the voice-over functions as one more asynchronous sound in a disjunctive soundtrack that conveys a partial view of Mariyam, just as the other narrative parts of Mariyam convey only a partial view of her.

When the director says of his concept of character that there is really no center anyway, this is not to say that Mariyam has no interior, only that she has no fixed and immutable interior, no single trajectory of identity that characterizes her. How is one version of this polyphonic character related to another? Not in any linear or single-minded way, not in any overarching narrative voice that polices what the viewer sees. Like the placement of the camera, the sound and the screen image convey partial perspectives, not an omniscient narration. Within the larger context of the narrative, this scene sequence is the first time the viewer sees Mariyam intentionally take her veil off in public. By placing such an important plot element in this complicated context, it prevents the viewer from assigning only one meaning to it, or making it definitive for the story. For a viewer like LC, who described herself as someone who usually follows a film through its dialogue, taking the meaning of the image for granted, the letter-writing scene was a dizzying experience. Mariyam, not controlled by words, becomes a moving black space, fluid rather than static, and even the buildings behind her seem to move because they are no longer reified images. When voice and image part company in the way they do in this sequence, words do not control the visual story and words do not function as a superior form of cognition. Moreover, the narrative is not linear. Instead it is polyphonic: Each moment is a unique synthesis of multiple communications that are always in motion, always changing. No single verbal or visual articulation can distill the meaning of any moment, much less characterize all moments in one meaning. Every part of the sequence is inherently multi-dimensional, a web of intersecting semiotic structures.

Ironically, Ali is the one who is isolated by this sequence. The sound of his sharp knock on the door, the noise of his feet on the hallway floor—these sounds are synchronic. His scenes do not participate in any way with the other scenes in the sequence. The boundaries are absolute. His scene does not overlap or share space, sound, image, or tempo with any other element of the sequence. From the perspective of Mariyam's liberty, he appears severely circumscribed—not only in what he thinks but also in what he knows. Although he bookends the sequence, the viewer has the impression that he has no idea of what has come in between. He talks patronizingly to Mariyam when she returns, telling her to put on her veil and not go out without him. Put another way, Ali lays claim to the conventions of the traditional male character of linear narrative, namely, the presumption of authoritative consciousness. He talks down to Mariyam like the omniscient narrator of her life. Like other Iranian suitors who visit her, he sees Mariyam as a marital object whose only identity is female sexuality. The veil expresses her value, but only in this way. Within the paradigm of Iranian Muslim fundamentalism, this is the veil's invariable signification. For Mariyam herself, as an Iranian woman she is covered up by the fact of her sexual identity. The physical encumbrance of the veil signals her entrapment in a system of meaning that pejoratively represents her individuality, her thoughts, and her emotions as excess.

The Suitors not only rejects the material practice of veiling through Mariyam's actions in the story. The design of the screen image also rejects the invariable signification that underlies the fundamentalist ideology of the veil. Like the veil she wears, Mariyam is a mutable image, not fixed in meaning, not a reified thing. Mariyam does not control the screen image, nor does she generate it. She does, however, fully participate in it, not as negative space but as the polyphonic character who emerges fully into view in the letter-writing sequence. The different versions of Mariyam are all her, but they cannot be reduced to any single identity, any single space, or any privileged transcendent voice, even her own.

THE STABBING

Murder scenes in cinema are usually definitive events. They can punish moral transgression, determine who has power, achieve narrative closure,

Ali.

define who is good or evil, who is knowledgeable, who is just or unjust, what is possible or not possible. Whatever its agenda, the murder scene typically accomplishes it with absolute clarity, with epistemological certainty. By contrast, *The Suitors* contains a murder scene that is controversial and diffuse in its meaning. While it is in many ways the most American scene in the film, its impact differs from the significance of murder scenes in most American films. Viewers offered many different motives for why Mariyam stabs Ali at the country house. They did not even agree on whether it actually was a murder scene. Some were sure it was a fatal wound, others were sure it was not. Far from bringing closure or certainty to the narrative, the murder-that-is-also-not-one is a complicated scene that spins off in many directions, all the more so because it is the last time Mariyam wears the veil.

The stabbing scene occurs about two-thirds of the way into the film, as the culmination of the middle section when Mariyam gains a measure of freedom for herself, only to find new suitors trying to put her back into a traditional wife's role. During the opening section of the film that concludes with Haji's death, the story of Mariyam and her veil is primarily about whether she can or will ever take the veil off. After she is on her own, the theme of the veil is reversed. It becomes a question of whether Mariyam will put *on* the veil, and what or who will make her do that. The letter-writing sequence is the moment when the reversal occurs, and this begins the middle section of the film. These scenes typically begin with Mariyam *not* wearing a veil, and at some point in each scene she puts it on. That point is invariably when a man enters the scene who is not her husband or her relative—all of the men in the film after Haji dies. Mariyam puts on her veil in conformity with Iranian prescriptive practice. As these scenes emphasize, it is a practice enacted by a woman, but evoked by the presence of any man who is not her relative. Although Mariyam seems to control the veil, in fact it is men who, by their presence or absence, control its use. Furthermore, while it may be isolating for the individual woman, it is not an isolated act. On the contrary, it is a very public act.

For example, when Haji's friends (who collectively killed the sheep) become Mariyam's new suitors, each visits her apartment. She puts on the veil before answering the door—an increasingly comical progression that emphasizes Mariyam's veiling routine and how she must treat her own home as public space. NJ recounted the experience of seeing this sequence in the theater:

> It wasn't individual people coming to propose. It was this woman being bothered by the doorbell ringing constantly. It was like one laugh at the first one, it kept increasing through the second and the third. By the fourth it was getting hysterical throughout the whole audience because it was the same thing. It's just reacting to one particular situation that kept getting translated into these different forms. You get up, put the veil on, bring out the coffee and sit down and talk to them. Their actions were individual, but it was clear that we were supposed to see it the way she did, as simply this bothersome, repetitive group of men.

The sense of repetition comes most strongly from Mariyam's repeatedly taking the veil from the hook by the door and wrapping it around her, pulling and tugging it to make it fit correctly before she opens the door for yet another suitor. The humor of it is indicative of how comfortable the audience has become in viewing Mariyam without her veil since the letter-writing sequence. In this section of the film, the audience sees the veil as a ridiculous and incapacitating encumbrance that Mariyam herself doesn't want or need. If she is belittled by it, the visiting men who provoke her to put it on are even more belittled by it. Having any of them as a husband would likewise be a ridiculous and incapacitating encumbrance. Where at the beginning of the film the audience had interpreted Mariyam as all veil and no woman, submissive to her husband, now she is all woman without a veil and in no need of a husband. The visits of the suitors establish the theme for the story of the veil in this section. The veil may be physically wrapped around a woman by her own agency, but a woman's veil is not her own.

Reza.

The only Iranian man who gains Mariyam's confidence is also the only one who does not behave in a traditional way. As JD put it, "Reza is really the only one who doesn't push her to come to him for guidance, protection, domination, or whatever." When Reza visits Mariyam, his intentions are more ambiguous than those of the suitors who have preceded him. He has dropped by to return some of Haji's books. He doesn't propose marriage, and he does not criticize Mariyam when she lets the veil fall away from her head as they talk. He tells her that he can't get along with Haji's other friends and is striking out on his own, planning to leave for Europe. When Mariyam asks if she can go with him, he accepts her offer but asks her to keep it a secret. She smiles and agrees. It is Reza whom she calls for help in making her escape from the country house after she stabs Ali.

After Reza's visit, Ali comes again to secure Mariyam's acceptance of his marriage proposal. Ali is a tentative and somewhat reserved man, acting on Mr. Amin's urging. Mariyam refuses to let Ali come in. Talking to him through the door, without her veil on, she tells Ali to go away and leave her alone, asserting her independence. In retaliation, Ali becomes coercive, returning the next day with his sister Zari and Mr. Amin. The viewer sees this group of Iranians from a distance, ushering Mariyam out to their car. She is fully veiled. It is a polite abduction—there is no physical roughness and Mariyam offers no overt resistance. Nonetheless, viewers saw Mariyam as being kidnapped at this point. She is taken to Mr. Amin's spacious and expensive house in the country, where she is then kept for the wedding to Ali. It is not clear who all these Iranians are at the country house, but viewers referred to them as "the Iranian community" or "those people" rather than a family.[37] One thing is clear: they are complicit in Mr. Amin's plan to have Mariyam wed Ali. The veneer of politeness continues as they refuse to acknowledge their control over Mariyam.

Although viewers disagreed on many other things, they were united in their view that Mariyam was being sorely mistreated. BW said: "I was so disgusted and upset with the assumptions they made! The way they had her all ready to marry this guy without her even being asked. It was appalling!" RL saw it as the motive for the stabbing: "They were holding her there against her will. That's the same thing as a rape or any other kind of attack. I thought just the fact that she was being kidnapped was justification enough for her to stab him." BT was more ambivalent, but also saw the stabbing as a defense against an insidious coercion: "When she stabbed the guy, I don't know—she could have knocked him out. I could see she didn't need to kill him, but for her there is such a building up of frustration and desperation. I can see she had to stop it. It was the only way."

The absence of any physical injury to Mariyam made the stabbing more problematic for viewers. What Mariyam has to stop is the workings of a culture, not the malignant, dangerous acts of one individual. As JD explained:

> I got a sense of conflicts between societal norms and individuals, and between people, but not evil. The people who were holding her back from freedom— that was indifference rather than evil. It was more indifference than malevolence that was the real foe there. That was the real darkness, I think.

Her frustration and desperation stem from the diffuseness of her oppressors and their indifference to her. It's not that they beat her up. It's that they profoundly ignore her as a person when she refuses to consent to the marriage and a way of life she does not want. NJ believed that escape rather than murder was the real solution:

> There wasn't any particular thing to fight against as much as these people that are acting out a cultural network. It makes her stabbing him not as much of a battle. He's just going to be replaced by the next ten people that come along unless she gets out of there.

Mariyam does get out of there after she stabs Ali, but this is why the stabbing scene functions more as a catalyst than as an image essential to the story. The middle section of the film illuminates a cultural situation that makes closure-by-murder impossible—killing one person would have little effect on the systematic oppression she faces. The belief of some viewers that Ali was not killed reflects this dislocation of murder from its customary function as a

Mariyam in the storeroom, brushing off her feet.

resolution of the plot in more conventional films. Viewers felt the lack of closure here—hence the belief that it could not have been a murder.

The failure of the stabbing to become a focal point of plot resolution is also strengthened by an unusual "slasher" scene that precedes the stabbing. On the eve of the wedding, before she stabs Ali, Mariyam steals the wedding dress and rips it to shreds. Moving stealthily around the house alone without her veil, she sees the dress lying on a chair in the living room. She grabs it, runs upstairs, and hides it under her bed. Sitting down at the vanity, she picks up a pair of scissors and starts to cut her own hair off. Changing her mind, she gets out the wedding dress and starts hacking away at it with the scissors, then tears it to shreds, curling her lip in anger. In Persian literary symbolism, the bride in a wedding dress is a common symbol of meaning. The dress symbolizes the poet's words and the bride herself is the meaning, and also the spirit, to which they refer.[38] Consequently, destroying the dress is symbolically weighted beyond its marital value. It is an iconoclastic act aimed at primary cultural meanings, even a destruction of meaning itself. As a plot element, it has far more symbolic resonance in Persian cultural tradition than a woman killing a man would have.

For some viewers, this scene was a more important act of resistance than the murder of Ali that follows it. For Iranian-American BH, "cutting the wedding dress was a strong enough statement" about how she felt and the predicament she faced. The murder was not needed and the stabbing did not make sense to him: "I had trouble with that. I didn't think someone like Mariyam would be capable of killing." He suggested a more culturally familiar plot: "A lot of women in Iran do run away with their lovers when they are expected to marry someone they don't want to marry." He saw this as the basis for Mariyam's plan to escape to Europe with Reza. LF, also an Iranian-American, likewise thought the murder did not make sense in relation to her own cultural experience as an Iranian: "That she just killed him with a pair of scissors—I have not heard of those things. It seemed strange. I don't think very many women in our [Iranian] society are into that kind of behavior, to kill easily. That was a little bit off, that killing part." For LF as for BH, tearing up the wedding dress and making her escape made sense, but the act of murder did not make sense. The stabbing, which they both interpreted as a killing, was a disruption of an otherwise viable plot-line for them.

American viewers, and particularly women viewers, also thought the destruction of the dress was a compelling symbolic act. They were very surprised by it and found it a deeply gratifying scene. For TN, it was the high point of the film: "I *loved* that scene! And the way she curled her lip—that was so good!" Unlike Iranian-American viewers, however, TN also liked the stabbing scene just as much. She construed it as premeditated murder, acting on the intention (as she understood it) that was expressed in destroying the wedding dress. For most American viewers, however, the stabbing was understood as a separate scene, whose symbolism was much deeper and more meaningful than shredding the wedding dress. GA described her sense of considerable escalation when Mariyam turns her iconoclasm on Ali using the same weapon (the scissors): "And then it was like, wow! This is not just about a dress anymore!"

With the stabbing of Ali, the film shifts cultural registers to a distinctly American crisis of meaning. NJ sensed this shift very strongly. She said she was "shocked" when Mariyam tore up the wedding dress, but the symbolism of a woman killing a man by stabbing him did not surprise her. On the contrary, this was culturally familiar territory, something to be expected. As an American viewer, she felt more experienced and knowledgeable than the immigrant Mariyam, as if she were helping the character through an initiation into American culture:

> The weird thing is, you're on the edge of your seat, but in a sort of mentor position. It's like, I know how to deal with these things. I would know how to deal with this. "No, stupid, don't shove him into that." I mean you got to the point where you were like taking over as being a kind of cultural guide through there. I felt very protective of her.

The film juxtaposes two kinds of slasher scenes: first the Persian version, in which Mariyam slashes the wedding dress, then the American version, in which she stabs Ali.

Without significant Iranian precedents, the murder scene borrows from American and European film precedents. For instance, a woman stabbing a threatening male in the back with a pair of scissors occurs in *Dial M for Murder* (1954). *The Suitors* draws on the classic thriller rather than the slasher for its mood, tempo, dialogue, and music. But this is not to say that *The Suitors* merely leaps from Persian to American ways of thinking. These American film elements are deployed differently in *The Suitors*, giving the viewer a sense of familiar American themes shifting into a fundamentally different register, one that finds its meaning within the film's own narratives, the story of the sheep and the story of the veil. Far from assimilating Mariyam into a thoroughly American plot, the film carefully differentiates itself from familiar American themes of the thriller, the slasher, and, as well, the genre of made-for-television domestic-violence dramas—in effect offering a different way to think about violence and the image of a woman.

In the stabbing scene, the veil figures as the focal point of dispute between Mariyam and Ali. Beginning with an exterior shot that shows the house in darkness at night, the film cuts to Mariyam in her bedroom, seated at a desk, still wearing the black-and-white print dress she had on when she stole the wedding gown and tore it up. She hears a knock at the door and asks, "Who is it?" We hear Ali's voice: "It's me." As with previous scenes in this section, Mariyam puts on her veil before she lets him in. The veil seems more than ever like a shroud, as Mariyam is literally hidden by it. With the camera behind her, she appears as a faceless black mass when she approaches the door of the stark white room. When she opens it, the camera, now placed in the hallway, shows her face with the veil pulled closely around it. She greets Ali with reserve, and then asks nervously, "What are you staring at?" These are the last words she speaks in the scene. Ali replies as he enters the room, "I'm staring at your veil. In my presence you need not cover yourself anymore. . . . No need for that. . . . The time for covering yourself from me is over. . . . We're going to get married. . . ." Mariyam's silence is notable as she fails to respond each time Ali pauses for a response from her. Viewers understood her silent refusal to unveil as an attempt to protect herself. As BT described it, "The veil was a wall. She was trying to put him out." In putting on the veil, Mariyam is trying to defend herself by appealing to cultural tradition—she is not yet his wife. Ali is also making an appeal to tradition when he asks her to remove it—she's going to be his wife. Ironically, Mariyam wants the veil on, Ali wants it off—yet another reversal in the story of the veil that emphasizes again that the veil is worn or not worn at the behest of men, rather than by the choice of women. The veil has its female symbolism, but it is a male-coerced symbolism, and this proves to be a flimsy defense for Mariyam.

Mariyam veils herself when Ali (shadow left) comes to her room.

Mariyam backs into the room, slowly retreating as Ali advances. When she sits down, he politely hands her a wrapped gift, then moves around behind her and takes the veil away from her head. Mariyam cringes as he rests it on her shoulders. Telling her that it's time "to talk about our plans for the future," he then takes the veil away from her shoulders, too. Mariyam is now unveiled, but not by her own choice. Although his actions are not violent, the sinister nature of them is unmistakable. In coming to her room and removing her veil before they are married, Ali has assumed an unwarranted familiarity with her, transgressing the cultural tradition he claims to uphold. As DS described it, his removal of her veil seems like rape:

> It's intense! It's incredible! I thought, I could feel that thing around my shoulders, and he pulls it down even further. I felt like he had her totally undressed at that point, and all he'd done was take her veil off. And I thought right then he had already violated her. He didn't have to do anything else.

With an anguished look that is emphasized by the camera, Mariyam gets up with a start—without her veil. Ali sits down, taking her place on the chair. Presuming her consent to their marriage, he then becomes obsessed with his description of their future domestic life. He has found a house nearby, he tells her, and carries on about it in an artificial and poetic manner: ". . . As far as the eye can see, there are trees, hills, water, and the vast sky. Don't call it a house. Call it paradise. . . ." Completely taken with himself and obsessed with a domestic ideal that will make Mariyam his sexual property, he continues more precisely, "The living room and the kitchen face east, the bedroom and nursery face west. . . ." Oblivious to Mariyam, he is unaware that she has circled around behind him and picked up the scissors. She suddenly stabs him, and he breaks off in mid-sentence. Clutching his neck and his back, he groans miserably and falls forward as Mariyam draws back against the wall, aghast at the sight of him.

Mariyam does not kill Ali because her life is threatened. Viewers agreed that Mariyam was not in physical danger, that this was clearly *not* a case of kill-or-be-killed. For many viewers, this was an important and welcome difference. For example, VL commented, "It was good to have that guy stabbed in the back for arrogance and presumption! He deserved it! That's so much better than having physical abuse be the motive." When I asked DS whether self-defense from actual assault would have made for a better plot, she responded:

> I think it would have diminished the movie's message, personally. Because we've already seen so many stories about women who find courage only when they're about to be raped. Or women who find the strength only when they're about to be done in. Then we can say, my god, in the fear of the moment she grabbed the first thing, the frying pan, the gun, or whatever, and that dilutes her role as the heroine. To—just—have—enough. To have him be in a moment of excitement and description, and this is what we're going to do, this is what we need, but he's constantly repeating, you don't have to wear the veil around *me*, you don't *have* to wear the veil *around* me, you don't *have* to wear the veil *around* me. He must have said it ten times and she went over the edge. That was it. No more veil. It wouldn't have mattered who said it. It could have been one of the women. She was not going to do the veil again. I thought the way she did it, pushed to that point, made her more of a heroine and a worthy lesson than just another woman who fights back because finally it hits her she's going to be raped. I'm really sick of those stories.[39]

Her critique of American films about women who kill in self-defense weaves together elements of both slasher and domestic-violence films. What they have in common, what she critiques, is the repetitive focus on life-threatening self-defense, a focus that she found "diminishing" to the woman character, something that "dilutes her role as the heroine." *The Suitors* opens up rather than dismisses the complex issues for women that surround such acts. As DS moved from conventional American stories about rape and self-defense, back to the scene in *The Suitors*, she interpreted the stabbing as part of the story of the veil. Mariyam's motive for action is a refusal "to do the veil again," regardless of whether that means putting it on or taking it off. DS also saw this issue as something different from the gender polarization of women and men that characterizes physical self-defense scenes: "It wouldn't have mattered who said it. It could have been one of the women." For DS, the idea of a culturally imposed symbolic image that is alien to the woman herself is what the story is about and what Mariyam rejects. DS understood the significance of the stabbing in *The Suitors* as the refusal of a cultural ideology rather than a rejection of Ali as an individual or as a man. For DS, the crucial victimization was the ideology of a woman and her image.

By situating Mariyam's act of violence outside the interpretive framework of physical self-defense, dislodging it from its traditional context, *The Suitors* exposes the inadequacy of simple binary oppositions. *The Suitors* is disruptive of traditional polarities, especially that of innocent victim/guilty perpetrator. There was no agreement among viewers as to who was guilty and who was innocent in the stabbing scene. For CM, the guilty one was Ali because, through his actions, he aligned himself with cultural tradition: "Ali tells her not to wear the veil anymore around him. She says okay, and then she kills him. He brought it on himself." She added, "The culture is what killed him—you know, the rules." BT concurred: "Ali was a martyr to tradition." VR saw Mariyam as rejecting the categories of innocence and guilt altogether: "She felt no remorse. That was great!" GB found vindication for Mariyam in her rejection of objectification:

> He was objectifying her so completely. She could have been an inanimate object in his life. The male force, the male domination and objectification of women, that's really what I saw her kill. I didn't really see her kill him as a human being. She was killing the whole idea of it.

GB evoked the earlier parallel of the sheep and Mariyam to make the scene a symbolic self-defense. Observing that Mariyam was being treated the same way the sheep was, GB pointed out that the sheep could not "fight back," but Mariyam could, and did. Her interpretation of physical self-defense, in drawing on the innocence of the sheep, implied that Mariyam does not have this vindicating innocence in her own right.

The evocation of the sheep did not necessarily lead to the conclusion that Mariyam was innocent. NJ condemned the stabbing as "a stupid move," explaining, "it was like she was the sheep killer at that point." Simply reversing the roles of perpetrator and victim could not lead to Mariyam's liberation. Like NJ, HT thought the route to liberty had already been marked out in earlier scenes, that Mariyam "stopped being a sheep" when she went out alone, took off the veil herself, and started learning English:

> I thought there was more drama in her stalking around the apartment learning the language tapes. I mean, that was a deliberate defiance of the role they wanted her in, acquiring that knowledge. That struck me more than the actual murder.

For viewers such as this, the murder itself was only a demonstration of how deeply Mariyam was culturally trapped at the country house in a traditional symbolism without efficacy. KL's interpretation also drew on this perception: "That killing—it's breaking into the world of action." Mariyam breaks out of the role of the victim, but she is still constrained by the simplistic terms of the binary opposition. To cease to be a victim by becoming a perpetrator is not freedom because, KL added, "sacrifice is a rotten basis for action." CK shared this view. She was emphatic about Mariyam's guilt, drawing out the analogy of the sheep-killing as a ritual cruelty without efficacy: "I felt sorry for the poor guy she killed. I'm sorry, but I felt sorry for him. I thought that was kind of cruel. He was a blood sacrifice and there was blood all over." CK rejected Mariyam's act of violence as strongly as she had rejected the violence of the men who killed the sheep. For NP, the most salient moral issue in the stabbing scene was her own sense of contradiction as a viewer: "I feel guilty! When they killed the sheep, I felt really bad, but when she killed the bridegroom, I kind of liked it." The role reversal in *The Suitors* brought out an awareness of the double standard of more conventional perceptions, in which a killing perceived as a role reversal is justified by the role reversal itself.

Far from providing closure or epistemological clarity, the stabbing scene was controversial, both among different viewers and even within the interpretations of individuals. Viewers sympathized with Mariyam's plight, yet found it difficult to justify her violence without the motive of physical self-defense. At the same time, few were willing to wholly reject her actions. GA summarized the most common stance of the viewer, a moral ambivalence about Mariyam's act mixed with a strong sympathy and understanding of why she did it: "I was torn, but I still wanted her to escape." Some said she didn't have to do it, or she shouldn't have done it, but viewers were not willing to abandon her because of it. If they rejected her act of violence as wrong, they did not reject Mariyam herself, distinguishing between Mariyam's actions and her person.

Their ambivalence reflects the use of cinematography and color symbolism in the stabbing scene. In keeping with the film's development of character in terms of how events affect the character, the cinematography throughout the stabbing scene privileges Mariyam's face and her expressions of pain and disgust. In this sense, it is her scene rather than Ali's, even though Mariyam is largely silent. Ali's disregard for Mariyam's responses to him is emphasized when Ali twice moves in front of the camera, blocking out the view of Mariyam—the viewer gets a direct experience of the symbolic obliteration that characterizes Ali's attitude toward Mariyam. Once Ali sits down, Mariyam's movement dominates and claims the space of the room as she circles around behind Ali. Although

Ali falls downward toward the camera after he is stabbed, the camera ends on Mariyam leaning against a doorway, dwelling on her anguished expression as the final image of the scene.

While the camera encourages sympathy for Mariyam, its emphasis on her is not a moral vindication of her act or her perspective. The black-and-white color symbolism of the scene, emphasized by the strong geometric design within the frame, plays out across both Mariyam and Ali. It begins with the almost fully abstract image of Mariyam's solid black angular shape framed by the geometrics of a white room as she approaches the door. Black window panes and white wood frames constitute the background for Mariyam as she opens the door. As Ali enters the room, he passes so close to the camera that the viewer sees only a dehumanizing extreme close-up of the back of his head and neck—a visual montage of black and white lines and shapes: his black hair, the rim of a white shirt collar, and his black suit. Stark black and white contrasts are dominant as the two confront each other, but neither Mariyam nor Ali is exclusively associated with good or evil, white or black. Despite several changes in camera placement, both the images of their persons and the backgrounds that frame them continue to be a mixture of black and white. Ali's black suit and white shirt are matched by Mariyam's black and white geometric print dress, which the viewer sees both at the beginning of the sequence and after the veil is removed. Preventing the symbolic personification of either character as the embodiment of good or evil, the cinematography also rejects the equation of masculinity with power, or femininity with victimage. Mariyam is empowered by the camera's emphasis on her expressions, while Ali is dis-empowered by his lack of physical movement as soon as he sits down. Though he engages in a good deal of arm-waving as he sits and describes their future house, these gestures seem disengaged from the space of the room itself. Mariyam, in circling around behind him, dominates the real space of the room, while Ali sits in his own imaginary, fictitious space.

Just as important, the colors of black and white evoke the scene of the sheep's stabbing—also a black and white scene (though still in color)—inviting a comparison between the two scenes of violence. However, there is also an important difference. When the stabbing of Ali occurs, it is a bloodless crime. The color red is used in this scene on both characters, but its use is ancillary to the central plot. Ali wears a red-and-white striped tie, and there is also the large red bow on his gift for Mariyam, which the viewer sees as a prominent foreground in a shot of Mariyam's distressed face. The camera does not show Ali lying on the floor, and when Mariyam drags his body down the hallway to hide it in a store-room, it is too dark to see anything more than his silhouette. Even when

After the stabbing, Mariyam has blood on her hands.

Mariyam shoves him into the chair in the storage room, the bright light bulb hanging overhead does not illuminate any blood on his body or hers.

The viewer does not see any blood until after Mariyam has closed the door to the storage room. Then the viewer sees—and then Mariyam herself suddenly realizes—there is blood on her face, arms, hands, and dress. She runs to the bathroom to wash it off at the sink. When NJ remarked that "it was like Mariyam was the sheep-killer at that point," she specifically recalled Mariyam in the washing scene in the bathroom, not the act of stabbing itself. Mariyam takes off her bloody dress and returns to the storage room door to clean the floor in front of it. CK says "there was blood all over," but a viewer can see that only in the next scene after the stabbing. Because the stabbing and the sight of blood are separated—unlike the killing of the sheep, where they are simultaneous—the symbolic interpretation of Mariyam's action is enhanced.

Notwithstanding the analogy, the story of the sheep maintains a moral perspective that withstands the moral chaos of the stabbing, even allows that chaos to emerge. However its relevance is interpreted, the sheep's story retains its own meaning, its own statement about wrongful violence. Consequently, Mariyam as a character is freed from the personifications that are frequently forced on female characters in American genre films—namely that they be innocent or guilty, good or evil. Without the pressure to affirm the reductive polarities that diminish or dilute a character, viewers have the latitude to be ambivalent and conflicted about

Mariyam's actions, to see her as a complex individual and not simply as the embodiment of a moral category or the epitome of victimage.

Unlike *Thelma and Louise*, where the women's rebellion against patriarchal coercion ultimately leads to their entrapment and death, and unlike traditional noir films that punish moral transgression in women, Mariyam is not captured or punished for stabbing Ali in *The Suitors*. Stabbing the bridegroom and successfully escaping victimage are evocative of the female heroine of American slasher films, a genre that experienced rapid development in the decade prior to the making of *The Suitors*. Like most slasher films, *The Suitors* evokes the famous shower scene in Hitchcock's *Psycho*, in which Marion Crane (Janet Leigh) is brutally stabbed to death at the Bates Motel while she is in the midst of taking a shower. However, Ebrahimian is an admirer only of Hitchcock's cinematic techniques, not his social values or his plot-lines. *The Suitors* substantially critiques the ideas informing the Hitchcock shower scene by telling it as the story of the sheep-killing. The slaughterhouse atmosphere of slasher films is ironically invoked in the killing of the sheep in the bathtub, and the sheep-killing sequence ends with the film's most explicit allusion to *Psycho*, a shot of bloody water running down the bathtub drain. *Psycho* employs a dubious match cut from the circular drain to the circular dead eye of Marion to end the shot sequence of the killing. As a touchstone of the contrast between the two films, *The Suitors* ends its scene with a cut from the purling drain to the blood dripping down on a bingo card in the fundamentalist's apartment below, beginning the sequence that will end with Haji's death in the SWAT team raid. Where *Psycho*'s match cut closes off a consideration of larger social issues, staying within its fetishistic obsession with the dead body of a young woman, *The Suitors* opens outward to the complex social, political, and religious issues that surround the sheep's killing. Through the symbolism of the story of the sheep, and its complex relation to Mariyam and the story of the veil, *The Suitors* continually asserts its difference from Hitchcock's prototype. After Mariyam stabs Ali, the allusion to a blood-filled bathroom is only vaguely evocative and mainly humorous—Mariyam does not take a shower, washing up at the sink instead. Unlike the killer Norman Bates (Anthony Perkins), who takes great care and deliberation in cleaning up the blood and disposing of Marion's body, Mariyam is hasty and rather careless in disposing of Ali, dumping him in a chair in a spare room without even caring whether or not he's dead. As a last, witty aside to Hitchcock, Mariyam sits perched on the edge of the bathtub as she calls Reza on the phone—in contrast to Hitchcock's Marion, who sprawls naked and dead over the edge of the bathtub, ripping the shower curtain down with her as she falls. Mariyam, by contrast, is very much alive and busy planning her successful escape with Reza.

Carol Clover has described the American slasher genre as a particular kind of horror film that features a female heroine, the "Final Girl," who successfully turns on her male aggressor in violent triumph, reversing a progression of victimage by killing her tormentor.[40] Mariyam, it would seem, has the makings of a Final Girl in stabbing Ali. Her anger and frustration and sense of claustrophobia in the country house evoke significant parallels with the cornered Final Girl who strikes back, reversing a course of victimage that gives her control and makes her the dominant character.[41] Wresting control of the plot-line through her own murderous act is what makes a Final Girl a heroine, the main character and not just another object of violence. However, Mariyam utterly fails in the sexual identity attributed to the Final Girl. Clover has capably analyzed the Final Girl, in the moment she kills, as a "masculine female." As Clover says, the slasher film "regenders the woman" as male. She is "manned" by her actions. When she kills the male villain, she is "reconstituted as masculine." Clover emphasizes throughout her analysis that the transformation of the Final Girl from potential, feminine victim to "unfeminine" masculine hero is a figurative one.[42] This regendering is the culmination of the plot in the slasher film: "The moment at which the Final Girl is effectively phallicised is the moment that the plot halts and horror ceases. Day breaks and the community returns to its normal order." By contrast, viewers described Mariyam in *The Suitors* as a beautiful woman, not a girl, and not masculine. GB described the *other* women as masculine, the women who *don't* resist as Mariyam does:

> In the hostage situation, the women went along with it. They were part of keeping her there. They stopped being women to me after awhile. They just had a feminine look of masculinity.

In contrast to this figurative masculinity, the most important thing about Mariyam at the end of the film is her womanliness. GB explained, "The Iranian-ness is what's most important about her at the beginning. Being a woman is what's most important at the end." Mariyam's resistance, though superficially like the Final Girl's, is not a figuratively masculine act. On the contrary, she is distinctly perceived as a woman in her action.

When Clover says that the Final Girl is "effectively phallicized," that effectiveness comes from the fact that the genre is metonymic in its defining moment. The heroine is renamed masculine to describe her significant actions, and this masculinity is both defining and figurative—privileging the figured rather than the literal body. Masculinity is the spiritual and cultural essence of this physical—and saved—female. The female body, like the bread of the Calvinist sacrament, must be real, ordinary, yet it does not have the power of sanction. It must be a real female body for the slasher film, but the sanctioning of that self is always masculine, transforming the female body as the bread of the sacrament is transformed in the salutary act of renaming. Attaining a sacrosanct subjectivity, the iconoclastic wrath of the Final Girl is enacted in the violent destruction of the psychopathic killer, whose image of authoritativeness in the plot she proves to be false.[43] However, this is not a triumph for women. One kind of masculinity is traded for another, the killer's for the Final Girl's. Clover's analysis itself employs the discourse of phallic symbolism, ascribing masculinity to the female hero who kills the threatening villain. The idea of a public, dominant discourse of sexuality that is fundamentally female instead of male is unheard of in American public culture. Neither the slasher film nor Clover's analysis does anything to challenge this. Clover's essay demonstrates instead how masculine terms are used to conceptualize and describe female main characters in films.

The Suitors is a radical departure from the American slasher genre because, in the Iranian semiotics of the veil, there is no contradiction between Mariyam's sexuality and her positioning as the main character of the film. She is under the aegis of a female sexual symbolism that has no counterpart in American culture.[44] Consequently there is no struggle against her own sexual identity, as there is for the Final Girl, in her struggle to assert her authority over her life. At this symbolic level, the semiotics of the veil intercedes to reinterpret the slasher moment in The Suitors as a moment when Mariyam asserts herself as a woman. It has nothing to do with a girl becoming masculine.

Hamid Naficy has justly pointed out that psychoanalytic theory is inappropriate to the study of Iranian film because the Iranian veil signifies value rather than lack. The phallic symbolism of psychoanalytic theory has no vocabulary or concepts for talking about the value that the veil represents. On the face of it, this seems a very attractive alternative for women—to be symbolized as valuable rather than lacking, to have the sexual symbolism of public culture be female rather than male, to have female sexual symbolism be the idiom of sexuality. However, since the idea that the veil expresses value is also what LF was told by the Iranian fundamentalist revolutionary government when she was forced to wear a veil, it is questionable whether this expression of value is really of any benefit to women. As a symbolism imposed by men on women, as in modern Iran, the symbolic value expressed by the veil is the value of the female body as property—the property of an individual man, father or husband, or the property of the state. To wear the veil literally and materially, not just symbolically, is incapacitating, dis-empowering. As comments by Iranian women make clear, women such as LF and SR felt *devalued* by the practice of veiling. And no American woman walked away from The Suitors thinking it would be a good idea to move to Iran or wear a veil. The symbolic power and value of the veil for women lies outside Iranian culture, not within it, and at the imaginative and epistemological level, not the literal one. For the American viewer, the veil's power in *The Suitors* lies in what it symbolically allows a viewer to perceive about a woman and her image.

The Suitors takes the general notion of the Iranian veil as expressive of value and gives it a very different kind of value than Iranian clerics assign to it. Ironically, as the symbol of a "foreign" culture for an American audience, the veil gives expression to the foreignness of female sexuality within the American system of phallic symbolism. It states the problem for American women. In the development of the story, the veil asserts the reality of female sexuality and gives it recognition in public culture's symbolism of sexuality. The veil also presents an alternative way of thinking because it shows that female sexuality can be figurative without becoming masculine. The veil is not identical with the body, as the image of woman is in Mulvey's thesis. The more times Mariyam takes off the veil—something that can't be shown in films in Iran—the more the film emphasizes that the veil is a figure that gives material shape to the idea of sexual symbolism as an arbitrary semiotic *about* the body that is not itself a *part* of the body. Unlike the body that typifies cinematic realism, the *figura* of Mariyam and her veil evokes an awareness of the shapes on screen, the design of the film image, and the reality of the film image as image. The dynamic of the veil disrupts the sense of her as confined and controlled by the reified image of realism. The character of Mariyam, who she is, includes these diagrammatic forms of the screen image. Her cinematic image in *The Suitors* de-fetishizes the screen image of the woman. Mariyam brings into conscious perception that the film image of a woman is not fixed, reified, naturalized as it is in American realism, but instead mutable as the shape of Mariyam's veil is mutable. Consistent with this mutability, Mariyam challenges the fusion of innocence, victimage, and female sexuality. She acts not to acquire something she doesn't have, but instead to reject Ali for attempting to own the power of female sexuality for himself.

EXIT THE BLACK SCREEN SUITCASE

Although Mariyam has rid herself of the veil when she leaves the country house, she has yet to confront the problem of the American image of a woman. She finishes the stabbing scene in a black slip, the same attire that had caused American viewers to think of her as being just like an American woman in the film's earlier scenes. When the veil is the image of a woman, it is potentially separable from the woman herself.

Mariyam watches as Reza puts air holes in the suitcase.

One can imagine getting rid of the material veil altogether, as Mariyam does. However, when the material body itself is the image of a woman, as it is in American culture, the same idea of getting rid of the image of a woman seems inconceivable—or at least inconceivable short of death. At its culmination, *The Suitors* conceives a solution without extinguishing its heroine in the process, liberating Mariyam—and consequently the viewer as well—from the oppressive symbiosis of woman and image.

In this last section of the film, the plot itself is minimal. The director described it as a process of "taking everything away until it's just her." Reza is the only other character of significance, and he becomes tangential. The sequence begins with Reza and Mariyam driving away from the country house in darkness. At dawn, when they arrive at an airport to buy tickets to Europe, the airline won't issue a ticket to Mariyam because she doesn't have her passport. Mariyam decides to smuggle herself onto the plane as baggage. Reza buys a large black leather suitcase, and Mariyam tries it out in a motel room. She has now become thoroughly Westernized in her attire, wearing blue jeans and a close-fitting black sweater. Because the literal plot is so simple, the figurative plot easily dominates the viewers' sense of what is happening. For example, GB used a sustained metaphor to describe Reza's return to the motel with the suitcase:

> I loved the line, "I got the biggest one I could find." But it's still a suitcase, you know. You'll have the most room in this one of any, but the fact is it's

Reza unzipping the suitcase (Mariyam's perspective).

still a suitcase. He was even willing to give her air holes so she could breathe, but it was *still* a suitcase! Even life with him, even though it would probably be the best by far of any of the four, would still be living in a suitcase, and it was unacceptable.

The suitcase *as metaphor* is what conveys the meaning of the plot for GB because the progression of figurative meaning *is* the primary plot. Viewers were aware that the literal plot was in some respects unrealistic but considered those lapses unimportant. For example, VR mentioned with a smile that "if you take an international flight, they always check your bags." I asked her if that detracted from the film and she assured me it did not, that she still thought it was "an amazing movie." The amazing dimension of the film rests with its figurative import, and especially with the black screen sequence that closes the film.

The sequence begins when the film cuts away from the motel room where Mariyam has just tried out the suitcase. The viewer sees a black screen that seems like a gap for dramatic emphasis. With the music poised at a climactic moment, the viewer waits for the final sequence of escape to begin. After a long four seconds of anticipation, the viewer is astonished when the black screen suddenly zips open at the center from top to bottom! It discloses Reza's face and shoulders as he looks down at Mariyam— what Mariyam sees from inside the suitcase. The black screen has not

Mariyam inside the suitcase (Reza's perspective).

been a blank space between scenes. It is part of the story, a representational image of what Mariyam can see from inside the suitcase. Reza has unzipped the suitcase/the screen, and his hand is holding the parted suitcase open. DS described her intense reaction to this scene:

> The biggest scene for me was when she curled up inside that suitcase and after he had clearly transported her from the motel room to the airport parking lot and the camera was like inside the suitcase and he opened it. So it was total blackness and then this zipping, the unzippingness, and then his face in the sunlight, inquiring on her state of health and was she going to do it and was she going to make it. I will remember that part forever!

The gendered shot/reverse shot sequence that occurs here is especially striking: her inside the suitcase and him outside the suitcase. It states a theme that will be developed further in this final sequence of the film. Here it ends on Reza, who takes one last look at Mariyam with obvious apprehension. Then he zips the suitcase shut, from the bottom of the screen to the top, and the viewer is again faced with a black screen.

This use of the black screen, unprecedented in dramatic film, brings off-screen space on screen. When Reza zips open the screen image, he discloses the existence of what has been off-screen: Her. Suddenly the black screen represents on-screen how she has been obliterated in representational cinema and in Western representational systems in general. For GB, it was a gratifying experience to see this idea on screen: "It was such a powerful symbology! A woman in this culture is like a woman in a suitcase." The film's demystification of the representational image changes the significance of the black screen. When Reza zips up the suitcase and the viewer sees the black screen again, the viewer knows that while the screen may be black, it is not empty. Mariyam is there and very much alive. In unzipping the screen/suitcase, the film has symbolically redefined the black screen, transforming absence or negation or a gap into a substantive presence.

The film cuts to a long shot of Reza struggling with the weight of the bulging, heavy suitcase—more affirmation that there is someone inside—and then back to the black screen again. This time it has a live soundtrack, Mariyam breathing inside the suitcase. CK said, "The sounds of her panting inside the thing just took on a wonderful dimension there." The sequence develops the opposition of shot–reverse shot as an outside/ inside opposition, and through this process it relocates the emphasis from him to her, reversing the sense of inside and outside. That is, the film develops the sense that Mariyam is inside the main story and Reza is outside it. When the film cuts again to a long shot of Reza, still struggling through the parking lot, he is in conventional representational cinema, outside in bright daylight with the sounds of normal life around him articulating representational space, but separated from the black screen. The film emphasizes his exclusion when it again cuts back to the black screen for the duration of the last conversation between them. He asks her if she's still okay—she says, yes—and he tells her he's now going inside the terminal so he can't talk to her anymore, that "I'll check you in soon." She says, "Alright"—her last words in the film. The camera stays on Mariyam for the whole dialogue—that is, the screen remains black for the entire conversation, showing her perspective instead of his.

This emphasis continues inside the terminal. The film cuts momentarily to Reza at the ticket counter, and then the screen goes black again, with Mariyam breathing heavily. The muffled voices of a dialogue between Reza and the ticket agent can also be heard, but the emphasis remains on Mariyam's perspective, as HT's description of this scene reflects: "I *loved* the blank screen with the breathing! And you can feel what it's like to be in the suitcase, and you can hear what's going on outside but you don't know what it is. I had an emotional stake in her." Mariyam is outside dialogue altogether at this point, and consequently there is an intensification of her isolation inside the suitcase. Nonetheless, it is the black screen that has become primary in the viewer's attention and that serves as the point of reference, an image intrinsic to the story. This is where the viewer's emotional stake is, not with Reza. The cross-cuts to Reza become subordinate images, the second kind of images that are added to comment on the story—in this instance, to let the viewer know where the suitcase is in representational space.

The suspense is heightened considerably when the film shifts back in a sustained way to representational images in the world outside the suitcase. Suddenly the viewer no longer sees the black screen and cannot hear Mariyam breathing. Reza is climbing behind the counter to place the suitcase on the conveyor belt so the ticket agent won't touch the suitcase. As it begins its baggage journey to the plane, the camera, placed on the conveyor belt, follows right behind, keeping the suitcase fully within the frame. As it passes into the back area of the airport, the viewer sees the suitcase, but the only sound is the harsh, grating machine noise of the conveyor belt. The sense of Mariyam's vulnerability is heightened as Reza leaves the ticket counter and walks through the airport. The camera continues to cut back and forth between Reza, in the bright light of the airport with the other passengers, and the suitcase, rumbling through increasingly dark spaces of the airport, its sleek black outside only faintly illuminated. Mariyam cannot be heard. At the beginning of this sequence the black screen had seemed strange, a shutting out of the image. Now the viewer is frustrated and increasingly anxious because there is no black screen and there is no sound of breathing. Viewers know what's missing from the representational cinema of Reza alone in the airport, with crosscuts only to a representational image of a suitcase moving along on a conveyor belt.

While the viewer fears Mariyam will die for reasons of science, the viewer also fears emotionally and semiotically that she will die because the viewer can no longer see her. This is why the black screen is so important. Because the black screen symbolizes a woman without her image, it has meaning. Conceptually it has become an image of the living woman distinguishable from her image. However, more disturbing shots about the separation of woman and image are yet to come. In the latter stages of her journey on the conveyor belt, there is a repeated shot where the audience hears her breathing, but they see the suitcase only from the outside. That is, the sound of her breathing returns, but not the black screen. With this variant, the representational image of the suitcase seems superimposed on the black screen image, treating the black screen as a transparency, as nothing rather than something—unlike the black screen that was visible. With the black screen, the viewer had conceptualized Mariyam inside the suitcase yet distinct from it, and analogously, as "inside" the representational image but distinct from it. For the viewer, the suitcase shown from the outside is not-Mariyam. It has now become a symbolic image of the stifling opaqueness of the conventional representational image, and all that it hides in its pretense of seeing. From the viewer's perspective, it is the representational image of the suitcase's exterior that now conveys absence, not the black screen.

Now she is perceived as a woman without her image in a way that seems deeply threatening. The image of her has indeed disappeared, has become nothing, a transparency. In Lacanian terms, this is the desired end, the extinction of her image altogether and the extinction of "woman" along with it. No wonder, then, that viewers thought that she was about to die, and that she could not avoid this fate. The Western symbiosis of woman and image would seem to demand it. Viewers imagined that she would suffocate or be crushed to death under other suitcases, or that she would flip the suitcase over and kill herself accidentally, or that she would freeze to death in the plane's hold during flight. No viewer anticipated that she would get out. As DS put it, "I never, never, *never* thought she would exit the suitcase into her life!" However, in *The Suitors* the meaning of these images continues to evolve through the sequence, consistent with the director's idea that every moment is different in its essence. There is one more important transformation to come.

As the suitcase reaches the end of the belt and daylight, a handler grabs it and puts it on a truck. Suddenly the black screen returns and Mariyam is heard gasping and heaving. The return of the black screen and the breathing reaffirms the existence of Mariyam inside the figurative suitcase, but now it also warns against the reification of this image of the black screen as a viable alternative to conventional representation—she sounds as if she is close to suffocation. The film cuts to its last outside view of the suitcase, close-up, as the sound of her desperate breathing continues. The suitcase wobbles and suddenly Mariyam's thumb appears at the bottom of the suitcase zipper, fumbling for a grip. As her hand slowly moves up to the top of the suitcase/the screen and Mariyam sticks her head out, the live soundtrack is taken off, replaced by the music of a string quartet that accompanies Mariyam to the end of the film.[45] The music allows the viewer's mind to take in the hope and imagination of these final moments. Emerging into this figurative world, Mariyam has finally completed her journey from the suffocation of metonymy to the freedom of metaphor and the act of imagination it predicates. As one reviewer put it, the suitcase has become "an elegant visual metaphor of confinement and liberation."[46]

The fact that viewers did not anticipate her getting out is suggestive of the oppressiveness of metonymic structures of representational meaning, which seem impossible to escape from. And yet the escape to metaphor is possible in reality. The film combines the figurative, musical dimension with the real time of Mariyam emerging from the suitcase. She sticks her head out and looks around. Her shoulders appear. She tosses out a purse,

Mariyam emerging from the suitcase.

a water jug, and her shoes. As she crawls out in this close-up, her torso, her legs, and her feet pass before the camera until there is nothing to see but the empty suitcase and its yawning opening—the place from where she has come but which she no longer occupies. KL appropriately described the scene metaphorically:

> She zips that womb open and steps out, or sort of hops out, sort of falls out as if she's falling into the world and then takes off. She's moved into freedom of some kind. It's a very dangerous, iffy sort of thing, but then I guess that's what freedom is.

This is the last essential image of the film.[47] Its emotional significance resonates through a brief closing sequence in which Mariyam quickly goes back through the airport to the street. She looks grim at first, and in a last brief gesture of veiling, she momentarily covers part of her face with her hand. Freedom will not be easy. This is not a utopian ending. Then she lets her hand drop and turns pensive as she watches a plane fly overhead, pulling her tumbling hair back so the viewer sees her face clearly. Then she hails a taxi and gets in. The last image is a long shot that shows the taxi leaving the airport.

   To see Mariyam initiate her own exit from the suffocating ideology of conventional representational film was the most exhilarating moment of the film. When Mariyam gets out of the image/suitcase and leaves on her

Mariyam hesitates—freedom will not be easy.

own, her liberation is also the viewer's, the culmination of the viewer's conceptual journey through the film. Viewers retrospectively described the journey as a wonderful trip. CK said of the final sequence, "Her idea of getting into that bag was just fabulous!" LL and DS echoed the most common response: "I was blown away by it!" The conceptual differentiation of woman and image, and the evidence that Mariyam is the living part of that differentiation, gives a great sense of release. GB described the undoing of the symbiosis of woman and image: "Being a woman is what's most important at the end. The woman has value, and that's the part that goes on out of the airport." What's the other part? When I asked her, she said "the veil part." Mariyam is without the veil/the suitcase, but she has value in her own right. GB continued, "It was such a freeing feeling—to walk away from being a hostage and walk out into this seething humanity with her hair blowing in the breeze." KL was more philosophical: "I see the ending—at the same time I have this feeling of great apprehension, I also see it as a tremendous release. Because she's really striking out into her own freedom, whatever it may be. Not necessarily power, but freedom."

Viewers did not describe Mariyam as free when she left the country house after stabbing Ali. She isn't described as free until she emerges from the suitcase. Viewers felt it was a substantive freedom, not a superficial one. LC said of her experience of watching *The Suitors*, "You're thinking about freedom and lack of freedom. The issues were different from American films. The emotional effect is more subtle than in American films." The kind of freedom Mariyam has does not derive from the clichés of American political culture. On the contrary, viewers saw the concept of freedom as originating with the film. DS explained, "The word *freedom* was planted in my mind with the movie. It evokes that ideal at a level you can take seriously."

Mariyam's experience of freedom is more than a refusal to read the representational image as an accurate idea of a woman. Or, to put it another way, that refusal can be attained only by the development of another way of thinking. The black screen is the pathway to the freedom of multiple meanings because, conceptually, it is a polyphonic image. It evokes and draws into itself both the story of the sheep and the story of the veil. Unlike the stabbing scene, the black screen merges these stories with coherence. The black screen ceases to be empty and becomes an image of her inside the veil when the suitor unzips the black screen, gendering the black screen as female but also evoking an interpretation of the black screen as a variant of the veil. It is another version of Mariyam as the "black space moving" that appears throughout the earlier part of the film. The cinematography has repeatedly displayed a black space, the veiled Mariyam, as part of the screen image. Because the viewer has repeatedly associated Mariyam with the black space in the image, when the black space completely fills the screen in the culminating sequence, viewers understand this within the film's terms, as an image of Mariyam—and still as a black space moving. CM remarked, "When she's in the suitcase, she's not moving, but she is moving—she's on the conveyor belt." The suitcase is readily viewed as a variant of the veil—it's black, it covers her up, and when Reza first looks at her inside it, his perspective discloses her face framed by the suitcase/veil. The suitcase emphasizes the veil's stifling control of women and how it cuts her off from social relations—a point emphasized further by the muffled dialogue outside the suitcase at the ticket agent's desk. The black space of the image also evokes an awareness of the composition of the image as image because Reza unzips the screen as well as the suitcase. The shot discloses that the screen image, whatever it is, articulates someone's perspective in a particular location. This is consistent with the photography throughout the film, but it is far more striking in this shot–reverse shot sequence, where in classical cinema the position of the camera is hidden and denied.[48] DS's awareness of where the camera is, even in this emotionally climactic moment, is part of what she found so memorable about this image. Both form and content flow into this black space that reveals the cinematic image as such.

Most important, the black screen as off-screen space creates a space for the return of the story of the sheep. The sheep's death off-screen has marked this space as the place of the sacrificial victim throughout the film. Literally absented from the screen in an act of gratuitous violence, the dark meaning of the sheep's violent death has haunted the story. In the black screen, the off-screen image-less death of the sheep comes on-screen, is fully acknowledged, and it is joined with the image-less black screen that is Mariyam. At the beginning of the film they were loosely paralleled by the formal analogy of each of them riding in a car into the city. Now their stories are conjoined, each reading the other as they occupy the same visual space: the black screen. The convergence of the sheep's story with Mariyam's story intensifies Mariyam's life-threatening experience, and viewers felt it acutely in their fear that she would die in the suitcase. Like the sheep, she seems to be utterly helpless and passive, and ignorant that she will die. The sheep's story, considered by itself, closes off the possibility that Mariyam could escape, could get out. However, it also provides an interpretation of her imminent death as martyrdom, not simply death. As BT described it: "If she stayed in the suitcase, that would be a horrible ending! She would be a martyr. That would be terrible!" While the sheep's story evokes the idea that death will be her fate, it also reads that death as something other than inevitable, as a gratuitous act. Unlike the numerous transgressive women who die in moralistic American films, the prospect of Mariyam's cinematic execution is perceived as horribly unjust even as it seems inevitable.

Inevitability gives way to another meaning because the story of the suitcase produces an off-screen space of its own. In the equivalence of off-screen space with the enclosure of the symbolic veil, the sheep's story of the victim is taken into Mariyam's own story and is rewritten. Through the convergence in the black screen, Mariyam enters the off-screen image-less space that has been defined by the sheep's death and where the sheep has continued to wander through the viewer's imagination. The presence of the sheep, a full acknowledgment of the sheep's story, is restored to the narrative and taken into it as Mariyam's own story. Now the wished-for resistance, not just for Mariyam but also for the sheep, is realized, and the sheep's story reaches closure. In the darkness there is no differentiation, and all the elements of the film's plot and iconography now flow into this image. The black screen becomes an image of the film's montage as montage, the image of juxtaposition itself and the third kind of images, the unrepresented thematic meanings of the story.

There is a further convergence in the symbolism of the suitcase itself. Unlike the veil, the suitcase does not refer to either Iranian or American culture specifically. It is a transcultural symbol, and a common image in transcultural plots, symbolizing a crossing between cultures.[49] In *The Suitors*, however, the suitcase symbolizes a crossing between systems of gender representation that leaves *both* cultures in its wake, abandoning American viewers' presuppositions about images of women in addition to the Iranian veil as the image of woman. Although Mariyam gives up the material veil before she confronts the American version of women, the film avoids any representational scene of Mariyam definitively discarding the veil—because she hasn't discarded the veil semiotically until she moves through the black screen sequence and emerges from it.

This is a story that is fundamentally composed in images, and is about images, and not surprisingly, it seeks its compelling resolution at the level of cinematography, in the concept of the film image itself, not just in the plot or dialogue of the film. In the resolution of the black screen sequence, the film loosens the grip of the image on female sexuality by creating variability between them. What breaks the symbiosis of woman and image is not, finally, the disappearance of either one. The last essential image in the film is not the black screen. It is Mariyam getting out of the suitcase. Rather than staging the permanent disappearance of either woman or image, the film considers both possibilities and rejects both. It creates instead a semiotics that allows 'woman' and 'image' to vary in complex and changing ways in relation to each other. This is what it means to have semiotic freedom of movement. To be persuasive, it has to occur at the level of the film image itself and the viewer's own experience of seeing the film. It can't just occur at the level of the dialogue or the representational plot—that would be the equivalent of telling the viewer without showing the viewer. This is a freedom whose expression is grounded in the semiotics of the image, not in any speech that Mariyam makes at the end of the film.

To achieve her liberation, Mariyam faces down the culturally constructed threat that a woman ceases to exist without her image and discovers she can pass through that danger into something else. American viewers thought of her as a courageous woman. HT admired Mariyam for her bravery: "She had a lot more guts than I would have. I liked her. She had a really strong survival instinct. She's a strong woman who's fighting the odds and asserting herself even though it's potentially disastrous." In the end it is not disastrous because the threat of extinction lies in staying in the suitcase, believing the culturally sanctioned image will assure safety and validity and being. To get out of the image/suitcase is freedom. This last essential image is the resolution of the film's narrative in all its dimensions. As NC put it, "The big moment came when she emerged from the suitcase. She burst her bonds, and that was very interesting." The film achieves its interesting closure through its cinematography, in a climax without dialogue and in an action by the main character that is utterly simple at the level of plot, but very complex in the forty-five shots of cinematography and montage that tell the story.

The theory of the image that informs Mariyam's freedom is different from the typical American or European film, not only in the artistic ways I have already described, but also in a philosophical sense. When I asked Ebrahimian what he thought film was about, he said, "Film is about light, because without light there can be no images." This is very different from saying, without women there can be no images! Philosophically—not just scientifically—light is the generative source of the image in *The Suitors*. For this director, whose own background is Zoroastrian, not Muslim, both the nature and the prominence of the image in his film theory draw on Persian cultural beliefs about light and darkness.[50] The result is a theory of cinema in which women do not have a privileged relation to the image. The idea that light is the source of the image allows the concepts of woman and image to move, to vary in relation to each other. Unlike American woman characters, who are perceived as the source of the image, Mariyam is liberated from the onerous burden of maintaining and protecting the existence of the film image at an ontological level.

Speaking further about his interpretation of Zoroastrian light and darkness, Ebrahimian continued, "Light gives you the image, so you know what you are dealing with." The image is given by light, not created out of itself as a fetish seems to be. Nor is the image understood to be created by human beings. The image given by light enables knowledge—so you know what you are dealing with—and this is why the cinematic image gains such importance in its own right, and is not subordinated to dialogue or treated as a suspect, inferior source of knowledge. The light-given image does not evoke the devastating fear of deceit that characterizes Protestant iconoclasm, that makes the Protestant image the target of righteous violence or the object of fetishistic adoration. In Zoroastrianism, light is associated with knowledge, with truth, with life, with what is good. Light "stands for the hope of having meaning," where darkness signifies "ignorance, not knowing what is around you." Not knowing is quite different from not existing. While darkness carries a negative connotation, it is not itself negation. It is not nonexistence. Darkness is a state of mind, a particular condition—as when GA described a "feeling of not-knowing-ness" early on in the film, a feeling generated by the film's drama. The viewer is there, thinking and wondering, not absent. And in the black screen sequence, Mariyam is there—you can hear her breathing—even though she is in darkness, and like the sheep, not knowing what is around her. Her alive-ness contradicts the conventional Western reading of darkness as absence or nonexistence, and American viewers were riveted by this.

They did not look away from the black screen sequence at any point. For them, there's something important and complicated on screen even though the screen image might be described in Western terms as absolutely blank. Although viewers do not anticipate the black screen sequence, they were ready to read it because the film has prepared the viewer for this moment. The veil, as black, marks her there-ness, but at the same time marks her as unknown within the darkness of the veil. JH and other American viewers initially equated that darkness with nonexistence, thinking at first that there was nothing under the veil. As Mariyam takes off the veil, American viewers understand that darkness is not nonexistence and, by extension, that Mariyam is not characterized by "lack"—that particular form of absence or nonexistence that is used especially to characterize women in Western systems of thought such as psychoanalysis.

The opposition of light and darkness is not only epistemological. It is also social and ethical. In the Zoroastrian worldview, human beings have free will, the freedom to choose, and especially to choose between the light and darkness. Zoroastrianism does not, like Calvinism, have a concept of an omnipotent, all-determining, omniscient, totalizing deity that preordains what people do and what they are. In Zoroastrianism, human beings are seen instead as having been placed at the center of a flawed world, where their choices affect what the world becomes and what experience they will have within it. Free will is seen in this context, making it important to choose light for the social good as well as the good of the individual. Within the Zoroastrian worldview, freedom is about choice rather than control, as KL noticed when she said Mariyam had gained freedom, not necessarily power, but freedom. Part of that freedom is the freedom to live without the veil. Although the film is about veiling, the literal veil as the image of the fundamentalist Muslim woman does not hold the film together, does not ground the meaning of the film. Semiotically as well as politically, the story doesn't validate the veil as a viable image, as American films validate phallic symbolism. For Ebrahimian—and for LF—this is instead what state terrorism does: it validates the image of the veiled woman, but not the woman herself. In *The Suitors*, as the veil becomes more symbolic/arbitrary, less and less connected to Mariyam's shape and identity as a woman, it becomes itself the signifier of a semiotic system based on ignorance (the 'mystery' of female sexuality) that arbitrarily entraps her, enclosing and confining her—like the suitcase. When she gets out of the darkness, she chooses the light. That choice is emphasized by the shot of her unzipping the suitcase herself, a lengthy eight seconds of real time.

In watching the film, viewers experienced what it was like to think in terms of Zoroastrian ideas, particularly the concepts of light, darkness, and free will—the aspects of Zoroastrianism that Ebrahimian described as the most important to his understanding of Zoroastrian thought. As with the Persian narrative structure, viewers had a sense that they were seeing something different, but not that they were seeing something unintelligible. For example, here is DS's retrospective interpretation of a scene in the last sequence, when Mariyam is alone in the motel room, waiting for Reza to return. Mariyam is silently looking out the window:

> I think she was taking in all the different ways she could achieve freedom. I felt like she was observing the whole puzzle of humanity for the first time from up above rather than being sunk down in the walls of the culture where she couldn't see anything. She was coming out of a maze and a tunnel life and looking from an eagle's view down on the world and the options it held for her. Each and every thing and person is a choice.

Mariyam sees with clarity "rather than being sunk down in the walls of the culture where she can't see anything." This metaphor associates the darkness with conventional women's roles, which are nothing but "a maze and a tunnel life," a life lived in darkness and ignorance, in a suitcase. The emphasis on choice, rather than power, as well as the awareness of choice, is reflective of Zoroastrian ideas. Mariyam is not the source of the light, not the source of the images she sees. She is, however, the source of the choices she makes.

The Zoroastrian idea of free will also informs the basic structural relations between the film-maker, the film, and the viewer, and the way this narrative is constructed to activate the audience. This is reflected in the viewers' continuing awareness of the director's design of shots and especially of where he chose to place the camera. Viewers were attuned to the director's choices and to the fact that, as viewers, they were making choices, too. Viewers were especially aware of this at the end of the film. TG said she liked the ending because "it lets you put in what you feel the film has led you to." I asked some viewers what happens to Mariyam after the film is over, to see if the idea of Mariyam extended beyond the material film image itself. Was Mariyam permanently stuck in the images of the film, circumscribed by what the director had chosen to show? Or did woman and image acquire a variability in relation to each other that would allow viewers to imagine a future for Mariyam on their own? Viewers were not surprised at the question. They had already thought about it and told stories that they described as their own interpretive choices. Here is GA's version of what happens to Mariyam after the film is over:

> The idea that she's going to get in a suitcase and make it—it's like, well this is a long shot! And the credibility seems like it's slipping away here. And then when she gets out and walks out of the terminal, I'm like, well you're

not so stupid after all! And I'm thinking, well that boyfriend's really in for a surprise when he gets to Europe with empty baggage. And I'm thinking, how will she hide herself? And I'm thinking, well, she'll figure it out. My mind assumes that she makes it. She'll disappear and she'll make it and they'll look for her all over the place and they won't find her. She survived the entrapment and she escaped. Then I started wondering, how long will it last? How will the grapevine handle it? Will their political connections and their tight-knit community find her out? I chose to believe that it wouldn't, that her freedom is real and it's permanent—because I have this penchant for a happy ending, so I put it in there.

A few were skeptical that she could maintain her freedom, but they acknowledged that they, themselves, had chosen to interpret the film in that particular way. Most viewers envisioned an optimistic continuation of the narrative, that one way or another "she makes it."

Not only were viewers able to imagine a Mariyam beyond the last image of the film. Their own conversation about the film also displayed a sense of liberation in their use of metaphors and analogies. The veil of skin, the invisible veil, the sheep and the sheep-killer, the cat in the cage, feeling torn about the stabbing that follows the tearing of the wedding dress, the sense of being sunk down in the walls of the culture, the observation that a woman in this culture is like a woman in a suitcase—all these and many more were interspersed in the comments by viewers. Although they draw on particular scenes in the film, these metaphors express an interpretive free will, the viewers' own set of juxtapositions that articulate the meaning of the film for them. They are the viewers' articulation of the unrepresented images in the film, juxtapositions they create in "experiencing" the film. Viewers selected elements of a screen image, not an intact, reified image. For example, the prison bars of marsh grass that surround Mariyam outside the country house borrow only the image of the bars and the general notion of a person behind bars, not their particular context in the story or the men incarcerated behind them.[51] The viewers' metaphors and analogies evoke selected aspects in the design of a screen image, not a whole reified image intact. When images move in this sense, it suggests a complex variability between the viewer and the film. There is movement between the viewer and the film, a continuous shifting of the elements of the images in the minds of viewers as they interpret the film, an imaginative act of free will expressed by analogy and metaphor.

It has been said that cinema is not compatible with metaphor, that it does not lend itself to metaphor, that it is not about metaphor.[52] This may be true only for certain kinds of films. When cinema is considered as montage, then cinema appears far more hospitable to metaphor because metaphor, too, is a montage, a juxtaposition that creates meaning. Metaphor is the transfer of meaning from one place to another (symbolized by the journey in the suitcase), and in a way that produces a striking image, a figurative meaning that is discernible as such, a creative use of language that is different from customary expression.[53] To say that it is striking is to say that it retains the sense of having moved from one place to another, from there to here. When it migrates, the concept of more than one place remains discernible. The metaphor of the prison bars of marsh grass takes the prison bars from the early jail scene and transports them to the marsh grass on the shore of Long Island to render, as the viewer said, her sense of the "entrapment" of Mariyam at the country house. Something is juxtaposed with something else to create a meaning different from what is materially depicted in each image, in each location. A film that conceptualizes montage as juxtaposition and emphasizes those juxtapositions in the film, as *The Suitors* does, lends itself to metaphoric interpretation. Indeed the film itself might be described as juxtaposing American and Iranian cultures to express ideas that differ from each taken by itself. To be able to use metaphors, to think of them, to think with them, liberates the viewer from the workings of metonymy, the favored trope of capitalism, Calvinist iconoclasm, and Lacanian psychoanalytic theory. Metonymy, through its assertion of ownership, suppresses the idea of two conceptually distinct places. The proprietary claim that metonymy expresses obliterates the variability of movement that characterizes cinematic montage and metaphor.

Mariyam in the suitcase—there could hardly be a better image of the renamed object of metonymy, the owned thing that is the object of metonymy, carted around as baggage in a trope that makes metaphoric thinking impossible. *The Suitors* offers the liberation of metaphor in the viewer's imaginative experience of the film, reasserting the reality of more than one location conceptually—in popular parlance, it affirms that "there is a there." To be stuck in one location, stuck in a suitcase—this self-concept cannot access metaphor because metaphor takes something from one location and employs it in another. The concept of more than one place, of a transfer, a movement of meaning from one place to another, also played out across a different spectrum, the film and the viewer as distinguishable places. Viewers commented on the social reality of their own lives at the same time they talked about the film. They talked about themselves in relation to people they knew, provided a sense of their own social network and themselves within that network and how they perceived that network. Interspersed among their comments about the narrative in the film, viewers told me their own personal stories that elements of the film had brought to mind—about marriage, courtship, divorce, death of a spouse; Iranian friends, clients, roommates, or lovers; about members of their own family; about childhood and growing up; about their own differences from their parents; about women and men from countries in the Middle East other than Iran; about their own experience of immigration. These vignettes were not separate from their ideas about the film. They were interwoven with the metaphors and analogies and narrative interpretations I have quoted throughout this essay. The film was not an escape from their lives, but reminded them of experiences in their own lives. In the rhythms of their discourse, then, they spoke both literally and figuratively—expressive of the liberation of metaphor.

Essay Three
Relief from the Production of Certainties

Overview: Peirce, Eisenstein, Manchevski

Although set in Macedonia and London at the time of the Bosnian war in the 1990s, *Before the Rain* (1994) is a film that could be about social conflicts in many places. As writer and director Milcho Manchevski explained, "The story was inspired by the events unfolding in Yugoslavia, but it was *not about* them. It was about people in any country who stand in front of large events that are about to engulf them."[1] Reflective of the director's concept of his work, people in just about any country have been interested in seeing this film. *Before the Rain* has been screened throughout the world. From Italy, where it garnered the first of its more than thirty international awards, to Australia, Peru, the Philippines, the U.S.—these are just a few of the many countries where the film has been shown. Manchevski is even a prophet with honor in his own country. The nation of Macedonia bestowed its highest civilian award on the Skopje-born filmmaker for *Before the Rain*, his first major film.[2] The worldwide commercial success of *Before the Rain* demonstrates that art cinema does not necessarily mean abstruse films for small audiences and cult-followers. This film has defied the usual distinction between art cinema and commercial cinema. A truly international narrative, it also exceeds the boundaries of nationalist and ethnic cinema. Like the phenomenon of globalization that is refracted in its story, this film shakes up traditional categories of thought in many ways.

The purpose of this essay is to develop an approach to the film that can address the theory of the image informing its most prominent characteristics—the "cubist" structure with its compelling dislocation of linear narrative; the unusual attention to documentary photographs; and the innovative deployment of women characters who are crucial to understanding what is socially and artistically innovative about this film. To do this involves a reconsideration of basic ideas about the photographic image, and especially a critique of the general cultural presumption that a photograph records an image. Two theorists who confronted this issue of the photograph, what it is and what it isn't, are Sergei Eisenstein and Charles Sanders Peirce. Wollen and Deleuze both have recognized the potential importance of Peirce's philosophy of signs and Eisenstein's theory of montage.[3] Unlike linguistic theorists, both Peirce and Eisenstein developed complex theories of the image that did not derive from either linguistic models or psychoanalytic structures. However, this advantage has also been a disadvantage in contemporary theory. Neither Peirce nor Eisenstein has been carefully considered with regard to their theories of the photographic image.

A comparison and contrast of the theories of the image in the work of Peirce and Eisenstein can open up major questions about the politics of the image in photography and cinematography. Each brings out what is most distinctive in the other, but it would be reductive to cast them as a binary opposition. Their theories of the image are paradigms that hold some ideas in common, but diverge on the matters most crucial to each of them. Eisenstein's primary emphasis was on the social character of the film image as an iconic sign, a socially constructed image with variable possibilities. While Peirce also had a concept of the iconic sign, his crucial social idea was his concept of the index, which he developed into a theory of the photograph as a recorded natural image. The discussion of Peirce and Eisenstein is the basis for the primary distinction I make in this essay between "indexical" and "iconic." The second half of this essay undertakes an analysis of *Before the Rain* as an iconic film. *Before the Rain* actively seeks new political and intellectual ideas, articulating its own theory of cinema that critiques a belief in indexical meaning and develops an iconic cinema that goes beyond anything Eisenstein imagined. The theory of cinema articulated by this film rivals previous cinematic theories in its importance for the international, global society of the twenty-first century.

THE ICON AS A SET OF RELATIONS

The theory of the icon in the work of Peirce (1839–1914) was an aspect of a more comprehensive semiotics whose primary focus was scientific logic and philosophy. His initial ideas about the icon were formulated about 1867, and he returned to them intermittently, developing them further in the later part of his life, at a time when still photography had gained wide acceptance as an important cultural invention.[4] Eisenstein (1898–1948) wrote more than a generation later than Peirce. Although educated as an engineer, Eisenstein soon turned to theatrical production, and then to film-making, as his life's work. His theory of the cinematic image was born in the crucible of the Russian revolution, which the young Eisenstein supported strongly (though later he was often at odds with the government). He developed his theory in essays he wrote and published while making the films that earned him international acclaim. Socially and politically, these two men were vastly different. Peirce was an American Victorian, a descendant of an elite, pro-slavery, Boston Puritan family who supported himself by doing scientific measurements for the government.[5] Eisenstein, the son of a renowned architect in Riga, Latvia, was a modern and cosmopolitan revolutionary who also traveled extensively outside Russia.[6] That these men held any ideas in common seems strange. What they shared may be due to the fact that both received an education in science and mathematics. They both developed a theory of the icon as a set of relations, rejecting more conventional notions about the icon as a static image. However, they reached profoundly different conclusions about the significance of this theory.

Peirce's theory of the icon was part of a semiotic triad that consisted of three kinds of signs: the symbol, the icon, and the index. Symbols were arbitrary or conventional signs, such as language. Indexes were signs that were non-arbitrary. Icons occupied an ambiguous middle ground whose touchstone was the quality of resemblance or likeness.[7] At times, Peirce was a careful idealist in his concept of an icon, explaining that an icon "strictly speaking, can only be an idea" (2.276). Then again, he could be more casual, extending "icon" to include material images as well: "For convenience in ordinary parlance and when extreme precision is not called for, we extend the term *icon* to the outward objects which excite in consciousness the image itself" (CP4.447). Even in this more casual usage, "the image itself" remained an idea, distinguishable from any concrete object or signifier.

Peirce seems to have struggled with finding a description that was suitable to his concept of the icon. Although the icon was based on the idea of a resemblance or analogy with what it signified, Peirce was insistent in his assertion that the icon is not any kind of natural sign. That is, the icon has no inherent relationship to what it signifies. The following passage is typical of his thinking:

> The icon has no dynamical connection with the object it represents; it simply happens that its qualities resemble those of that object, and excite analogous sensations in the mind for which it is a likeness. But it really stands unconnected with them. (2.299)

Although Peirce was often unclear about what "resemblance" might be about, he was clear about what it was *not* about: "A pure icon can convey no positive or factual information; for it affords no assurance that there is any such thing in nature" (4.447). The icon had no utility at the level most people think of as a conventional function of signs, to represent things in the existing world, to refer directly to the world one lives in. The icon's relationship to the world was provisional, problematic, possibly nonexistent—a hypothesis rather than an assertion of fact. Since the icon was not predetermined by the material world, it also presupposed the possibility of motion and change in relation to that world.

As his theory developed, Peirce's concept of the icon became more expansive than what is usually meant by "images." In the process, the notion of direct visual resemblance became secondary. Although his definition of the icon continued to include such things as representational painting, it also came to include diagrams, graphs, and especially algebraic equations (2.277–78). In this expansion, the icon came to be first and foremost about its own internal characteristics as the basis of its quality of resemblance:

> An icon is a representamen [a sign] of what it represents and for the mind that interprets it as such, by virtue of its being an immediate image, that is to say by virtue of characters which belong to it in itself as a sensible object, and which it would possess just the same were there no object in nature that it resembled. (4.447)

While representational art continued to be one kind of resemblance, other kinds of resemblance interested Peirce much more. For Peirce, good examples of icons were *not* direct visual analogies, *not* things that could be said to look like other things in the way that a portrait resembles a person. For example, "a geometrical diagram is a good example of an icon" (4.447). He elaborated, "many diagrams resemble their objects not at all in looks; it is only in respect to the relations to their parts that their likeness consists" (2.282). The icon was distinguished by its relations among its parts. This shift was very significant because it conceptualized the icon as a dynamic sign and as an act of imagination whose value lies in articulating relations within itself. What relations are expressed in a particular equation? How are its parts related to each other? The icon as a set of relations distinguished it from the older and more ordinary concept of the icon as a static thing, a statue or a painting that drew its claim to resemblance from the person or thing it represented. Peirce's concept of the icon freed it from the burden of mimesis, the icon as a derivative copy or representation of the existing material world. He granted originality to the icon itself as a creative idea about the world, one whose relation to the world was open to question because it was not constrained to imitate or represent the already existing world. The icon can be a means of changing that world, of imagining different relations than those that exist.

This idea is not as unfamiliar as it may seem in its abstract definition. Take this example from ordinary life: A pie chart of a monthly budget is a diagram that visually expresses the ratios, the relations, of monthly expenses—such as 30 percent for housing, 20 percent for food, and so on. The iconic thinking involved is about *the relations expressed among the parts.* The pie chart does not convey factual information in that it does not distinguish between one absolute amount of money and another. It can only resemble relative figures, ratios. For example, interpreter A spends $700 a month on housing and that is, for them, 30 percent of their income. Interpreter B spends $2,000 a month, and that is also 30 percent of their income. The pie chart looks the same for both interpreters, expressive of the same ratio of 30 percent. The pie chart does not distinguish between the absolute dollar amounts that A and B spend, but that does not mean that it has no relation to the material world. It is expressive of particular *relations* in the material world, and it allows the interpreter to imagine alternative relations among its parts. An interpreter might change the amount spent on housing to 25 percent, or change jobs, or move to a different city. The diagram is potentially dynamic because it allows its interpreter to imagine different relations, other ratios, even another way of life. The interpretation of a present way of life can also change significantly— an interpreter might not have been aware of what proportion of their income they were spending on housing, even if they knew the absolute amount. The icon has dynamic capabilities as a sign because it can be ideationally manipulated. It isn't necessarily otherworldly just because its relation to the material world is not absolutely determined. Its relation to reality is complicated and variable, encompassing the hypothetical as well as the representational. This idea of the icon emphasizes as well that people actively think in icons. They don't just passively receive them.

Peirce developed and articulated his theory of the icon through his interest in mathematics and logic, apart from consideration of representations of the human form. Peirce's "good" examples of icons were those that did not include the potentially confusing element of visual art. Instead he turned to mathematics, which he thought was primarily iconic:

> The reasoning of mathematicians will be found to turn chiefly upon the use of likenesses, which are the very hinges of the gates of their science. The utility of likenesses to mathematicians consists in their suggesting in a very precise way, new aspects of supposed states of things. (2.281)

The algebraic equation was his paradigmatic example: "every algebraical equation is an icon, in so far as it *exhibits,* by means of the algebraic signs (which are not themselves icons), the relations of the quantities concerned" (2.283). The notational signs themselves are *not* icons. The icon is the equation taken as a whole, as it expresses "relations" or "patterns" among its parts that can be "manipulated" (3.364).[8] Patterns and rules of manipulation, such as "multiplication is distributive," are "the *icons par excellence* of algebra" (3.364). Peirce makes his strongest statements about the value of icons in the context of discussing algebraic examples. For instance: "A great distinguishing property of the icon is that, by the direct observation of it, other truths concerning its object can be discovered than those which suffice to determine its construction." It is the icon that has "this capacity for revealing unexpected truth" (2.279). The icon is about the discovery of new concepts, finding something unexpected. It is about thinking in new ways, discovering "other truths" beyond what is known. "Given a conventional or other general sign of an object, to deduce any other truth than that which it explicitly signifies, it is necessary, in all cases, to replace that sign by an icon" (2.279). An iconic sign may have no utility as an expression of fact or even as a conventional sign in ordinary discourse, but that is precisely its value. Iconic signs are dynamic signs—speculative, hypothetical, experimental, crucial to the creative imagination.

Eisenstein shared with Peirce the idea that iconic thinking was first and foremost about a set of relations. In Eisenstein's theory of the image in cinema, the basic unit of cinematography is montage, not the material photographic image per se. Montage is the creative juxtaposition of images, and the distinctive quality of montage is juxtaposition, the *relating* of images to each other. In contemporary film theory and criticism, Eisenstein has often been described as a proponent of a "montage of attractions," an early idea of his that was based on an awkward combination of theatrical and industrial production.[9] However, this was an idea he largely rejected when he turned to film. Eisenstein's important essays on cinematography begin with those he wrote in 1929–30, after the international success of his film, *Battleship Potemkin*.[10] Here he articulated his theory of film montage as the cinematographic principle, the basis for a theory of the cinematic image. Like Peirce, he conceptualized the icon as a constructed set of relations.

Eisenstein's "The Cinematographic Principle" went beyond the shot in its opening declaration. Cinema is not simply the shot, the material image taken in itself. "Cinema is montage," the relationships among shots, the juxtaposition of shots. To explain this idea, Eisenstein evoked the concept of the Japanese ideogram. While Eisenstein here asserted that film was like a language, it is crucial that the language he selected was pictorial. He explained how an ideogram is a montage in its composition: "by the combination of two depictables is achieved the representation of something that is graphically undepictable" (30). Two images that are in some sense representational, which can be visualized, are, when juxtaposed, united to generate another, "undepictable" concept. He gave quite a few examples of Japanese ideograms, such as "a knife and a heart signifies 'sorrow'" (30). When juxtaposed, graphic images do not remain bound to the graphic level. They yield undepicted concepts, abstract ideas initially generated by perceived images but distinguishable from them. Resorting to a mathematical concept, as Peirce had, Eisenstein explained that the combination of images that constitute an ideogram "is to be regarded not as their sum, but as their product, i.e., as a value of another dimension, another degree; each, separately, corresponds to an *object*, to a fact, but their combination corresponds to a *concept*." This was the basis of "intellectual cinema" (30).

In his idea of cinema as the creation of undepicted meaning, Eisenstein sought to articulate how images can express abstract concepts, how it is possible to think with images. For Eisenstein as for Peirce, the juxtaposition of images conceptualized the icon as fundamentally relational. Like Peirce's algebraic equations, Eisenstein's montage was about the relationships among its parts. He called the parts "montage pieces" to emphasize that the relation among them is what formed the montage. It was montage that went "beyond the shot," montage that was the basic unit of cinema, *not* the individual image. Montage yielded concepts that were the results of relations. To go "beyond the shot" was to recognize a capability in cinema that freed the cinematic image from its tethered thing-for-thing resemblance to the existing material world.

In "The Cinematographic Principle," Eisenstein explicitly rejected the idea of montage as an assembly of images, images put together and immobilized "like bricks." This idea, which initially had informed the "montage of attractions," was cast off as a "make-shift analysis" (36).[11] Now the "attractions" had become more sophisticated in their dynamic interactions and more complex in their results. In saying that "cinema is montage," Eisenstein went beyond the shot, beyond the idea of film as simply a picture show, by placing the key emphasis instead on the relations between shots rather than the shot itself. Deleuze, discussing Eisenstein's theory of montage, wrongly attributed to Eisenstein a belief in "the identity of concept and image," in which "the concept is in itself in the image, and the image is for itself in the concept" (161).[12] This was not Eisenstein's theory. It was the theory Eisenstein *rejected*. For Eisenstein, the concept that constituted the intellectual cinema was not *in* the image. It was in the juxtapositions, the montage. Eisenstein's basic concept of juxtaposition has also been mistakenly described as an association.[13] While he did discuss association as one possible kind of montage (57–58), he also considered it a poor use of montage because it was easy to lose the "emotional dynamization of the subject." Association did not necessarily involve the idea of "a value of another dimension," and without this higher level of meaning, the montage "ossifies into lifeless literary symbolism and stylistic mannerism" (58). In general, his concept of montage was more complicated and more dynamic than "association" suggests to a modern reader.

Eisenstein described how the value of another dimension was created in a variety of ways. It could be a "collision" of images that exploded into something else. In a subsequent essay, "A Dialectic Approach to Film Form," he stated the idea of the icon in terms of dialectic: thesis and antithesis yield a synthesis akin to the "value of another dimension" in the ideogram. But Eisenstein was not always a dialectical materialist in his explanations of montage. In another instance, he referred to the lines of *haiku* as "montage phrases," as shot lists, suggesting that the imagery of poetry was a suitable analogy—though he was careful to underscore that the ideogram was the basis of *haiku*, again fending off a directly linguistic analogy (32). Among his most interesting ideas about the dynamics of montage was the notion of "incongruity." He explained, "Degree of incongruence determines intensity of impression, and determines that tension which becomes the real element of authentic rhythm" (50). Montage, by constructing how much incongruity exists between adjacent shots, determines the conceptual development of the film, its rhythm, its movement in the conceptual sense. The more incongruity in the juxtaposition, the more emotionally intense and intellectually striking it will be. He explained incongruity another way in a reference to Kabuki theater and its "acting without transitions." He also quoted Renoir and Baudelaire on "irregularity" as a crucial dimension of art, any art, and offered as examples the use of "spatial disproportion" and "temporal disproportion" (as would occur in close-ups or slow motion) (51).

Montage as Eisenstein understood it was about creating juxtapositions that would provoke thought. He strongly contrasted his own theory of montage with the work of film-makers who depicted transitions and avoided striking juxtapositions, thereby eliminating the undepicted meaning that typified Eisenstein's iconic dimension of cinema. Eisenstein sought to create irregularities in perspective rather than regularity and order—anything to avoid the predictable movement of "linkage." Eisenstein thought that a juxtaposition that was only linkage—an association of the simplest kind—was only one example of montage, and not a good one. He drew an analogy with physics to explain this:

> Recall what an infinite number of combinations is known in physics to be capable of arising from the impact (collision) of spheres. Depending on whether the spheres be resilient, non-resilient, or mingled. Amongst all these combinations there is one in which the impact is so weak that the collision is degraded to an even movement of both in the same direction. (38)

Note that Eisenstein's references to "collision" were not literally about violence or shock, as some Deleuzians might think, but instead meant figuratively to convey the importance of dynamic and unexpected juxtapositions for an intellectual cinema.[14]

As Eisenstein developed his theory of montage, he extended the iconic theory of juxtapositions to the shot itself. That is, he conceptualized depiction itself as montage. He called this *intra-shot montage*, a montage within the frame that honed in on the dynamic tensions, conflicts or incongruities of lines, scales, volumes, depths, masses, lightness or darkness—the diagrammatic, geometric, or tonal aspects of a shot on the plane of the frame (39). In a manner analogous to Peirce's inclusion of diagrams and graphs among his good examples of icons, Eisenstein interpreted all these aspects of the shot as iconic. For some he included diagrams of his own to show how diagonals in separate shots could build up a particular perspective or emphasis through a series of frames. In a sense, Eisenstein's theory presupposed that, conceptually, every shot has an open frame. As he put it, "conflict within the shot is potential montage, in the development of its intensity shattering the quadrilateral cage of the shot and exploding its conflict into montage impulses *between* the montage pieces" (38). The dynamic tension within the frame generated conceptual motion between different iconic aspects of one shot as well as between shots. With this development of his theory, Eisenstein extended his iconic theory of montage beyond the juxtaposition of independent shots, interweaving it with juxtapositions within the depicted image itself. Nonetheless, the image as a material thing, such as one frame on a filmstrip, remained a "montage-piece," understandable only in its relation to other montage-pieces. Because iconic thinking was intrinsically dynamic, the concept of intra-shot montage set in motion even the apparently static depiction. It was indeed a theory of the moving image, and extended even to images that appeared to be static. Stasis in film could be achieved, but only by using particular kinds of iconic structures. Analogously, there was no structuring lack inherent in film. If one wanted the abstract idea of a structuring lack in a film, it had to be composed like anything else.

With admirable consistency, Eisenstein recognized that his iconic theory of film was not unique to film, that it also described other kinds of arts. His many references to theater are well known, but he also drew examples from painting, drawing, and other seemingly static visual images. For example, he asked,

What comprises the dynamic effect of a painting? The eye follows the direction of an element in the painting. It retains a visual impression, which then collides with the impression derived from following the direction of a second element. The conflict of these directions forms the dynamic effect in apprehending the whole. (50)

Some paintings generate four or five impressions, or more, and it was all of them together, the montage, that constituted the apparently single image that was called the painting. To clarify his point, Eisenstein evoked some examples from art-history kinds of art, among them:

> The secret of the marvelous mobility of Daumier's and Lautrec's figures dwells in the fact that the various anatomical parts of a body are represented in spatial circumstances (positions) that are temporally various, disjunctive. For example, in Toulouse-Lautrec's lithograph of Miss Cissy Loftus, if one logically develops position A of the foot, one builds a body in position A corresponding to it. But the body is represented from knee up already in position A + a. The cinematic effect of joined motionless pictures is already established here! From hips to shoulders we can see A + a + a. The figure comes alive and kicking! (50)

The film-viewer underwent a similar experience when seeing a sequence of film images. Eisenstein argued against the idea that people see images one after another when they watch a film. He insisted instead that the viewer sees images one of top of another. What happens in the mind when "placed next to each other, two photographed immobile images result in the appearance of movement"? He says,

> Each sequential element is perceived not *next* to the other, but on *top* of the other. For the idea (or sensation) of movement arises from the [mental] process of superimposing on the retained impression of the object's first position, a newly visible further position of the object. (49)

The fact that frames materially appear next to each other on a filmstrip does not tell us how the viewer perceives them. Eisenstein rejected the mimetic conclusion that the mind imitates the filmstrip. Rather, the mind combines or even rearranges the images in various ways through the iconic process of montage.[15]

Eisenstein extended his theory of the icon to images in the common-sense use of the term, even to photographic representations of people in dramatic film. That there was hesitation in interpreting the photographic image as an icon is evident in Eisenstein's own statement about it: "In painting the form arises from *abstract* elements of line and color, while in cinema the material *concreteness* of the image within the frame presents—as an element— the greatest difficulty in manipulation." The photographic image seemed at first to be unlike the visual figures of paintings and drawings, where the abstract elements were readily apparent.[16] He queries if, in cinematography, he is dealing with a "combination of two concrete denotations of two con-crete objects" (60), but concludes that he is not. Why? Because "the differ-entiation in montage-pieces lies in their lack of existence as single units. Each piece can evoke no more than a certain association" (60). Here, "asso-ciation" refers to the way an icon relates to a concrete object. It is because the icon's relation to the material world is problematic, *not* a simple substitution of image for thing, that the juxtaposition of images in cinema is fundamen-tally different from the denotative naming of a concrete object.

He demonstrated his iconic theory of the photographic image by taking the "film clichés" of a murder scene montage: "1. A hand lifts a knife. 2. The eyes of the victim open suddenly. 3. His hand clutches the table." And so on (60). Eisenstein pointed out that "in regard to the action *as a whole, each fragment piece* is almost *abstract*. The more differentiated they are, the more abstract they become" (60–61). And therefore the more they depend on juxtaposition for their intelligibility. The iconic qualities of the film related the montage pieces to each other. It was the semi-abstract qualities of pho-tographs that, taken together, conveyed the feeling and the idea of murder, that made the sequence more than a means of conveying murder "as infor-mation" for the audience. Iconic thinking in cinema extended to photo-graphic representations of people and their actions, and had to extend to such images if the audience was to be moved by what they saw, if they were to grasp "an idea of murder—the feeling of murder" rather than simply murder as plot information. Eisenstein took care to point out that montage sequences like this need not appeal only to the emotions. They could also be used to "serve the ends of new concepts—of new attitudes, that is, of purely intellectual aims" (61).

Eisenstein concluded that photographic images of people and things in cinema functioned in the same dynamic way as other kinds of artistic pictorial images, that the cinematic icon was not a uniquely static image, but was dynamically engaged in a set of relations within itself and with a larger set of relations among montage pieces. This may sound like it involves the fragmentation of the body, but it does not. To read it in that way would transform Eisenstein into an iconoclast, and he was anything but iconoclastic. Eisenstein's theory is about iconic images of the body, *not* the physical body itself, which he conceived as distinct from those images. In the same essay, Eisenstein goes into more detail in articulating what kinds of juxtapositions could be found within the image, in intra-shot montage: conflict of planes, conflict of volumes, conflict of light and dark, and so on. He conceptualized these properties of the photographic image in a relational way, the relation between one plane and another, the rela-tion of one volume to another (54). He also included diagrams that show the changing relation between angles in successive shots—intra-shot montage was part of inter-shot montage. Indeed, the purpose of intra-shot montage was to explode the quadrilateral cage of the shot, to allow images to move dynamically in relation to each other. His examples of the iconic in film are like Peirce's equations and diagrams.

Importantly for film, Eisenstein developed what Peirce did not, an iconic interpretation of images that specifically addressed the issue of images of people. Peirce's general theory of icons overlapped at some points with Eisenstein's ideas, and particularly Eisenstein's analysis of pictorial images such as drawings and paintings. Although Peirce did not explore such images in the same detail, or with the same enthusiasm for this subject, he did account for it in a brief passage on the customary, ordinary idea of images:

> Turning now to the rhetorical evidence, it is a familiar fact that there are such representations as icons. Every picture (however conventional its method) is essentially a representation of that kind. So is every diagram even although there be no sensuous resemblance between it and its object, but only an analogy between the relations of the parts of each. (2.279)

Picture and diagram could be mentioned in the same breath because they had the same qualities as they composed a set of relations. One can see how unimportant the notion of "visual resemblance" in the traditional representational sense had become for Peirce. He grants its rhetorical usage in common parlance, but he does not give it philosophical weight in defining an icon. It has meaning only as one set of relations may resemble another set of relations.

However, Peirce shared Eisenstein's concepts only up to a point. In the above quotation, "every picture" means pictorial representations such as paintings or drawings, and moreover, such pictures taken one at a time, each as a separate instance. Unlike Eisenstein, Peirce thought in terms of a single instance of an image, a single picture, a single painting. Peirce did not extend his iconic theory to the relation of multiple pictorial images to each other, except in discussing the use of photographic images in map-making. Peirce shied away from discussing pictures of people—in the sentences following the quote above, he went directly to algebra to expand his idea, not to instances of pictures such as Eisenstein's sequence of murder scene shots. Peirce consistently developed his general theory of the icon through an analysis of diagrams and equations, icons that did *not* involve representations of the human figure or, indeed, any kind of "visual resemblance" in the customary sense. And finally and crucially, Peirce did *not* make the leap from pictorial art to the photograph, as Eisenstein did. On the contrary, he pulled back from it. For Peirce, the photographic image was something altogether different. In a paragraph following the quotation above, Peirce expressly *excluded* the photograph from his theory of icons, arguing that the photograph is fundamentally different in its making, and consequently, fundamentally different in its connection to what it pictures (2.281). For Peirce, the photograph, picture though it might be, was something else, an index. Because Peirce's semiotics of the mathematical icon had freed itself from the constraints of "visual resemblance," the fact that photographs seemed to be about visual resemblance was not important to what they were, not a reason to consider them icons. Peirce's primary ideas about images of people developed as an aspect of his concept of the indexical sign, not the iconic sign.

INDEXES: THE NATURAL IMAGE, RACISM, AND PHOTOGRAPHY

In Peirce's triadic scheme of signs, the place of images within it has usually been treated as obviously iconic. However, his theory of indexical meaning also generated a theory of the image, one that conflicted with what he said about the iconic sign. In effect, these two different theories of the image, the iconic and the indexical, described two different ways of thinking. Oddly, although Peirce was a chronic inventor of new terms, he seems not to have coined any new words to distinguish his different concepts of images. Consequently I have used my own term—"the indexical image"—to denote the theory of the image that grew out of his analysis of the indexical sign. Of particular importance for film is why Peirce considered the photograph an index, why this supported his social conservatism, and why the indexical image as such went unnamed in his own discussions of it.

Peirce defined the index as a non-arbitrary sign, a sign with an inherent relation to what it signified, what has often been called a "natural sign." Although natural signs are generally regarded as pre-modern,[17] Peirce was not unique in his modern belief in natural signs. For example, Saussure believed in natural signs, too. Saussure has functioned as the gold standard, so to speak, for modern theories of the arbitrary sign, an idea that Saussure developed into a theory of difference that emphasized the arbitrariness of the linguistic sign. What has not been sufficiently recognized is the context in which he did this. Notwithstanding his theory of arbitrary linguistic signs, Saussure not only believed in natural signs, but he predicated his theory of language on the existence of natural signs. His "first principle," that the linguistic sign is arbitrary, also asserts his belief in signs that have a "natural bond" between the sign and its referent:

> The word symbol has been used to designate the linguistic sign, or more
> specifically, what is here called the signifier. Principle I ["The linguistic sign is

arbitrary"] in particular weighs against the use of this term. One characteristic of the symbol [the natural sign] is that it is never wholly arbitrary; it is not empty for there is the rudiment of a natural bond between the signifier and the signified. The symbol of justice, a pair of scales, could not be replaced by just any other symbol, such as a chariot.[18]

This is a bizarre contrast for so many reasons that it's hard to know where to begin. The scales of justice, with its obvious cultural import, seems an odd choice if Saussure's purpose was to clarify what a natural sign is, as distinct from arbitrary signs. His choice bespeaks an unacknowledged anxiety about the arbitrary linguistic sign and a concomitant need for a natural sign that would ground his otherwise unstable system of linguistic signs. He secures truth in a figure that has power by virtue of being *outside* the arbitrary system of linguistic signs. Saussure did not discuss this, nor did he acknowledge that he picked a visual image to typify a natural sign. He does not say why he believed that "symbolism" should be understood as natural rather than cultural. Having abruptly secured the natural sign as one pole of a massive binary opposition that underwrites his theory of language, he simply dropped the matter of natural signs. In effect, he treated the semiotics of the natural sign as self-evident, and went on to develop his theory of difference as it applied only to the arbitrary signs of language.

Wendy Brown, in her critique of liberal political thought, argues that the idea of equality in liberalism was formulated only as an abstract idea. Once the multiplicity of material identities are considered—such as race, gender, ethnicity, and so on—the abstract idea of equality is not maintained.[19] As to why this is so, Saussure's semiotics is suggestive. Saussure was a liberal in the sense that he believed in the abstract equality of languages. He has also been criticized by sociolinguists for omitting the social conditions of language use from his theory.[20] Saussure's statement about the arbitrariness of all linguistic signs, accompanied by his belief in natural signs, suggests that social and material reality was relegated to the category of the natural sign. Take his example of the scales of justice. It is not difficult to see how Woman fits into this scheme of things once the full symbol of justice is considered. It isn't simply the scales that represent justice. It is the Roman goddess Justitia who holds the scales.[21] Without her, the scales would be indistinguishable from a trader's scales. It is the female figure of Justitia holding the scales that has served as the symbol of justice for two thousand years in Western culture. Justitia is a figure with a long imagistic history in Western culture—both in her Roman goddess form on the architecture of many public buildings and in recent liberal realist films as the arbiter of true and false images.[22] The natural bond in Saussure's example, when fully considered, is a natural bond between female gender and justice—and one that very strangely makes her the arbiter of justice at the same time that it relegates her to an exemplary exclusion from linguistic signs and places her in the realm of the visual.

Peirce's theory of the indexical sign is important because Peirce, unlike Saussure, paid much more attention to natural signs. Where Saussure left the natural sign untheorized, Peirce explored this idea in great detail, developing his idea of the index as a modern theory of the natural sign. Peirce gave it equal importance as one of the three kinds of signs in his triadic semiotics. And it was Peirce who recognized the importance of a theory of the image that would account for the (at the time) recent invention of photography. As I will show, the photographic image, understood as a recorded image, was a crucial dimension of Peirce's theory of the index. Photography became his exemplary instance of the index, fusing the new technology of photography with the semiotics of the natural sign to produce a modern theory of the natural sign that is still widely believed—not because everyone has read Peirce, but because Peirce codified the widespread assumptions of his culture regarding photography. To understand the role of the photograph in legitimating natural signs, making them credible in modern society, it is important to consider the general context of Peirce's concept of indexical meaning.

In Peirce's philosophy, the meaning of an indexical sign was bound to a specific material locale. The index "depends upon association by contiguity, and not upon association by resemblance or upon intellectual operations" (3.306). Peirce meant contiguity in a material, physical sense. The index must involve "existent individuals" (people or things). It was tied to a particular material place and/or a particular material person. Illustrating this necessity for physical contiguity, Peirce offered the indexical sign of a pointing finger as "the type of the class" (3.362). Peirce ranged among different kinds of signs and different kinds of physical contiguity when offering more examples of indexes. The gesture of the pointing finger did not mean indexes had to be nonverbal gestures. Words used to orient the body in physical space, such as "over here" or "over there," or "on the left" or "on the right," were also indexes (2.290). The index was not limited to words or references to the body's orientation. It could be something heard or seen. Among other examples Peirce gave: a rap on the door, a weathervane showing the direction of the wind, a footprint, a sundial, a barometer (2.286). The indexical sign was in some way physically connected to what it signified. This is what made it a non-arbitrary sign, "a real thing or fact which is a sign of its object by virtue of being connected with it [the object] as a matter of fact" (4.447).

Epistemologically, the index differed from the icon. Where an icon afforded "no ground for an interpretation of it as referring to actual existence" (2.251), the index did precisely that. Continuing to contrast the iconic sign with the indexical sign, Peirce asserted, "The value of an icon consists in its exhibiting the features of a state of things regarded as if it were purely imaginary. The value of an index is that it assures us of positive fact" (4.448). Unlike the iconic sign, the index offered an assurance of positive fact, an absolute point of reference, contact with the real through its physical connection to its object.

Belief in the validity of the natural sign as Peirce defined it is far more current and widespread than has generally been recognized—even among theorists themselves. In contemporary life, indexes are easy to find and enjoy considerable credibility. For example, the most popular current television series, *CSI* (Crime Scene Investigation), is primarily about indexes. Cases are solved through the analysis of physical evidence—indexes that are used to determine the identity of the criminal, and often to determine what the crime was. The rightness of the solution to the criminal case depends on the indexes used to solve it. The TV series dramatizes how different the index is from the icon. Iconic thinking opens up possibilities of interpretation at the beginning of the show, engaging speculation about the crime and its perpetrator. At the end of the show, determining indexes have shut down the possibility of alternative explanations and point with certainty to the criminal and the exact nature of the criminal act. The physical contiguity of indexes, the evidence, is the epistemological guarantor of the truth of the explanation on *CSI*, the evidence that is certain and gives closure to the episode. In fictional stories such as *CSI* as well as in classical detective stories, the validity of the natural sign is never questioned, although it may take characters a long time to understand what its validity is, what has been physically contiguous with what. When they do finally understand it, the index stands out as incontrovertibly true. This constitutes a solution to the case.[23]

Indexes have also had credibility outside fictive circumstances. For instance, DNA is widely regarded as an index of identity—not arbitrary and not socially constructed, but naturally true as indexes are true. Yet indexes, and even DNA, can become problematic in society, and when they do, societies seem ill-prepared to step back and consider whether natural signs exist. When an index is challenged, it produces considerable controversy, partly because the immediacy and material specificity of an index makes it difficult to see that a general concept—the natural sign—is its basis. For example, in the O. J. Simpson criminal trial in Los Angeles, a media event as much as a legal event, the defense attorneys became famous for their ability to turn indexical evidence back into iconic speculation.[24] Faulty collection processes had interfered with physical contiguity, introducing problematic interpretations. The prosecution demonstrated that DNA evidence, when closely examined, involved a great deal of mathematics, and mathematical probability resonated with iconicity, not indexicality. Near certainty was gradually recast as uncertainty, as iconic speculation. The suspect was ultimately judged not guilty, a highly controversial decision. It is not so surprising that *CSI*, also produced in Los Angeles, began its highly successful run just a couple of years later, offering a fictive version of the guaranteed viability of indexical evidence that the Simpson case had seemed to repudiate.

Perhaps the predominantly African-American jury in the Simpson criminal case also refused to convict the African-American defendant because to do so would have validated the idea of indexicality as a legitimate determinant of criminality. Indexical thinking has long been the basis of racial profiling, where physical characteristics are treated as weathervanes pointing to criminality. There is no better example than the thinking of Peirce himself on this matter. Where for Saussure the natural sign was prejudicially symbolized by female gender, Peirce associated the natural sign with racism instead. In an essay on indexical meaning, he digressed to tell an illustrative story about the loss of his watch and overcoat on a boat.[25] Peirce assumed it was theft and, ambitious to find the thief, he began his search this way: "I then made all the colored waiters, no matter on what deck they belonged, come and stand up in a row" (271). Peirce did not argue for the validity of his racism. He took for granted that race was a natural sign, an indexical sign, and expected the reader would do so, too.

That indexicality as a way of thinking is still an underlying principle in contemporary criminal law is reflected in the exoneration of the police officers in New York City who killed an innocent African man, Amadou Diallo. In this notorious case of police murder, the courtroom arguments displaced the issue of racial prejudice by focusing on the interpretation of a physical gesture. The police claimed that when Diallo reached for his wallet in his pocket, they thought he was reaching for a gun. Diallo actually had another purpose, to get out his identity card. The police acknowledged that they had misinterpreted his gesture, assuming it was an indexical sign of a gun being drawn when there was another possible interpretation. The police refusal to recognize other possible meanings for Diallo's action led to Diallo being shot and killed in an instant. Amazingly, when the police were put on trial, they were exonerated. Their vindication in court validated and demonstrated the privileging of indexical meaning in criminal investigation and enforcement. The police were judged to have been behaving properly as police because they were thinking indexically. As one journalist explained it:

> In a typical murder trial, prosecutors have to prove that the defendant killed the victim. In this trial, they had to prove that it was unreasonable for the officers to claim that they shot Mr. Diallo because they believed he had a gun.[26]

In effect, the exoneration of the police made Diallo's death his own fault because his gesture was unclear by indexical criteria. The Diallo case shows that the idea of an indexical sign is a very political idea even when it seems innocuous. That the concept of the indexical sign may have some validity when one is talking about "right" or "left," "up" or "down," in relation to the physical body—it was this kind of validity that was politicized in an instant for Diallo. Shoe prints are made by someone's shoes, as fingerprints are made from someone's fingers, but physical contiguity does not produce the epistemological certainty that Peirce attributed to such things. Whether one calls it a natural sign or an indexical sign, it can only assert what is culturally believed by someone to be true.

Or is it even belief? An act of belief grants more subjectivity than Peirce did in his theory of the indexical sign. Peirce described the impact of indexical truth as an experience that happens without thought. Indexes operated by "forcibly intruding upon the mind, quite regardless of its being interpreted as a sign" (4.447). The index was a very one-sided affair—described solely in terms of reception. Where the icon was based on a concept of the subject as a composer of signs, a maker of signs, the index eliminated both subject and sign. In the indexical way of thinking, the subject was cast as a passive recipient of something whose sign-ness was not even recognized as such. Forcible intrusion occurred "quite regardless of its being interpreted as a sign." Emblematic of authoritarianism, the index was specifically understood as being *not* of the subject's own making and being beyond the subject's control or apprehension. The index came about through its connection with the object, not the subject: "The index is physically connected with its object; they make an organic pair, but the interpreting mind has nothing to do with this connection, except remarking on it, after it is established" (2.299). An index was made by and in the material object-world. The subject did not think about indexical signs. Instead a reaction overtook the subject, who might be said to simply register a significance rather than interpret it, and even that occurred only after the fact, after the index was already lodged in the mind. Because he thought the subject had nothing to do with it, Peirce in effect defined the indexical sign as something that was discovered rather than created. The index was self-evidently credible, beyond manipulation and interpretation, *because* it originated outside the mind. There was no concept of the mind's construction of an indexical sign as there was with Peirce's iconic sign. Instead, there was a bizarre inversion of the typical hierarchical connotations of the subject/object relation. In Peirce's theory of the indexical sign, it was *the object, not the subject*, that generated the indexical sign. The object engaged in the activity of sign-making, and the subject was the passive recipient of the sign made by the object. Did this theory empower the object? It didn't empower the object Amadou Diallo. It did, however, exonerate the police subject, as it has exonerated most cases of police brutality. In the indexical way of thinking a subject without subjectivity cannot be at fault, but an object with sign-emitting powers can be.

Visuality began to enter into Peirce's discussion when he elaborated on how the forcible intrusion into the mind occurred. Although, according to him, indexes could have been anything heard, touched, smelled, or seen, Peirce privileged vision: "The index asserts nothing; it only says 'There!' It takes hold of our eyes, as it were, and forcibly directs them to a particular object, and there it stops" (3.362). The index's forcible intrusion on the mind occurred by forcibly directing the eyes, controlling the subject's act of seeing in its recognition of the existence of the object. To call this an act of perception might be misleading insofar as that would imply an act of interpretation, and Peirce did not call it that. What he described was more on the order of an automatic response to visual stimuli. Indexes "direct the attention to their objects by blind compulsion" (3.306). "Blind" was an interesting choice of terms—suggestive of the notion that something was seen, but not perceived. With eyes wide shut, to borrow a phrase from Stanley Kubrick, the subject became aware of the existence of the object.

Did the subject see an image or not? Peirce was a bit squirrelly on this matter, and perhaps he himself was confused. In a cryptic acknowledgment of the problem, Peirce wrote:

> In so far as the Index is affected by the Object, it necessarily has some Quality in common with the Object, and it is in respect to these that it refers to the Object. It does, therefore, involve a sort of Icon, although an Icon of a peculiar kind; and it is not the mere resemblance of its Object, even in these respects which makes it a sign, but it is the actual modification of it [the indexical sign] by the Object. (2.248)

There was a "sort of Icon" involved. It was an icon "of a peculiar kind." The sort-of-icon of a peculiar kind is what I am calling the "indexical image" because this sort-of-icon did not have an iconic relation of resemblance to its object. What was peculiar about the indexical image, what made it "sort of," was its non-iconic relation to the object. The iconic sign had a relation that was problematic, speculative, not a certainty. The icon was "external" to the object, not physically connected with it. The index, by contrast, was physically connected. The index's relation to its object was not resemblance, and not analogy.[27] Rather, the index experienced "actual modification by the Object." That is, the object controlled the relationship between the object and the indexical image by infusing the indexical image with qualities of the object itself. This was what made the indexical sign natural, and not cultural, for Peirce.

That the indexical image was not only indexical but also an image is apparent from Peirce's description of the crucial epistemological role the image played in the subject's experience of an index. Peirce implied that indexes did not inevitably "excite in consciousness an image," but when they did, the subject received a positive assurance as to truth of fact. He wrote of the index:

> It may simply serve to identify its object and assure us of its existence and presence. But very often the nature of the factual connexion of the index with its object is such as to excite in consciousness an image of some features of the object, and in that way affords evidence from which positive assurance as to truth of fact may be drawn. (4.447)

An index might only offer assurance of existence and presence, of hereness. Peirce distinguished this ontological kind of index from the index that excited an image in the subject's consciousness. This latter index, the image, became the "evidence" for adjudicating what was true or false. Certain truth arrived in the conscious mind through an indexical image that mediated between the object and the subject. It was indexical because the image in the subject's mind was caused by the object—in this sense, the subject's mind was passive. The evidence that allowed the subject to positively conclude (not just guess or speculate or infer) a truth of fact about the object—that evidence was imagistic. To say, however, that the mind interpreted the resulting image is not accurate, because the indexical sign dictated how it would be received by the passive mind it forcibly intruded upon. The indexical image, emitted by the object, dictated the conclusions that would be drawn from it. Otherwise the unique certainty that defined the indexical sign would be lost.

Peirce's own story about the loss of his watch and overcoat bears this out. We left Peirce with the usual suspects rounded up on deck. He had now to determine which one was the thief. Peirce was proud of his indexical, thoughtless solution:

> While I was going through the row, chatting a little with each, I held myself in as passive and receptive state as I could. When I had gone through the row I made a great effort to detect in my consciousness some symptoms of the thief, and this effort, I suppose, prevented my success. But then finding I could detect nothing I said to myself, "Well, anyway, I *must* fasten on someone, though it be but a random choice," and instantly I *knew* which of the men it was. (281; emphasis in original)

Peirce tried to be the receptive subject, but found that in consciously looking for symptoms, indexes of guilt, his consciousness was interfering with
receiving the indexical sign he wished for. He wasn't being passive enough.
Only when he abandoned thinking altogether was he able to know spon-
taneously who the thief was—or so he claimed. When the investigator
from Pinkerton's asked him to explain his choice, Peirce replied, "I have no
reason for thinking so; but I am entirely confident that it is so" (273).
Indexical thinking was not about reasoning, and not about consciousness.
Unfortunately for Peirce, but fortunately for the valet, Pinkerton's investigator did not share Peirce's beliefs about indexical signs and refused to
have the valet arrested. Peirce, steaming with frustration, later found his
watch at a pawn shop and offered the following as the evidence that his
indexical selection had been right: The pawnbroker "described the person
who pawned the watch so graphically that no doubt was possible that it
had been 'my man'" (275). Although Peirce argued that indexes and the
inferences drawn from them should be investigated and verified scientifically, this example shows how flimsy the so-called verification could be,
and how graphic.

The object of philosophy's subject/object relationships is frequently a
person, another subject. When Peirce's examples of the index involved
people, when his "Object" was a human being, the conservative and insidious import of his semiotics emerged quickly. To critique this idea simply
by pointing out that conventional signs are used to interpret a natural sign
does not go far enough as a critique because it leaves the idea of the natural sign intact, even strengthens it by implying it can be distinguished from
the cultural signs used to interpret it. The major issue is the designation of
something as a natural sign in the first place. What is needed is the recognition that this designation is itself a deeply political choice. Academic
semioticians have talked about barometers, sundials, and animal tracks to
explain the index. It would be considerably more enlightening to talk
about fingerprints, mug shots, and police line-ups as examples of indexes,
or the recent Patriot Act in the U.S., which has led to the systematic
detainment, fingerprinting, deportation, and incarceration of many people
in the U.S.[28]

Peirce's efforts to develop a modern theory of the natural sign in his
concept of the indexical image brought the natural sign into relation with
the developments of industrial capitalism, for his theory shows that
fetishism, reification, and the Peircean natural sign were all basically the
same thing. Lukács' essay on reification, which took Marx's theory of the
fetishized commodity as its starting point, showed how reification was
extended through all aspects of capitalist society. Still, for Lukács, reification remained a characteristic of capitalist labor, and "nature" remained

elusively outside this structure, co-opted by the bourgeois philosophy of "natural law." The social character of Peirce's indexical sign crossed this boundary between capitalist society and nature, and in both directions. Reification, by means of the natural sign, was extended outside the specific social structures of capitalist labor—and back into it as something that seemed not to come from it. Like the dehumanizing labor of the assembly line, Peirce's natural sign trapped a human being (the "Object") in a claustrophobic physical immediacy as the totality of identity. It conceptualized a person as a thing without consciousness whose physical being involuntarily emitted signs. Peirce's theory shows how fetishism can be understood as a technique for attributing the power of reification to the object itself, because it projected all the attributes of this semiotics onto the object too. The indexical sign was supposedly of the object's own making. Peirce's concept of indexical meaning sanctioned a massive projection of the sign-maker's own social values and sign system, rationalized as natural, as an "indexical sign" that emanated from the object, denying the subjectivity of the subject. Peirce hypothesized a world in which indexical signs pointed back to the fetish objects they emanated from, not to the perceiver whose constructions they were.

The photograph entered into the milieu of Peirce's semiotics as the paradigmatic example of the indexical sign that "excited" an image in the mind of the subject.[29] Peirce explained, "A photograph, for example, not only excites an image, has an appearance, but, owing to its optical connexion with the object, is evidence that that appearance corresponds to reality" (4.447). Peirce was making two points about the indexical sign here, not just one. His example of the photograph constructed an indexical chain in which there were two identical indexical images: (1) The photograph recorded an image of (2) an object emanating an image. It was the photographic *process*—this is the "optical connection"—that made the photograph an index. The scientific process of making the photograph required that the camera be physically contiguous with the object being photographed. The photograph, the material result of this process, was an index (and not an icon) for this reason. Peirce's second point was directed toward the criterion of the indexical image as it afforded evidence of "truth of fact," namely, its image-ness as such. Peirce did not consider the photograph an interpretation. It was indexical, without interpretation, because it was a passive *recorder* of the image, not altering the image emanating from the object but merely transmitting it with transparent accuracy. In Peirce's theory, the photograph's own physical contiguity with the object guaranteed the truth and certainty of the image to the person who saw the photograph—just as if the viewer of the photograph had seen the object itself.

The photograph "excited" an image in the mind both because it was an object originating an indexical image itself and because it transparently contained and recorded an object's indexical image. Both images were the same because the photograph itself was also an index, guaranteed by the physical process of photography. The indexical image that originated with the photographed object passed through the photograph unaltered to the viewer of the photograph. In other words, Peirce argued that the photograph as material object "excited" the same mental image that a direct view of the object would excite. In this sense, the photograph was transparent, like a windowpane. The camera did not create images (that would be iconic). It only recorded them, transmitted them—it was indexical.

Peirce's descriptions of the photograph acknowledged an image but actively suppressed all the iconic properties of an image that involved thought. On the one hand, the photograph was a mixed sign, involving both an index and an icon, because "a photograph is an index having an icon incorporated into it, that is, excited in the mind by its force" (4.448). On the other hand, Peirce's description showed that the indexical qualities of the photograph, created by physical connection with the object, were in control of the icon, determining what the photograph was and how the apparent icon would be understood indexically, not iconically. Peirce explicitly differentiated the indexical image in the photograph from his theory of the icon in several ways. He strongly contrasted the icon and the index in general: "Of a completely opposite nature [from the icon] is the kind of representamen [sign] termed an *index*" (4.447). In the context of discussing icons, he made it clear that he did not consider the photograph to be an icon. Citing the example "by means of two photographs a map can be drawn," he made clear that it was *the map* that was the icon, expressing the *relation* between two photographic images. As for the photographs themselves, Peirce added that the photograph's image, because it was established by "physical connection," was *not* what he meant by iconic resemblance, that a photograph was *not* a good example of an icon (2.281).[30]

And why not? Because the icon "incorporated" into the photograph was without the icon's capacity to have a problematic, variable, and imaginative relation to the object it signified. Peirce's theory bears consideration as a corporate theory of the image. Incorporation—that is Peirce's choice of terms (4.448)—had a coercive effect, forcing this image to stay put, to not change or vary. It immobilized the image in its quadrilateral cage. Stasis was important because the indexical image was peculiar in its epistemological value: "If the Sign be an Index, we may think of it as a fragment torn away from the Object, the two in their Existence being one whole or a part of such whole" (2.231). This was what Peirce meant when he said that the index had an "internal" relation to the object it signified, where the icon's relation to its object was "external." If an indexical image was perceived as "mere" visual resemblance, the viewer misunderstood what the photograph actually was. The photograph actually captured the essence, the identity of something. As such, it needed to remain separate from other images to maintain the purity of its truth value. The visible image of the index was the mark or trace that disclosed what might otherwise remain unknown—like the dark skin color of the waiters on the boat that the racist Peirce believed was an index of their moral character, the color of a thief. Politically, the concept of the indexical image forced definitive identity to the surface. Identity was worn on the material surfaces of the body, on what could be photographed.

The value of the photograph as a paradigmatic example for Peirce was its capacity to serve as an objective correlative of the indexical process of thinking. The photograph recorded the object/subject relation of indexical meaning. Although only the object, not the subject (the photographer), was depicted in the photograph, that was part of what made it such a good example. It captured both the object's visibility and the subject's invisiblity, the subject's passive reaction to the image. The photograph was an index of indexical thinking, an image of the mind at work receiving the image that had originated from the object. In other words, the indexical mind functioned just like a camera. As Roland Barthes would later explain in *Camera Lucida*, a book heavily infused with Peircean semiotics, the photograph uniquely prompted an "arrest of interpretation" in the mind of the viewer, effectively stopping the act of interpretation.[31] And similarly the camera itself might be understood to accomplish the same thing with regard to the object photographed.

Peirce's theory of the photograph, the indexical image, was in effect an imagistic Cratylism.[32] The photograph, with its special kind of physical contiguity with the object, offered an indexical image that captured the essence of the object and contained it within the photograph. The indexical images of photographs offered not the right names of things that Cratylus had sought, but instead the right images of things—right because they were made through physical contiguity with those things, because they were images that had originated with the things themselves. One need only consult the image to know the thing itself because the image could epistemologically substitute for the object itself. The fallacies of Cratylist thinking in language studies have long been recognized, but the fallacies of imagistic Cratylism seem to be very much with us. Peirce's concept of indexical meaning underwrote what is still a widely held set of contemporary conventions about photographic images. For example, as Susan Sontag has pointed out, people typically have judged the authenticity of a painting (an icon) by its authorship—whether a painting signed with

Rembrandt's signature was really painted by Rembrandt. The photograph (an index) has been judged by a different criterion, the authenticity of what is depicted in it.[33] Consistent with Peirce's theory, the authenticity of the object is the defining criterion of the authenticity of a photograph because the object is believed to generate the image, and the photograph merely records it. A documentary photograph is discredited if the object is posed or composed, or if the photographer was not physically at the location with the camera in physical contiguity with the object.

It seems unwise to attribute such a widespread cultural acceptance of the theory of the photograph as a recorded image to a widespread reading of Peirce! Rather, it seems far more likely that Peirce's semiotics of the photograph itself tapped into widely held cultural beliefs, developing a theory that reflected general cultural beliefs. That this was so is suggested by Peirce's refusal of his own evidence of scientific experiments with photography that he conducted in 1869. François Brunet has carefully analyzed Peirce's findings regarding his photographs of a solar eclipse. Peirce determined that his photographs of the eclipse were not scientifically viable and that "regardless of the method used, the photographs could not be relied on."[34] In other words, Peirce determined that his photographs of the solar eclipse were iconic, and not indexical as he anticipated they would be when he made them. He further decided that it did not matter what method of photography was used, that it would have made no difference if he had corrected his technical errors. He drew his conclusions about photographs as icons "regardless of the method used" to make the photograph. When Peirce went on to construct his theory of the indexical image, with the photograph as its exemplary case, he contradicted his own earlier scientific findings in his photographic experiments. This suggests that Peirce himself was drawn to a set of cultural beliefs about the photograph, so much so that he repudiated his own scientific work in favor of them. Those cultural beliefs were the legacy of iconoclasm as it intertwined with capitalism.

Like the privileged metonymy of the Protestant sacrament, Peirce's index was defined by contiguity, which he presented in contrast to the iconic sign. Peirce's semiotics echoed the iconoclastic belief in a concept of a true image. In Peirce's theory, this was the index. That there could or should be a true image, offering assurance of positive fact, reflected the iconoclastic preoccupation with true and false images, and the image itself as a privileged sign. Although Peirce's examples of indexical signs included things that were not imagistic, when he defined the truth value of the indexical sign, he did so in terms of the image. The passive subject received its so-called evidence by means of an image. The fetishistic idea that the indexical image originated with the object, that it was produced

by the object, reflected the old iconoclastic abhorrence of humanly created images as false. It was important for the iconoclast that the true
image *not* be an image that was humanly created—hence the ideological
need for an indexical image that came from the object, an object that was
not perceived as human even if it was human. Peirce's theory of the
indexical sign also dehumanized the human object, so its creation of
an indexical image would not be an engagement with humanly created
signs. The iconoclastic wish for violent mutilation of the object was
reflected in Peirce's choice of words to describe the index as "a fragment
torn away from its Object"—to describe the indexical sign's epistemological relation to its object.[35] In these passages that resort to descriptions of
violence to conceptualize the making of an indexical sign, it is unclear
who commits the violence, the subject in an assault on the object or the
object in an acquiescent act of self-mutilation to extract the indexical sign
for the waiting subject. Since the subject was a passive receiver of the
image, by definition unaware, the photograph was also valuable because
it affirmed and materially recorded the image-ness of things, something
the passive subject could not otherwise conceptualize. That is, the camera
photographed, and thereby proved, the existence of the image "in" the
object. It verified that the visually experienced stimulus from the object
was indeed an image. For the iconoclast, the image-ness of the true image
was just as critical as the truth of the true image.

In the context of his theory of the indexical image, Peirce diminished
the theory of the icon that he praised so strongly in his discussions of
mathematical equations. In describing the index, Peirce did not say the
iconic sign was false, only that in the context of indexical meaning it was
useless because it was not a relation of material fact. The icon's capacity to
express relations, and to have a problematic relation to its object that
allowed for creative thinking—the sources of its intellectual power and
value—were recast as weaknesses in his theory of the index. Peirce understood the photograph as first and foremost an indexical sign rather than an
iconic sign, metonymic in its structure. Recall that the deployment of
metonymy generates a mental blank rather than a mental image, directing
the mind to look away from the figure itself and back to the material thing
or person that has been renamed. Analogously, the photograph as a record
of the image was itself transparent, invisible, calling attention not to itself
but to the person or thing that was imaged within it. Understood only as
a recorder, the photograph eliminated any awareness of a subjective or
political perspective in its composition, appearing to be pure objectivity.
The social conditions of its making and its viewing were made to seem
irrelevant to its content. This is what Peirce meant when he described the
photograph as having an icon incorporated into it. Acknowledging the

visual element of the indexical sign, he placed it under severe constraints that eviscerated the features of iconic thinking, reducing it to an indexical image whose only iconic feature was the sheer fact of its image-ness.

That he did so is not surprising, given the iconoclasts' simultaneous adoration and fear of images. The photograph offered the truth of the image, but at a safe distance, enabling control without epistemological loss. As an objective correlative, Peirce's interpretation of photography also offered assurance that, by the *mental* process it described, the subject could take an object out of context successfully because the object's essence was retained in the indexical image. The photograph (and the photographic mind of the subject) retained the truth of the true image in the absence of the material object itself. Once the contiguity of camera and object had resulted in a photograph, the object could be dispensed with. Subject, object, and political, social, and economic conditions were all jettisoned along with it. Barthes looked at a photograph and mused on the resulting "arrest of interpretation," but it would be more relevant to consider the arrest of people, and the incarceration of "objects" in prison cells to enact the sense of physical contiguity as the totality of the prisoner's identity. This is how indexical meaning functions in modern society. This is the "message without a code" in action. Obviously there is a code, the indexical semiotics of prejudice, based on an imagistic concept of the natural sign whose exemplary instance is the reified image of the photograph.

In Peirce's semiotics of the modern natural sign, the photograph as transparent recording became the paradigmatic fetish, the exemplary reification. The paradigm of the artistic idea of visual resemblance, of representational images, was supplanted by the mathematical icon on the one hand and the indexical image on the other. In Peirce's thought, representational arts of whatever kind were relegated to a minor place in his theory of icons, as not very interesting and not very good examples of iconicity. According to Peirce, the photograph was not a good example of iconicity either, but for quite a different reason: appearances notwithstanding, it was not about "resemblance." Indirectly, however, it was very much about resemblance—in the sense of controlling the variability of iconic resemblance to the point of eliminating it. Peirce's semiotics of the photograph extinguished the cognitive motion of the icon as visual resemblance and remade the icon into a static material thing. However, the icon remained, in a dormant condition, threatening to break the bonds of indexicality because, when all was said and done, Peirce's theory of the index was itself a theory about a relation. In other words, it required iconic thinking to arrive at it. The relational concept of the index, the icon-that-was-not-one, had at its foundation an unacknowledged and unresolved contradiction.

WHY EISENSTEIN HAS BEEN A THREAT

To be the transparent recorder of the natural sign, to render the image emanating from the object without interpretation, the photograph had to not call attention to itself. It had to be seen through, like a window, rather than seen. To take an iconic view of the photograph, to understand it in terms of Eisenstein's iconic theory of the visual image—this yields a very different idea of what a photograph is, namely that there is no such thing as an objective photograph, a photograph that is not composed. If the photograph is understood iconically instead of indexically, painter and photographer are very much alike, even though they create images by different methods. Every photograph has diagonals, verticals, or horizontals that weight certain aspects of an image. These interpretive aspects of composition, as well as the nature of the focus and the deployment of light and shadow, are part of what is depicted and cannot be separated out from the perception of the object photographed. As well, every photograph has a fixed frame, whose interpretive power is important. These are just some of the elements of a photograph that have to be suppressed when a photograph is interpreted indexically. They are also the elements of Eisenstein's intra-shot montage. Eisenstein consistently called attention to these interpretive aspects of the visual image as a substantive part of understanding what an image is and how it is perceived. How are these aspects related, and what does that relation yield—these are the kinds of questions Eisenstein asked, and they are the kinds of questions that Peirce eliminated from consideration in his theory of the photograph as indexical sign. In effect, Peirce refused even to acknowledge their existence. For a Peircean semiotician, Eisenstein's essays on intra-shot montage would be very threatening indeed. Intra-shot montage brought attention to all the variable qualities of photography—its iconic aspects, its artistic dimensions—to all the ways that the photographer's subjectivity and the material conditions of the shot construct the image. Because Eisenstein recognized the social and material dimensions of the shot, his theory led outward to the larger social and political conditions of the photograph, to the photograph as a cultural sign and not a natural sign. It also led outward from the image itself, for the iconic aspects of any film image combined with those of other images. Eisenstein saw every frame as an open frame. For the image to stay within it was to confine it to a quadrilateral cage—exactly where Peirce had put his indexical image. Peirce's indexical image dis-empowered the icon within it, shut down the variability of interpretation, and created the stasis that reification creates. Peirce feared the power of visual resemblance, but Eisenstein did not. Eisenstein sought out the power of images. Unlike Peirce, who severed his concept of iconic relations from visual resemblance, Eisenstein developed his iconic theory of cinema to fully include images perceived as resembling people and things in society.

Eisenstein's larger theory of montage, from which he derived the theory of intra-shot montage, was even more threatening. It directly violated the most fundamental premises of the natural image. Eisenstein's paradigm of the ideogram directly contradicted Peirce's theory of the natural sign. The cinematic image in Eisenstein's theory was juxtaposed with other images in a montage construction. For Eisenstein the mixing of images in montage yielded ideas beyond the image, breaking open the image to discover undepicted images, new ideas—much as a mathematical equation could open up new interpretations, or a dialectic could yield a new synthesis. Whether superimposed, varied, recombined, made disproportionate in relation to other images, or involved in any of the other possibilities of dynamic relations—montage broke up the sacrosanct realist image, destroyed the purity of the image, violating Peirce's epistemology of the natural sign in every way possible. For Peirce, because the image captured the essence of the object photographed, such mixing was a violation of essences, an adulteration and desecration of the true images he cherished as the pictured real. For Eisenstein, images were composed and created, not found. Eisenstein's concept of the unrepresented image, constructed through the juxtaposition of images, was inimical to the process of indexical thinking, which presupposed a reified image that must remain intact, and a concomitant belief that what is seen is all there is. Eisenstein's creative juxtaposition of images extended the mind beyond the material image.

Eisenstein's theory of montage was a threat to the theory of the film image as a recorded image because, in the latter theory, the image that the photograph recorded was 'out there,' outside cinema, outside the mind, outside the variations of motion and figurative thinking—in other words, its social character as well as its formal properties were completely inaccessible. Whether it was described as static, reified, natural, true, or real, the indexical image maintained its integrity only by remaining isolated and separate, even and especially from other indexical images. Its objective correlative was still photography, emphasis on still. The icon incorporated into the indexical image was not capable of conceptual movement—that was its advantage for iconoclasm and for capitalism. It might as well have been concrete. This was the theory of the image that was capable of building films only brick by brick, one brick cemented into place after another. The result was a brick wall in which nothing moved, in which cinema was believed to induce conceptual movement simply because the images moved mechanically through the projector one after another. This was the theory that Eisenstein rejected, and he rejected it because there was no idea of *conceptual* movement, no understanding even of what that might be about.

For Eisenstein, the cinema's relation to social and material reality was indirect, problematic. The camera was not a recorder of natural images. The film-maker using the camera (and quite a few other things) made images, created images. There was no such thing as a "natural image" in cinema, either intellectual cinema or any other kind. Naturalness and realism were an effect of art, not an alternative to art: "Absolute realism is by no means the correct form of perception. It is simply the function of a certain form of social structure" (35). The film-maker was an active composer of iconic signs. While the camera recorded the camera's *relation* to the object it was photographing through a particular lens, including the material conditions of the shot, there was nothing sacred about the resulting images in themselves. In his own work, Eisenstein often relied on drawings of shots to plan the photography, so the resulting photographic images might just as well be understood as representations of drawings.

Analogously, montage did not represent an event out there. Montage represented "our relation to the event" (34). This was a capacious "our," including both film-maker and audience because both the film-maker and viewer participated in the creativity of cinema. As Eisenstein remarked that it was the reader of *haiku* who completed the poem, similarly it was the viewer of the film who completed the film. Cinema was a dynamic network of relations, and those relations kept both film-maker and viewer involved in the very concept of film itself. Eisenstein took as axiomatic that people do actually think in images as creative thinkers expressing complex ideas and that, given the opportunity, they would respond to cinema as conscious, reasoning adults, not as thoughtless, submissive viewers paying homage to the world as it is. Eisenstein thought of film-making as a dialogue between the film-maker and the audience. The material film itself was the medium through which that dialogue occurred. The viewer was an active participant, a conscious thinker when looking at a film on screen. Eisenstein sought the viewer's *conscious* recognition of a film's meaning and significance, not the viewer's intimidation or submission or loss of consciousness. *The Suitors* is an iconic film, and one that was made with similar assumptions about the audience—that they would be "activated" by the film. This is why viewers of *The Suitors* had so much to say about the film.[36]

For Eisenstein, the social relation between film-maker and film-viewer was ultimately an egalitarian one, not a patronizing one, because film explored not only the relations between images within the film, but as well the relation between images and the viewer's own social conditions. Eisenstein explained, "I also regard the inception of new concepts and viewpoints in the conflict between customary conception and particular representation as a dynamic—as a dynamization of the inertia of perception—as a dynamization of the 'traditional view' into a new one" (47). He rejected "officially decreed harmony" for the disruptive and dynamic juxtapositions that could move (and change) the viewer's conscious mind as well as engage the viewer's emotions. Eisenstein developed a theoretical grounding for films as creative works of art, not just in the formal sense, but also in the social and political sense. Like other arts, film can generate ideas about the world that are different from the ideas one already has. By means of film images, an audience can imagine a different political reality than the one that presently exists.

Eisenstein's theory of the film image, as he expressed it in his ground-breaking essays from 1929–30, seems almost uncanny in its refutation of Peirce's concepts of the natural sign, the photograph, and the semiotics of reification that Peirce developed and embraced. Yet there doesn't seem to be any indication that Eisenstein read Peirce's essays or even knew of them.

What Eisenstein was likely to have read, or at least known about, was Lukács' essay on reification, published in 1922, which was widely distributed and widely read in Europe.[37] Lukács brought to the foreground the problem of reification, beginning with Marx's comments in *Capital* concerning the fetishism of commodities. Lukács did not address questions about the image or questions about film, but he did establish the problem of reification as central to the revolutionary movements of the early twentieth century. Reification as a cultural and political issue is the meeting ground of contradiction for Eisenstein and Peirce. Peirce liked reification and Eisenstein disliked it. Peirce theorized the natural sign in a new way, producing a modern, reified nature that was suitable to the expansion of capitalism, extending the concept of reification outside the immediate structures of capital, and naturalizing the photographic image in the process. Since Peirce was a social conservative and proud of it, one could hardly have expected him to do otherwise. Eisenstein theorized images in a new way, too, producing a theory of the cinematic image that was most of all dedicated to the revolutionary power of art rather than the revolutionary power of the Russian state.

Eisenstein's theory of montage refuted the concept of the recorded image as a reified image, regarding the idea of the recorded image as a conservative social construction. He introduced into film theory a concept of iconic dynamics that offered a different and far more creative understanding of the photographic image. Eisenstein was controversial in his own era, but more misunderstood than controversial in ours. Rather than understanding how Eisenstein's theory offered an alternative to socially conservative theories of the image, later theorists from Bazin to Deleuze simply aligned themselves with the indexical theory of the photograph as a recorded image.[38]

When the iconic qualities of the photographic image are brought forward, however, one can see how inadequate indexical theories are for the increasingly international society of today. The inadequacy of critical theory is most apparent when confronting transnational film because the indexical meanings of any particular culture are necessarily rendered problematic from an international perspective. Contemporary films, and especially transnational films, require a critical approach that can articulate what it means to think iconically, rather than indexically, about the film image.

BEFORE THE RAIN: AN ICONIC FILM

A European co-production, *Before the Rain* straddled a major cultural and political crisis, the breakup of the former Yugoslavia in the early 1990s. The intervention of both the United States and the United Nations in the conflicts within the former Yugoslavia transformed a regional ethnic conflict into a major international crisis. *Before the Rain* emerged in the midst of these complex social conditions, which seemed to shift continuously almost overnight. The individual experience of writer and director Milcho Manchevski was at least as complex. Born in Skopje, Manchevski went to film school in the U.S. and spent a decade in the U.S. media industry before he began work on *Before the Rain*. He wrote the first version of the script as a citizen of Yugoslavia, obtained the first support for it in Britain, and made the film as a citizen of the new country of Macedonia, which also provided funding for the film. It is not surprising, then, that *Before the Rain* is a transnational film that is grounded in iconic meaning rather than indexical meaning.[39] The indexical image is evoked in the viewers' expectations for the purpose of exposing it as a fiction that exploits rather than respects people. Through its highly imaginative narrative composition and cinematography, *Before the Rain* dramatizes the social construction of indexical thinking in many different forms, including documentary photographs and linear narrative as well as ethnic conflict and prejudice against women.

In its openness, this film's iconic way of thinking gave it a relation to the events in Yugoslavia that was different from the docudramas and documentaries about these conflicts.[40] As Manchevski explains, it was important that the film have "realistic detail"; the "concrete" aspect of filmmaking required that it take place somewhere, among specific people living in specific places.[41] Nonetheless, the events portrayed, the stories told in the film, are fictitious: "What is important is that I do not mean my film to be taken as a documentary of actual events."[42] A "fable" rather than a historical or journalistic work, the film is "not a documentary about contemporary Macedonia."[43] The iconic quality of the film was part of its original conceptualization. British Screen's Simon Perry, the film's first backer, recognized the difference between this film and realist films about the Balkan conflict even in the earliest version of the work: "It was a very topical story but it wasn't a piece of realism. It was always a piece of poetry."[44] The artistic director of Slovene Cinematheque, Silvan Furlan, who screened the film in Slovenia when it was released in 1994, also saw the difference. With Slovenia awash in television documentaries and journalistic reports—"we are full of those pictures"—Furlan saw something else in *Before the Rain*. Manchevski's work "opens a new imaginative register, even for the public of ex-Yugoslavia, which lives this reality every day."[45] As Furlan's comments imply, the film's relation to its audience is different, too. Because it is not just about the former Yugoslavia, it challenges the perspective of the audience as much as it challenges the viability of ethnic conflicts in Macedonia. It is in its imaginative, iconic register that the film is distinctive, both politically and artistically.

For Manchevski, the iconic, artistic dimension of storytelling is not merely a question of aesthetics. He asks through this artistic dimension: How does someone determine what is real to them? Not in a secure environment, not in distanced philosophical speculation, but on the edge of a social crisis of great magnitude from which there can be no escape. The film begins with the foreboding voice of a poet that sets the tone: "With a shriek, birds flee across the black sky. People are silent. My blood aches from waiting." It is a visceral feeling—"my blood aches"—but unlike Peirce, whose visceral feelings translated themselves into reductive indexical certainties, this poet takes in the surrounding uncertainty. He hears the eerie silence of people who wait, as he does, for what may be a cataclysmic shift of meaning and reality. The present moment has already been emptied of its familiar certainties, and so also of its comfortable present-ness. The present has reality only as a moment "before" something else still unknown, radically contingent on new meanings yet undisclosed. Manchevski has described it as a "before the rain feeling," as "a feeling of impending something—a change, an explosion, something bad, but also perhaps something promising and optimistic."[46]

The idea of alternative realities has often implied both a dominant, stabilizing point of view and alternatives to it that may be sought out. *Before the Rain* is more radical in its conceptualization. Every reality one can imagine is an alternative reality, and these realities collide with one another in unanticipated juxtapositions that change the lives of the people to whom they happen. How do people react when what they thought was real suddenly collapses? The film's imaginative register dramatizes not only the contingencies of people's lives in the collapse of what is familiar, but also the feeling of shock and surprise when it happens, a surprise that the viewer is drawn into as well. "I was stunned!" wrote one critic in describing his reaction to the final events in the film.[47] The response is all the more intense because the primary characters in this film are not naïve. They are acutely aware of social fluctuations and conflicts. They try to protect themselves from crisis—they think they are thinking. Nonetheless, they don't know how their own lives will suddenly be engulfed beyond all expectation, and the viewer is no more able than the characters to anticipate what will happen next.

"Thunder always gives me a jolt," remarks the old priest in the film's opening scene, an apt metaphor for the experience of the colliding juxtapositions in this film. The montage of the film moves the characters through juxtapositions of images that jolt the viewers into recognizing the limits of their initial impressions. Lightning doesn't strike in the same place for every viewer, but these jolts do happen in any viewer's experience of watching the film. They are the viewer's experience of a montage of collisions, and their effect is quite different from Eisenstein's concept of them. The collisions in *Before the Rain* have a centrifugal force, preventing closure or a unified system of meaning. Conventional expectations might lead one to assume that the film is therefore a descent into chaos, but as I will discuss later, that is to seek another kind of certainty that this film avoids with equal adroitness. This film presents something more complicated that was eloquently reflected in the words of critic Andrea Morini:

> I can still remember exactly how I felt at the end of that film: It was a mixture of intense joy and bitterness, the thought of what I had seen pained me, and—yet—at the same time, I was exhilarated by the way in which the story had been presented. This film was not a simplistic reproduction of reality, it was much more. It had distilled, interpreted and given its audience reality in the form of a refined language with a series of metaphors producing infinite variations of meaning.[48]

These variations of meaning typify what the exhilaration is about: a feeling of imaginative freedom in the experience of iconic openness and variation itself. "It comes as a relief to drown our certainties," comments Morini on the feeling and state of mind the film inspires in the viewer. This feeling is not a fantasy that rejects reality, nor does the film reject its realist elements in an allegorical leap to a 'higher' level of thinking. Rather, *Before the Rain* takes an iconic approach to its subject, finding its political significance in the discovery of its imaginative register and the complex, seemingly contradictory feelings it draws out. In this director's refusal to drown his stories in certainty, even the temporal flows of the stories are drawn into the speculative and variable dimensions of iconic thinking.

The film says at the outset that the story is "a tale in three parts," but the telling of the story interweaves this montage of three stories so deeply that, as the film progresses, it becomes difficult to say what is the beginning or ending of the tale, or to assign a definitive meaning to any of the three stories, even to the point of saying what the plot is. Nonetheless, there is an order of presentation, the order in which the viewer sees the stories. The first is set in rural Macedonia and begins very simply. A young priest, Kiril (Gregoire Colin), is picking tomatoes in a hilltop garden. As storm clouds gather, an elderly priest approaches and tells Kiril, "It's going to rain. The flies are biting"—an indexical truism of rural Macedonian life. The old priest observes that it's already raining "over there" on the horizon. Like many lines of dialogue in the story, the old priest's words take on a greater significance very quickly. As Kiril and the old priest leave the hilltop together and go to their church at a monastery, they hear children throwing bullets into a fire. The sounds of exploding bullets make them flinch as they have their religious service. The seclusion of the monastery suddenly seems very fragile, as does the peace of Macedonia, the only part of the former Yugoslavia that has not broken out in open warfare. In the surrounding villages, ethnic antagonisms pit Orthodox Christians against Albanian Muslims, two groups that had formerly lived peacefully together but have now armed themselves against each other.

Later that night Kiril is shocked to discover a fugitive hiding in his room—a young Albanian Muslim woman, Zamira (Labina Mitevska), who has been accused of killing a Christian man. Kiril gives her food and tries to conceal her presence, lying to his fellow priests the next morning. Zamira's presence in the monastery disrupts its seclusion, and the boundaries of Kiril's life rapidly fall away. The monastery is ransacked by the local Orthodox Christians searching for her. They then stand guard outside, convinced she is inside even though they can't find her. When Zamira is discovered by the other priests, she and Kiril are evicted, leaving together in the middle of the night. Amazingly they get past the guards and flee on foot over the hills to a mountaintop overlooking a highway. His priesthood gone, his vow of silence gone, Kiril suddenly finds himself a citizen of the world, suitcase in hand. Zamira finds herself willing to flee with him to London, even though she seems never to have left her rural village until now. Suddenly they are accosted by a group of Albanian Muslim men, led by Zamira's grandfather. These men have been searching for her, too. When Zamira refuses to leave Kiril, her brother suddenly shoots her in the back. The group of Albanian men are in disarray, frustrated and confused by the sudden and deadly violence that has occurred. A montage of collisions typifies the lives and deaths of these characters. The montage of collisions is more than an editing of images in this film. It *is* the social realism of the story. The cinematography needs an iconic, provisional, problematic sense of relations just to narrate what happens in these rapidly shifting social juxtapositions.

Montage not only characterizes the shifting realities in the Macedonian countryside on the verge of war. It is also describes the second story, set in London, which focuses on a thirtyish British woman, Anne (Katrin Cartlidge), who is an editor at a photographic agency. The story begins with her at work, looking through photos. When she picks up some photographs about the violence in the Balkans, a thematic resemblance with the first story resonates. As she goes back and forth between work and telephone interruptions, her daily life emerges for the viewer. It is a montage of conflicts that involve her husband, her mother, her job, her pregnancy, and a war photographer who is her secret lover, Aleksandar (Rade Šerbedzija). When her mother and Aleks collide on a London street, her carefully compartmentalized life begins to unravel. Her mother finds out about her affair and conveys her disapproval. Anne turns to Aleks, who convinces her to take a taxi ride with him so they can talk things over. During the ride, it becomes clear that both of them are anti-war, so when Aleks tells her he has come back early from Bosnia because he killed a man, they are both upset. Her compassion does not outweigh his disgust with himself. He tells her he has resigned his job as a war photographer, notwithstanding that he has just won a Pulitzer Prize. Anne is amazed, and although it is clear she has a strong emotional tie to him, when he asks her to marry him and leave with him that night for his home in eastern Europe, she pleads for more time to decide.

With Aleks suddenly gone, Anne returns to her office, where she broods over more photographs the agency has received. There are more disturbing scenes of violent conflict in the Balkans. This time they are photos of Zamira lying dead with Kiril sitting next to her—and United Nations personnel surrounding them. That evening, Anne meets her estranged husband Nick (Jay Villiers) at a chic restaurant for dinner. When she tells him she's pregnant and that he's the father, Nick is eager to reconcile with her. He also wants her to quit her job and suggests they move back to Oxford, but she tells him she wants a divorce. In the midst of their troubled conversation, an unknown man suddenly enters the restaurant and sprays it with bullets. Anne survives the screaming chaos but her grief and shock are acute when she finds Nick lying dead on the floor, shot in the face. Violent deaths have taken both Aleks and Nick away from her, each in a different way.

The third story is just as unpredictable, offering a new collision of juxtapositions even though it contains some familiar faces. The story focuses on Aleks, who, it turns out, is not only from Macedonia, but from the same

Aleksandar returns home.

Snapshot at the family dinner.

rural area where the first story took place. On the long bus ride to his old home, Aleks displays a morbid sense of humor when the soldier in the seat next to him warns him of the dangerous hostility now in Macedonia, that he might be killed. "It's about time," Aleks responds, words that will profoundly echo over the ensuing events. Aleks walks into his village and finds his family home, long abandoned and much deteriorated. Along the way, he meets men whom the viewer recognizes—men who were part of the gang that ransacked the monastery. Aleks's cousins welcome him, barely recognizing him. They've heard of his fame, and they find him much changed, now part of the culture of western Europe. They are amused and skeptical when he says he's come home to stay, but they take him at his word, invite him to dinner, and offer to help him fix up his house.

Aleks is distressed by all the guns he sees and refuses to carry one himself. He wishes to remain neutral in the local conflicts between Orthodox Macedonians and Albanian Muslims. When he asks after Hana (Silvija Stojanovska), an Albanian Muslim woman in a neighboring village who was once his sweetheart, he finds out how strained and divided the community has become. They tell him things are different now, and when he insists on going to see her, they warn him to be careful. It seems there will be another collision, but the ethnic conflict that is expected does not happen. Instead, Aleks is warmly received by Hana's father—whom viewers recognize as Zamira's grandfather. Here he seems a mild-mannered man, and he and Aleks lament the divisive hostility that has occurred in the community. Hana behaves as a traditional Muslim woman, her head wrapped in a scarf, speaking briefly to Aleks only when she enters the room to serve tea to the two men.

When Zamira suddenly peeks out from a curtained doorway for a look at the visitor, a collision occurs for the viewer. The "before" and "after" of the film's tale suddenly reverse themselves, unsettling the temporality of the entire film. Since Zamira is still alive, this third story must be a prelude to the first one—the ending of the tale has already occurred earlier. After Aleks returns home, his cousin is killed in the sheepfold, run through with a pitchfork. The demand for revenge mounts, but Aleks still refuses to join in. At night, Hana comes to his home and asks him to rescue her daughter Zamira, who is held captive by Aleks's relatives. Aleks knowingly courts death by taking Zamira from his relatives. As they walk away, his cousin fires, shooting Aleks in the back. He falls, telling Zamira to run. She does, evading bullets and escaping over the hills as the rain begins to fall. The Macedonian men pursue her, but Zamira is well ahead of them. She pauses to catch her breath, and turns her face into the wind, welcoming the rain as she is drenched by the storm. She then sets off for the monastery in the distance.

In the startling juxtapositions that disrupt the lives of these characters, the film shows how different groups of people rely on indexical meanings to understand what is happening. The most obvious one—and the one the viewer most expects to see in a film about violence in the Balkans—is ethnic conflict. The basis of ethnic conflict is an indexical semiotics that assumes biological identity, genealogy, is the determinant of character and social behavior. In the first story, the line of conflict is drawn between Orthodox Christian Macedonians and Albanian Muslims. Both sides arm themselves, presuming hostile intentions of the other side, polarizing the community into a binary oppositional structure. There are disparaging comments from both sides, akin to racial epithets. For example, when Zamira and Kiril are suddenly surrounded on the mountaintop by men from Zamira's family and village, the Albanian men denounce Kiril as "Christian scum." The viewer fears for Kiril's life because the logic of ethnic conflict would seem to demand his death. He is the only Orthodox Macedonian there, and when the Albanian Muslim men rough him up, his death seems eminent. Zamira pleads with her grandfather, telling him that Kiril hid her from the Macedonian men who were searching for her. Her grandfather denounces her, calling her a whore, but then, in a surprising move, he also orders the Albanian men to let Kiril go and they do. The grandfather tells Kiril to "clear off." Kiril hesitates, then walks slowly away. It seems that the conflict is over, that death has been averted. The lines of ethnic conflict are still intact, but its violent consequences seem to have been averted—at least for now. The narrative tension starts to dissipate, and there is a sense of closure to the episode. Suddenly Zamira yells to Kiril, "Don't!" and runs after him. Her brother Ali steps forward out of the crowd with his machine gun ready and yells, "Sister, no!" She doesn't stop. He shoots her in the back, pumping her full of bullets. The viewer sees her face as she is hit and falls to the ground. Kiril comes back to her and turns her on her side. He says, "I'm sorry," but she puts her finger to her lips, apparently gesturing him to be quiet. Her life ends with this enigmatic gesture—usually an indexical sign, but here an iconic one: Why she does this, what it means, is left open. Kiril stays with her, in effect refusing to "clear off." After she dies, Kiril sits on his suitcase, staring at Zamira. This final shot emphasizes how this supposedly ethnic conflict has actually turned out: Zamira has been killed by one of her *own* family, while Kiril remains unharmed.

It is because the audience expects Kiril to die that the murder of Zamira comes as a shock. Led along by the beliefs of the majority of the characters—surely they know who their enemies are?—the viewer adopts the explanation of ethnic conflict just as the characters do. When Zamira dies, viewers feel the sharp contrast between what they anticipated and what actually happens. That experience is reprised at the end of the third story, when Zdrave shoots Aleksandar in the back, again in a moment of crisis defined by ethnic conflict. In both murders, the threat of violence that circulates around ethnic conflict fails to explain what actually happens: each side kills their own. However, the film's narrative refuses to settle into a comfortable ironic reversal, as a more conventional film might do. Having shown that the categories of ethnic conflict do not explain the killings that occur, it then shows the characters' failure to see this. The film dramatizes how indexical certainty closes down any sense of alternative understanding, any possibility of thinking otherwise. For example, when Aleks is shot, his family gathers to pursue Zamira with renewed anger, as if she were the cause of their shooting Aleks. Because the viewer has followed the complicated lives of the characters who will become victims, when the killings occur the viewer sees how ethnic conflict, and especially the violence of it, is reductive and mistaken, that the real situation is much more complicated. The viewer also perceives that the characters, themselves, cannot or will not see their mistaken-ness. For the characters, the indexical certainties that form the basis of ethnic conflict are not lessened by their failure to explain the violent deaths that occur—they aren't even seen as failing.

The Western viewer may carry a sense of cultural superiority after the first story, a self-congratulating belief that ethnicity is a Balkan problem, not a Western European one. The second story dispels this. In England, simplistic binary oppositions of ethnic identity also fail to explain the deaths that occur. When Anne tells Aleks it's important to "take sides," she means take sides against war. Although this sounds like a more sophisticated cultural idea, in practice her binary opposition is drawn between 'we' in England who live in peace (conveniently omitting the "troubles" in Ireland), and 'they' in the Balkans who are at war. She believes London is safe as the Balkans are not, even warning Aleks that he shouldn't return home to Macedonia because it is a country that "isn't safe." Her own understanding proves just as illusory—as the mass killing at the upscale London restaurant demonstrates. Her belief in this simplistic binary opposition is shown by her failure to recognize the dangers in London. The radio news in her office reports that "a bomb went off in Oxford Street," but she pays no attention. At the restaurant, there is plenty of warning that violence is likely to occur, but she ignores this, too. The man who ultimately terrorizes the restaurant appears first as a customer who walks in, stands at the bar having a drink, and starts a fight with a waiter—angry words in a foreign language.[49] After a fistfight he leaves, and the owner fires the waiter as if he were the cause of the fight—despite the bilingual waiter's protest of innocence. Many patrons of the restaurant leave; Nick, Anne's husband, also wants to go, but Anne begs him to stay, and they sit down again. She's not thinking about danger because she's in London, where it's peaceable because it's London and not Yugoslavia. To calm himself down, Nick tries to joke with the owner that "at least they're not from

Ulster," but the owner is not amused—he's from Ulster, he says—yet another case of ethnic conflict as misperception. When the stranger returns with a gun and starts shooting, people scream and dive for cover, Anne among them. As she is engulfed by terrorism herself, it has finally become clear to her that London is not safe either, that it is just as subject to arbitrary violence.

The film portrays cultural ignorance and provincialism on all sides, so that no cultural viewpoint is privileged in this film.[50] In all three parts of the film, characters project the threat of capricious violence onto a cultural 'other,' unable or unwilling to recognize their own act of imagination in doing so. As a consequence, other people literally fall victim to their illusions. Those victims are not just people who threaten the viability of these cultural boundaries, like Aleks and Zamira. The victims include Nick, a white male English conservative who wants to go back to Oxford, who wants a stay-at-home wife, who sees just about everyone as a threatening 'other.' No individual viewpoint is privileged in this narrative, as no cultural viewpoint is privileged. There are neither outright heroes nor outright villains. Because there is no authoritative, unifying perspective from within the story, the effect of the film's narrative is to foreground the cinematography and montage for its semantic value in constructing a viable perspective on the plot. Unlike the rigid polarities of ethnic conflict, the cinematography opens up the possibilities of variant interpretations and meanings by foregrounding the problematic relations among images. Through its cinematography and montage, the film constructs an iconic perspective that allows the viewer to question and challenge the deadening certainties of indexical meaning.

Just as indexical categories such as ethnicity do not fit the characters, the images of this film are not identical with the characters. The cinematography in this film is highly visible to the audience because it creates and maintains an iconic sense of juxtaposition between the camera and its subject. While Eisenstein could imagine the work of the camera as it generated a semi-abstract image, as a creative engagement with the action being performed in front of it, he ultimately conceived the camera as something to be used to tell the story, as a method of storytelling that was subordinated in importance to the story itself. Manchevski does something else. For him, the camera is more than a method. He values the cinematography in its own right, as a storyteller that is just as important as the story, and always distinguishable from the story though still related to it in some way. The camera is not devoted to any character's point of view, it is not omniscient, and it is not stationary. What the viewer sees is a filmed juxtaposition of the storyteller and the story. That is, the story and the storyteller are juxtaposed, but they never match up exactly—or if they do, it is an unusual moment, distinctive for its sense of matching-ness. More often, there is a sense of a shifting fault line, between the story and the image. This is a concept of montage that opens up another dimension of film-making. For Eisenstein, the montage on screen generated another dimension, the undepicted image. Manchevski's cinematography adds yet another conceptual dimension of montage, between the story-as-story and the camera that tells the story. The story moves, and the storyteller moves, too, so the nature of the juxtaposition is always changing. There is no way to look through the camera to the story without seeing the camera. The viewer is always aware that the camera is there, composing images. These images tell the viewer something about the story and something about the image as image, the camera as composer. This is what makes the cinematography cubist. The montage works in a similar way, announcing its presence at every cut. There is no way to see the film without seeing the cuts.

For example, early in the first story there is a funeral scene that gives the audience their initial view of the Macedonian community outside the monastery. It occurs after the sequence of night scenes in which Kiril discovers Zamira in his room, but where the scene actually begins is left open. The film cuts from shadowy close-ups of two individuals in the dark interior space of Kiril's room, to an ancient gold cross against a bright daytime sky. Next there is a soft-focus shot of a rural hillside village in a closed frame. The image looks like an old landscape painting—with little attention to perspective, no people, and a geometric emphasis on the curvature of the roads and the shapes of grouped houses. The montage then cuts to a point-of-view shot, the perspective of several women walking uphill, making a strong diagonal across the screen that draws the eye to a distant group of people as their destination, but the viewer still doesn't know why the group of people are gathered or what they are doing. There is no linear sense of how the funeral scene relates to the prior narrative in the way the film cuts to it.

Following the point-of-view shot, the montage moves to the first image that seems sequential, implied by the previous image, as the camera is now close on the group of people who were previously in the distance. However, the cinematography is not attached to any specific character's perspective, instead suggesting someone walking around the perimeter of the group, looking in between people to try to see something of the burial rite. The camera moves continuously for the next two minutes of the film. Initially focusing on a cantor whose voice accompanies the cinematographic movement, the camera pans horizontally and diagonally, looking up and down and between the backs and torsos of people for glimpses of the cantor and the two men lying in open coffins. The camera's movement gives the viewer extreme close-ups of people at the

funeral, but not the kind that stops on individual faces to establish character. Instead, these are semi-abstract parts of bodies that are interposed
between the viewer and the burial rite, interspersed with other shots that
pass across faces in the way someone might look around momentarily at
the other people who are present. Although the camera moves continuously, this is not a single take by any means. There are as many cuts as
usual in a scene, but here the cuts emphasize both the differing angles
composing the shots and the content of the shot as thematic. For instance,
there is a horizontal panning shot of lower bodies—legs, shoes, skirts,
pants, food baskets on the ground, and a machine gun dangling at someone's side. The effect is to more strongly engage the viewer's interpretive
mind because the formal structure of the film image is brought out—the
shapes of the human form within the shot, continuously changing with
the moving frame, and the unusual angles of the shots in relation to their
subject, an activity of the camera that calls attention to the perspective
and imagination of the photographer composing the shots.

In a conventional film, this take might be simply an establishing shot—
with a still camera, a single take, and an inclusive shot of a group of
people all placed within the frame, to provide a sensation of orientation
and a unified, omniscient camera perspective. Here, however, the film's
treatment of its subject is quite different. The camera asserts a physical
closeness to its subject, but the meaning of the scene remains problematic. There is a provocative collision between the subject matter, largely
static, and the actively moving camera that searches the scene but without reaching any cinematographic conclusion about what is most important or significant. Legs, shoes, food baskets, wine bottles, scarves, jackets,
coffins, and escutcheons get equal attention. Although the camerawork is
suggestive of point-of-view shots, the cuts and the moving diagonals give
the viewer multiple perspectives rather than the point of view of a single
character, or even successive characters. The camera's movement is not
dizzying, even though it is continuously moving. It gives the viewer a
searching impression of the funeral scene. The women, an elderly one
grieving more than the rest, are dressed in black, their heads covered with
scarves. The men are bareheaded; some are middle-aged, some are
younger; each is dressed differently. No one seems well-to-do, but no one
seems truly destitute either. The escutcheons flapping in the breeze, some
of them tattered, suggest traditional identities of some kind. The viewer
glimpses the details of some of the burial rites—the faces of the dead are
covered with white cloth, and red wine is poured on the cloths.

Manchevski has described his film as a "cubist narrative," and in the
montage of this scene, this sense of multiple, colliding perspectives on a single subject is brought out strongly. At the same time, it conveys a physical

reality that prevents the scene from becoming abstract—if anything, it seems far more materially real than "realism." This is achieved through a lively sense of the image-ness of the image, an awareness of the complex act of seeing, that actively prevents a collapse into the content of the shot at the expense of an awareness of the interpretive qualities of the image.

The conventions of indexical camerawork have led to the belief that the form and the content of the shot are antithetical, that a viewer can look at one or the other, but not both at the same time. In this film, the viewer does see both at the same time because Manchevski's cinematography locates the construction of the image in the *relation* between the camera and its object, not in the object itself as indexical semiotics does. In keeping with its cubist interpretation, the cinematography also refuses the use of renaissance perspective. For instance, as the camera moves to a tall man on the perimeter with a machine gun on his shoulder, the viewer sees his face clearly, but the camera does not rest on his face or follow his gaze. In a more conventional, indexical semiotics, the next shot would be a point-of-view shot, scanning the horizon for the enemy, valorizing this man's gaze because he has the means of iconoclastic violence at hand, setting up the structure of a binary opposition between this man and the group of people he guards, and some enemy—two sides that will divide the designation of good and evil. Manchevski's cinematography treats this subject in a very different manner. When the moving camera leaves the man's face, it moves vertically up to a shot of the sky, then cuts to a high-angle shot looking down on the group and showing them gathered around two open graves.

What does the scene mean? It isn't located in a linear narrative. It is simply located in daytime on a hill. It seems to be primarily an ethnographic scene that shows a small rural community of Orthodox Christians in Macedonia engaging in a ritual practice they have performed many times—an implicit evocation of cyclical time. The viewer doesn't know who is being buried, nor does it seem to matter. The viewer sees—but does not feel—the sadness of the funeral. The cinematography has brought the viewer physically to the scene, but it has maintained an emotional boundary between the viewer and the viewed. The tone momentarily shifts as the camera pans the outer ring of the gathering and the viewer sees the man armed with a machine gun. The technology of modern warfare collides with the impression of old and enduring local customs. When the international idiom of machine guns provides entry, the viewer suddenly steps into the culture imaginatively, with a heightened emotional interest. Yet the cinematography does little more than pique the viewer's curiosity, because it passes on to other elements of the scene that receive equally deliberate attention.

Gathering at the funeral.

There is still more to the funeral scene. Near the end of the sequence of shots, something like an establishing shot is introduced, a long shot of the group of people gathered in a circle around the graves. However, it looks very different in this film because the camera immediately moves away from it in the beginning of a horizontal pan that radically opens the social frame of reference outward to include individuals whose relation to the scene is geographically established but otherwise inexplicable. In this long, long panning shot, a single take that includes seconds when no human being is in the frame, the camera moves horizontally away from the crowd across the landscape and finally stops on a woman standing far from the crowd, alone, looking at the funeral. The camerawork emphatically asserts the importance of this woman because, after moving continuously for two minutes, the camera stops on her face. This shot conveys a sense of vast space (but not time) between the funeral gathering and the solitary woman. The camera cuts directly to the priest, then cuts again back to a close-up of the woman. She has some relation to the funeral, but not as a member of the Macedonian community. Her gaze is emphasized when she removes her sunglasses, but the back and forth cuts also emphasize that no one in the gathering returns her gaze, or even notices her. What is she doing here? That feeling is heightened when she says out loud to herself—in English, with a British accent— "Oh my god." This is the only dialogue in the scene and it's a monologue, a dialogue only with herself. What is her involvement? What does she know?

Again, no answers. As she repeats the phrase, the camera leaves her face and starts moving again. Starting to retrace its long panning shot, it comes across a boy in a plaid shirt with a small camera—who aims it directly at the film's camera and snaps a photo. The film's camera recognizes him indirectly by suddenly altering its own direction, vertically panning up the hillside, taking its cue from the boy's gaze as he turns around and looks behind him. There is a priest with a flowing cassock starting down the hillside in the distance. The film cuts to a close-up of his face, and the viewer recognizes Kiril. Is he on his way to the funeral? No. In an extreme long shot, the camera follows him as he runs down a steep hillside in another direction toward a beautiful ancient church on a promontory at the lake's edge. He reaches it and runs around to the door on the other side. The film cuts to a close-up of Kiril coming into the church, out of breath. He's late—the other priests are already there, and their morning service has already begun.

The funeral scene is over, but where it has ended is even more problematic than where it began. In a way, the viewer realizes it's over only after the event, when the camera is already inside the church and a new scene is already under way. Up to that point, there is an expectation that the cinematography will return to the funeral scene, to finish its interrupted pan back to the burial, because the camera's movement has been deliberate, not impulsive, as the carefully drawn angles convey. As the camera continues to reframe its subject, in effect altering the conceptual frame of reference, the sense of a unified scene—the funeral—gives way to accommodate all that is happening in the same geographical area. The camera shows what might be seen from physically standing in different places in the same area as the funeral, but the geographical unity does not generate a sense of a unified story or a unified perspective. If anything, it thoroughly disrupts a unity of place by moving to characters whose relation to the funeral is problematic at best. Kiril is the only person in the scene that the viewer can recognize as an individual from previous scenes, but he seems wholly unconcerned with the funeral. The English woman is Anne, whom the viewer will know much more about in the second story, but who remains an enigma here. The boy with the camera remains anonymous, though his plaid shirt may identify him as one of the children who threw bullets into the fire at the beginning of the story. These three individuals have no relation to each other except the relation of geography, which has come to seem like an accident rather than a purposeful unity of place. Unlike the enclosed and unpopulated landscape near the start of this sequence, the successive shots at its ending open outward to a highly problematic, even contradictory, relation between the people and the land—a dynamic juxtaposition of people and land that undoes any simple equivalence between the unity of a people and the unity of place.

Narratively, the funeral scene disrupts any developing sense of a linear narrative because its temporal place in the narrative is uncertain. The viewer sees a great deal, but the iconic dimension predominates over the meaning of the scene within a larger narrative structure. The narrative open-ness of possibilities is strongly conveyed in every moment of the two-minute moving camera sequence, and by the way the scene stops ambiguously rather than ends. Consequently it remains wide open to interpretation, without closure, yet paradoxically suggesting an emphatic closure in its subject matter—the deaths of two men. As the narrative develops through the film, this scene remains available to the viewer's interpretation of events because it is not directly juxtaposed in a narrative way with the scenes that immediately precede and follow it. What happens to this scene in the minds of viewers is suggestive of how freely the viewer moves in the domain of the undepicted meaning of the film. Viewers reach for the funeral scene at the end of the film, when the temporal frame of reference is thrown wide open, inviting juxtapositions and sequences over large reaches of reel time. They think back to the funeral and reframe/reconceive the scene as the burial of a main character, Aleksandar. For those who remember there are two graves, his cousin who was killed with a pitchfork is mentally laid to rest beside him. Which is to say, Aleksandar cinematically dies before he lives in this tale of three parts. It is not that the viewer remembers what the bodies look like in the coffins, nor does the cinematography return to the funeral site. Viewers who think it's Aleksandar's funeral make that conclusion on their own, achieving closure by recollecting the scene and retrospectively making it the end point of a linear narrative about Aleksandar. The visual sign that confirms this reading—for viewers who take it—is the presence of Anne and her emotional response to the scene, that social place where the camera comes to rest after moving for two minutes. It is Anne's relation to this scene, not Aleksandar's, that clinches the interpretation that it's Aleksandar who is being buried. However, there is much more to it, as I will discuss later in the essay, for what is also being buried here—as the cinematography has disclosed—is linear narrative.

While every shot in this film is composed differently and functions differently within the story, the example of the funeral scene does typify how the cinematography opens up the meanings of what is being photographed. Juxtapositions occur in many directions, often surprisingly, drawing out the significance of each image in multiple ways across all three of the stories. Because the frame of reference is continually shifting, the viewer experiences multiple points of orientation while watching the film. Each act of perception reframes other elements of the story and gives them a different meaning. Typically, a major plot development takes the viewer through a sequence of conceptual as well as literal reframings. Every time the viewer does not anticipate what will happen next, the viewer reacts by reconceptualizing the story being told to include new meanings, new ideas about what is happening—just to keep up with the story. To an extent, this happens in any good film, but it usually happens through only one or two characters' perspectives. In this film, many more perspectives are in play, and moreover, they stay that way. There is no definitive conclusion to this film, no single character who finally figures it out. The viewer's perception of the film's images becomes a complex experience in its own right, a contiguous plot about how to perceive the film. Because the film engages the issues of juxtaposition at a reflexive as well as a representational level, the viewer shares the general problems of continuous misperception and re-perception with the characters in the story. At every point, the film is about its relationship with the viewer as much as it is about the relationship among characters in the stories. Not everything is in play at once—this is a carefully modulated experiment—but more is in play than the viewer is generally aware of at any given moment.

Manchevski's montage implies that there is no such thing as a pure indexical image in film, even when images appear to be simple and obvious shots. He creates a montage that questions the representational film image at the basic level of depiction, casting doubt on a viewer's ability to see any pure, objective depiction anywhere in the film, to say definitively what is on the screen at any given moment. He emphasizes that the film image is an iconic sign whose meaning is problematic. The shifting frame of reference affects entire scenes as well as individual images or characters. The same scene can take on different meanings, a change that can occur within a scene as well as retrospectively. Those meanings do not succeed each other in a series of negations—first this, no, then that. Rather, the viewer holds these varying meanings simultaneously. The idea that the funeral is Aleksandar's does not negate the initial perceptions of the community or the other individual characters in the sequence. Rather, it juxtaposes yet another dimension of the scene in the viewer's mind.

WOMEN, TIME, PHOTOS

The reviews and articles about *Before the Rain* treat it basically as the story of Aleksandar. While he is a main character in the film, there are also primary women characters who are crucial to the film, even crucial to the intelligibility of Aleksandar's story—as Anne is in contemplating whose funeral it might be. The young Albanian Muslim woman, Zamira, is a pivotal figure in the first story and the third. A photograph of her also plays a crucial

Zamira, beaten by her grandfather.

The youthful Father Kiril in his room.

role in the second story. She has few lines of dialogue in the film, but this is hardly noticed in the first story because Kiril's vow of silence—until he breaks it—gives him even fewer lines. Zamira is herself a juxtaposition of modern and traditional ideas about women, a woman whose gender identity is problematic to the viewer and to her family, though not to herself. The viewer first sees her as a fugitive in the monastery when Kiril discovers her at night in his room. Many viewers aren't sure at first whether this slender teenager is a girl or a boy. With crew cut and blue synthetic sports shirt, and with most of her body in shadows, she can easily be mistaken for a boy—especially when juxtaposed with Kiril, a boyish-looking young man. When he turns on the light bulb dangling on a cord from the ceiling, she crouches, covering her head in panic and urging, "Don't hit me, please!" He steps back and she turns the light off, urging him, "Don't give me away." When he makes no verbal reply, she thinks he's mute, then supposes that he simply doesn't speak Albanian. She herself does not speak Macedonian. The cultural gulf between them seems doubly ironic in retrospect, when the viewer later realizes that she has only traveled on foot to get here—hardly the usual idea of an international journey. She moves away from him to a corner of the room—not a long journey either—and pulls a blanket over herself. At first it seems that he will give her away, but he then changes his mind and her actions start to determine his. He goes to the garden (where the viewer first saw him) and brings back some tomatoes for her. She eats them ravenously and says softly to him, in a distinctly female voice, "My name is Zamira" and "You are good." In these initial scenes with Kiril, Zamira's appearance, assertiveness, and risk-taking as a fugitive all suggest a strong and rebellious person, despite her fear of being hit. A viewer could easily infer that she has a crew cut because she cut her hair herself in a rebellious act against traditionalism.

She seems resourceful, too. When the Macedonian men leave the funeral, they go to the monastery and insist on searching it. Ransacking every room, they fail to find Zamira, yet she reappears in Kiril's room that night. Now more confident of him, she takes his hand, then relaxes on the floor across the room, propped up on one elbow looking at him lying in bed. The camera behind her emphasizes her shapely figure, and the viewer can see her red print pantaloons as well as her blue sports shirt—her clothes are a juxtaposition of traditional and modern dress. Their eyes meet, but they are still far across the room from each other, as they also are at dawn when suspicious monks break into Kiril's room. Kiril is banished from the monastery for concealing her, and possibly because the monks also assume that Kiril has had sex with her. However, the viewer doesn't see Kiril and Zamira even embrace, and the impression they give is quite different—that they've stayed on separate sides of the room. Once they

Kiril and Zamira embrace on a mountaintop.

have traveled on foot some distance from the monastery and are alone in the mountains, he kisses her very awkwardly on the cheek, and she throws her arms around him. Kiril promises that he will take her to the city of Skopje, that he will protect her and no one will find her. Although she doesn't understand what he says, she is willing to go with him.

Kiril has scarcely spoken the words when they are surrounded by armed Albanian men. Among them is Zamira's grandfather, who, unlike most of the other men, is not armed. She is relieved and happy to see him, but her grandfather shows only anger and disgust toward her. He hits her hard on the face, knocking her down again and again. Although bloodied, she keeps getting up, arguing with her grandfather, protesting that Kiril loves her. Kiril tries to protect her from being hit, but he is easily overpowered by the other men, who pin him to the ground. The grandfather rages on at Zamira, calling her a "whore" and a "slut," and yells, "I locked you up in the house. I cut your hair. Should I shave it off?" He cut her hair short to punish her, and specifically to punish behavior that he considered sexually immoral—her going out alone to the sheepfold. Finding her with Kiril seems to be only more evidence of the same immorality. In her grandfather's view, the haircut is a sexless and humiliating punishment, an indexical sign of her disobedience that should shame her into staying home. Ironically, the viewer cannot help but think that if she were in a place such as London or the U.S., it would be a very fashionable, contemporary cut. Social context matters!

In the way Zamira's story is told, the film is sympathetic to her, expressing that sympathy by juxtaposing her as an individual with the assumptions made about her. For example, the film calls attention to her own reserve with Kiril in contrast to the accusations of promiscuity and violence made against her. In contrast to the certainties of prejudice, the film gives the viewer no answers as to what happened with Bojan at the sheepfold and who killed him with a pitchfork. Whether Bojan assaulted her, whether Zamira killed him in self-defense, remains hovering in the narrative, never resolved. There are hints that each of them was capable of the acts attributed to them, but no one seems to know for certain what happened, or even whether Zamira was involved in Bojan's death at all. Among the men, the antidote for this not-knowingness is the enforcement of their prejudice against Zamira as a young woman who has generated uncertainty because she went out alone. She went out of the house, went out of the village, went out of the culture by herself. Both Macedonian and Albanian men call her a whore. No ethnic conflict there!

Indexical thinking is perceived as authoritarian and narrow-minded whenever it loses its certainty. The old priest at the beginning of the story does not seem authoritarian, but only authoritative, when, evoking traditional wisdom, he says the flies are biting, so it's going to rain. Where social issues of human freedom are concerned, however, indexical truisms appear as authoritarian because they appear arbitrary—at least to people like Zamira. Indexical meaning emerges as the idiom of intolerance, recognizing only one meaning, denying interpretation as a function of naturalizing the sign. In contrast, Zamira herself has imagination. She thinks in iconic terms, she thinks about what may be possible rather than what is certain. When Zamira refuses the indexical meanings forced upon her, when she refuses to be an obedient object, she refuses certainty for herself and risks the unknown, in running away, in hiding in a Christian monastery, in leaving the community altogether with Kiril, a young man who has treated her with respect, but whom she hardly knows. This is the Zamira who turns her face eagerly into the driving rain at the end of the film, who finds relief and hope in its soaking, symbolic purgation of the culture that has intolerably bound her. This is how the film remembers and values her in its last portrayal of her, in her moment of hope and freedom—a moment that comes after the rain, not before.

Zamira is accused of a good deal more than the vague charge of uncertainty. Her grandfather shouts, "You'll start a war!"—but she doesn't start a war. She's the only one of them who dies. What has this latter-day Helen of Troy done? Her social crime is an epistemological one. *She has refused to engage in the production of certainty*. As an indexical sign, this is her special duty. In indexical semiotics, the object—not the subject—is the source of meaning, the source of certainty, the guarantor of veracity. This is why the obedience of the object is so important. Obedience is the only acceptable action because the indexical sign vacates the possibility of interpretation. But that obedience is more than an individual action. It serves a critical semiotic function as the culture's mythic origin of certainty. The belief in the natural image, the belief that the truth emanates from the object, irrespective of the subject's perceptions of it, comes into direct conflict with Zamira's own imagination. What for her is freedom, a variable relation to society, is for men like her brother an immense epistemological threat. Her grandfather seems less threatened because he is more confident that he can command her obedience. When he fails, Ali shoots, suddenly claiming the Islamic prerogative to defend the honor of his family from sexual impurity.[51] *Before the Rain* highlights the eagerness with which the men sexualize this semiotic problem. They understand the iconic imagination as promiscuity, and the epistemological purity of their indexical semiotics as the purity of blood lines.

As the narrative develops in the next two stories, the production of certainty turns out to include the production of temporal certainty as well—for the viewer who may feel very distant from this indexical prejudice but actually is not. This film is well known for the way it plays with time. The experience of watching the film involves many jolts, many reframings, but the reframing of temporality itself is one of the biggest jolts the film delivers. Many critics have pegged it as a "circular" narrative, but they neglect to say that the circularity they perceive is not apparent until late in the film.[52] Viewers typically see the film as a linear narrative until about fifteen minutes before it ends. Then a sudden reframing of temporal perception occurs, and viewers decide that "before" is really "after," that they have been traveling in a circle without knowing it. However, this circularity ignores many warnings—written in graffiti and also spoken by the old priest—that "the circle is not round." Such interpretations also ignore the importance of women characters in the film even though it is Zamira who is essential to the perception of a circular temporality in *Before the Rain*. It is easy for a viewer to see how Zamira is exploited to serve the indexical beliefs of "them," the violent men of the Balkans who hunt her down and believe they are preserving their culture in doing so. It is more difficult to perceive one's own indexical meanings, especially where concepts of time are involved. Zamira is equally exploited by "us," by viewers who try to make a circular narrative out of this film.

Zamira serves as the pivotal point for reframing part of the narrative as circular when the viewer gets a glimpse of her in the third story. She peeks around a doorway to see the guest sitting in the front room—Aleksandar—who has come to visit her grandfather. This brief glimpse emphasizes her haircut because the viewer sees only her head and face. Her brother Ali quickly shoves her back out of sight, but most viewers recognize whom they've seen. Since the first story ends with Zamira's death, when she appears in the third story very much alive, the viewer suddenly reconceives this third story as a flashback. Her death is yet to come. Zamira reappears again for a much longer time when Aleksandar rescues her. Finding her in the cabin at the sheepfold, he brings her out alongside him. The viewer sees not only the distinctive haircut, but also the blue sports shirt and red pantaloons she wears in the first story. Many other characters from the first story have reappeared in the third, but none of the other characters has the same effect on the viewer—because none of them died in the first story. At the end of the third story when Aleks is shot, he tells Zamira to run, and she does. It is Zamira who leads the viewer—or perhaps I should say, runs the viewer—in a circular way back to the beginning of the first story. The film appears to end where it began: Kiril is picking tomatoes, the old priest warns him of rain, they leave the hilltop garden, and the monastery with its church by the lake can be seen in the distance. However, viewers now see someone else as well: Zamira is running up to the hilltop from one direction as Kiril and the old priest are leaving it in another.

In the viewer's perception of the film, Zamira's appearance, especially her haircut, can function both as an iconic sign, with great variability of meaning, and as an indexical sign, a distinctive means of recognizing her wherever she appears in the film. The haircut as iconic sign varies with the cultural frame of reference—punishment in the eyes of some, stylish for others. However, the haircut as indexical sign, as the viewer's means of recognizing Zamira as the same individual, remains invariable throughout the film. Read as an iconic sign, it varies with juxtaposition, with social context, but read as an indexical sign, it does not. The iconic sign tells something about her as a person. The indexical sign is far more limited and reductive, having only to do with what she looks like physically. One might use indexical signs to identify a dead body. Insofar as Zamira is used as the reckoning point for establishing the temporal direction of the narrative, the sense of her as a person becomes secondary, even expendable. This is why the character of Zamira is often omitted from critical descriptions of the film. If constructing a temporal direction for the narrative is the viewer's priority, then Zamira functions only as an index that enables the viewer to construct a circular narrative. Zamira, as second- or third-world woman, goes spinning into orbit as the vehicle of idealized circularity, certainty, and nature.

Yet this circular narrative can be only partial. Zamira's death at the end of the first story ends the so-called circle. This is where the circle is broken, where it fails to be round. The circular interpretation simply feeds on its own illusions, leaving out the second story and its primary character, Anne, the British woman. Like Ali, the Anglo-American viewer who believes the film is circular cognitively shoots his (or her) own cultural sister—not to ensure sexual purity, but to ensure temporal purity. Like ethnicity, circular temporality may seem to carry explanatory power, to make sense of things in the most fundamental way. In this film, however, temporal purity proves to be just as hollow as ethnic purity.

It is worth asking why viewers thought the story was a linear narrative in the first place. The first story is constructed only loosely with regard to temporality. For example, neither the camera nor the cuts exactly follow the movements of the characters, Kiril and the old priest, as they walk down to the church at the monastery. There is a sense of openings between the shots, creating a sense that other things may be happening elsewhere at the same time—as the cuts in the funeral scene affirm. Events at the monastery are a ritual of daily routines, so one day is much like another. Temporal reckonings have more to do with night and day, and with seasons, dry and rainy. The viewer has a rough sense of one day following another, but the sense of linear time is rough, approximate, often hazy. This doesn't seem to matter very much because there is also a sense that the possibilities are comfortably limited: Everyone travels on foot in the first story. The range of possibilities seems conceptually and imaginatively limited, and therefore contained, by the pace of walking. Linear time is most prominent for events that circulate around Zamira, often geared to who knows what about Zamira and when they know it. For example, to comprehend Kiril's gestures such as the nod that constitutes a lie to his fellow priests, one must have a sense that the scene occurs after he has found her in his room, not before. However, since Zamira's relation to the other characters in the first story is problematic, to say the least, the elements of linear narrative that begin to accrue around her as a fugitive do not cohere to interpret the story as a whole.

The end of the first story is emphatically disruptive of the sense that one scene follows directly from the preceding scene. The image of Kiril sitting on a suitcase, looking at the dead Zamira lying on the ground, seems to be the last shot as it fades to black, but there is one more. The black screen gives way to a shot of a woman in a glass-walled shower. The image is filled with a medium shot of her through the marbled glass. As she takes a shower, she cries, but she doesn't speak. The woman is Anne, and the film hasn't shown her since the funeral. The hiatus of the black screen allows for the viewer's cognitive jump cut back to the funeral as the preceding scene that matters for understanding this one. The shower scene is also followed by a black screen, so it is enclosed in a black screen—a kind of cinematic glass-walled shower stall in itself. This shower scene projects a linear temporality only with regard to the history of American cinema, as an ironic commentary on Hitchcock's *Psycho* and the slasher genre. Unlike Marion Crane and numerous slasher victims, Anne is safe from attack behind that hard glass door, as the purling drain of transparent water on the whitest of shower floors makes very clear. She is not, and will not become, a victim of violence. However, in her protected glass-walled space she also seems trapped, isolated and alone, excluded from the world. The shot does not even offer a spatial orientation beyond the glass walls. This shower could be anywhere—Skopje, London, some other city—anywhere in the world where there's electricity and indoor plumbing. Daytime, nighttime—it could be either. It's wet, but not because it's the rainy season. Anne is portrayed within her own emotional world. She seems even more excluded from society than she was in the long panning shot at the funeral because this scene breaks the temporal and spatial reckonings of the first story altogether. When the film cuts to the second black screen and announces the beginning of the second story with an inter-title, the viewer becomes aware of having no sense of how the first and second stories may be temporally related. For viewers who expect a linear narrative, this nagging question intensifies as the second story progresses through a rapid collage of images and sounds of Anne's life in London.

The second story opens with Anne walking through the modern offices of the photo agency where she works. Everyone speaks English, and people walk busily through the space in all directions, as if the space impeded their purpose. There is no indication of where the office is, what kind of building it's in, where the building is, or whether it's day or night. For a Western, urban viewer, the first story generates a de-familiarization so strong that this sudden return to office life is a jolt, and its routine practices seem both familiar and bizarre to a Western viewer because the sense of spatio-temporal disorientation continues—though the space is now larger than the shower was. In Anne's editorial room there are long tables illuminated by fluorescent lights. The sense of time is of multiple, simultaneous orientations projected from bits of information as she works. She's on the phone with one photographer while looking at photos, listening to radio news, while the rap music of the Beastie Boys comes and goes, as does an office assistant who rudely throws a package in front of her. These numerous juxtapositions within Anne's daily life have no linear organization. They occur randomly, haphazardly—whoever calls, whatever is on the radio while she's at work, whatever photographs are pulled out of the next envelope, and so on. The camera follows her, shows us what she's doing, what she's looking at. Anne is in almost every

Anne at work at the photo agency.

scene in the second story, and in this regard it is her story, but her life is an intersection of many incomplete voices, sounds, and images in an apparently arbitrary collage with no meaningful progression.

Anne conceptualizes her life temporally, but her purpose in doing so is to prevent surprising juxtapositions in her life, so the people she knows will not collide with each other. She is thinking in a kind of linear time, but it's the time of a day, "her" day—her mother for lunch, her estranged husband Nick for dinner, her working hours in between—this is how she has arranged "her time." It is a largely subjective and proprietary time that makes use of clock time as a method of organization. Aleksandar's first appearance in the film comes in this milieu. He's "supposed to be in Bosnia," as Anne says with obvious irritation when Aleksandar surprises her on the street while she's with her mother. So much for Anne's organization of "her" time. The second story represents to the viewer the way Anne moves through "her" day, or days, in a montage/collage of juxtapositions that typify her perceptions and the illogic of her life. She has a husband, a lover, and a mother who all reject Anne's own priorities for herself and try to force her into a wifely role they each want her to play—though not with the same man. Nick sounds conservative when he suggests that they move back to Oxford and adds with a touch of contempt, "You could give up that job of yours." Aleksandar may seem more tolerant in his style, but he implies the same thing when he asks Anne to come to Macedonia with him, handing her a plane ticket he has already bought for her. Both men seem absurd, not logical, in their demands on her. Within this framework constructed by others, Anne sounds contradictory when she tries to reject their attempts to control her, to define who she is. For example, when she has dinner with Nick, she tells him that she's pregnant, he's the father, she really cares about him, and she wants a divorce. This makes sense to her, but he is astonished and feels betrayed.

The juxtapositions of the second story do not convey a logic of cause and effect, and neither does Anne as a character. "Her time" is much more a question of who "spends" time with whom, rather than what comes before or after what. For example, the viewer has the impression that it doesn't matter whether she sees her mother before or after seeing Aleksandar, as long as she doesn't see them both at the same time. This is why the viewer easily loses the sense of before and after in this section. The viewer watches Anne's apparently habitual actions, but no particular linear order suggests itself, much less a sense of cause and effect. Working in a room at the photographic agency, crossing the street, walking down the sidewalk, meeting her mother, spending time with Aleksandar, spending time with her husband, talking on the phone—these actions form a collage, but not a linear narrative. How is all this temporally related to the first story? The viewer has an increasingly unsettling feeling of not knowing.

Connections to the first story develop when the viewer starts to see documentary photographs of violence in the Balkans. The viewer sees Anne in the agency office viewing black-and-white documentary photographs early in the second story. Documentary photos emphatically assert their indexical meaning, their truth values as indexical images, an image-ness that originates with the object photographed. Anne first picks up the (now) famous photograph of the emaciated man in a Serbian prison camp.[53] Here it is one of a group of black-and-white photographs that also show little children maimed and crying, some lying dead in a corner. There are photographs of men with machine guns, among them a smiling man with a swastika on his arm, and pictures of mourners at gravesites.[54] As Anne makes her way through these images, each photograph in turn fills the screen. For more than a minute, the film screen is saturated with their indexicality. For most of the shots, the film's camera moves across the photos, making its way to different details, sometimes quite noticeably, as in a vertical pan of the man with the swastika.

The camera then focuses on Anne viewing the photographs. The film viewer, having seen documentary photos fill the screen, notices how Anne is now interposed between the photograph and its direct perception by the film viewer. Her body partly covers the photographic images as she leans over them. In a close-up shot, where Anne holds a photo up to study it, the film viewer sees only her eyes and the white backside of the photo. In the belief system of the indexical photograph, both the viewer and the photographer are not important for its meaning because neither engages in interpretations of the supposedly self-evident meaning emanating from the photographed object. The film's repeated inclusion of Anne in the same frame with a photograph insistently portrays her subjectivity as a viewer—she looks grim, troubled by what she sees in the photos—but this attention to her by the film's camera conflicts with the absolute indexicality associated with black-and-white documentary photographs. The sense that her subjectivity interferes with the presumed objectivity of the photograph is symbolized in the way her body often interferes with the film viewer's perception of the full content of a photo. In these moments, she seems expendable, especially to the viewer who is deeply committed to indexical meaning.

This conflict becomes acute when Anne is later portrayed viewing another set of photos. Here the film viewer in search of a linear narrative has a vested interest in what the photos portray. Unlike the first sequence of photos, which related only in a general way to violent conflicts in southeastern Europe, this second sequence of photos makes a far more direct connection with the rural area of Macedonia portrayed in the film. Anne is in her office again, and again the viewer also sees the documentary photographs she is looking at. As the camera pans four photographs spread out on a surface, the viewer recognizes the individuals in them: Kiril and Zamira. The viewer sees Kiril, sitting on his suitcase, then Zamira lying on the ground, dead, as uniformed investigators stand near them, one of them taking photographs. Film viewers suddenly believe they know where they are in the film's temporality. Photographs of Zamira's dead body place their origin firmly after the material fact of her killing, establishing an irreversible linear sequence: first the death, then the photograph of the dead victim. The film's linear narrative snaps into place: The second story follows the first in linear time. For those who think indexically, linear time seems to be outside the narrative, enclosing it, but actually it is the documentary photographs of Zamira's death that *generate* this concept of linear succession in the viewer's mind. The viewer extends the past/present implicit in the photograph conceptually over the whole film, assuming the third story will follow the second in linear time. Zamira's indexical features identify her dead body here as they identify her live body earlier and later. Her production of certainty includes the production of temporal certainty, the certainty of linear narrative, for any viewer disposed to see it.

While Anne is looking at the pictures of Kiril and Zamira, she gets a phone call from someone in Macedonia asking for Aleksandar. The voice sounds like Kiril's—he had told Zamira that he had an uncle in London who was a famous photographer. Anne does not realize—but the film viewer does—that she may be looking at a photograph of the man she is speaking to on the phone. The viewer, now armed with this superior knowledge, gains an epistemological and apparently privileged viewpoint, a dominance over Anne, as all the characteristics of linear narrative seem to fall into place, excluding Anne's subjectivity. The film viewer knows how Zamira's death occurred, what led up to it—but Anne is lacking that knowledge. Ironically, at the same time the photographs are appropriated by the viewer to orient the linear narrative, the film viewer is also reminded by the sound of Kiril's voice that the complex story behind this picture cannot be gleaned from the documentary photographs. Ironically, as indexical certainty is posited by the viewer who wishes to see it, the social incompleteness of what is depicted in the documentary photograph is emphasized.

The second story strongly emphasizes the contrast between the apparent simplicity of documentary photos and the confusion amid the colliding images of Anne's life in London. The photographs seem firmly united to what they depict, a clear and stable point of objective reference, not subject to interpretation or the multiplicity of meaning that the film's montage creates, and therefore not subject to misinterpretation either. Which is to say, the second story emphasizes how the documentary photograph retains a privileged place in a socially enlightened Western European contemporary culture—as the indexical meaning that is still believed without question. It occupies a privileged place as an indexical meaning that is believed to stand apart from the prejudices evinced by men embroiled in ethnic conflict, such as Zamira's grandfather. Anne's mother is not about to cut her daughter's hair because she finds out about her affair with Aleks, much less lock her up in the house. Neither is her husband, Nick, who volunteers to his wife, "I forgive you the photographer." Liberal tolerance, it seems, is everywhere, and Anne expresses her frustration at its slick surface when she angrily replies to Nick, "I don't want you to forgive me the photographer!" What Anne senses in Nick's social tolerance is the categorical rejection of her subjectivity. There is a categorical rejection of her subjectivity as well by the viewer who reduces her to a device that involuntarily supplies the incontrovertible evidence of documentary photographs that generate a linear narrative.

As this story shows, linear narrative involves a categorical rejection of subjectivity, and so does the documentary photograph. Like Zamira, Anne becomes insignificant as a character when the viewer uses her as a device to determine the linearity of the narrative. Her temporal task is to supply the indexical photographs that supposedly disclose and guarantee the linear narrative. Having done this, Anne seems even more expendable after her conversation with Kiril underscores her limited knowledge of what is depicted in the key photographs. Like Zamira, her life is effaced by her role in establishing the certainty of linear narrative. For Anne as for Zamira, her iconic way of thinking, her subjectivity and complexity are diminished to the extent that she becomes another pivot point in the construction of linear narrative. A darkly humorous riff on the theme of the female breast emphasizes what part of Anne's anatomy is the essential pivot point and how her breasts indexically substitute for her person in the minds of many. The theme is stated in the shot of her in the shower at the end of the first story. Unlike Marion Crane's anatomy in the *Psycho* shower scene, Anne's breasts are in full view. When Aleksandar and Anne take the long taxi ride, Aleksandar rummages under her clothes to kiss one of her breasts. In the restaurant, when Anne tries to console Nick as she stands next to him—he's still seated at the table—she pulls him closer until his head is leaning on her clothed—and more inaccessible—breast. Finally, after the terrorist has left the restaurant, Anne is slumped on the floor next to a dead waiter whose hand lies aimlessly on her still-clothed breast. The corpse's hand falls away when she moves—an appropriate metaphor for the futility of using the woman-as-natural-image as a point of orientation in the composition of the second story.

The indexical function of the photographic image in the second story conflicts with the significance and interest in Anne as a character, as her own subjective viewing of the photographs visually interferes with the film viewer's unimpeded view of the photos. In its portrayal of Anne, the film asserts her subjectivity, and in its cinematography, it shows how this conflicts with indexical meaning. For the film viewer who wishes to see a linear narrative, one way to resolve the conflict is to eliminate Anne as a significant character, as many critics in effect have done when they discuss the film. For both Zamira and Anne, the imposition of linear narrative works in the same way as Barthes' second order of meaning because it *is* a second order of meaning, in effect renaming the significance of who is shown and immobilizing the icon that becomes incorporated into the index.

"Have a Nice War. Take Pictures."

As a photographer himself, Aleksandar has a relation to the photograph that differs from that of the women characters in the film, but his relation is also substantially changed by an iconic way of thinking.[55] Recall that the theory of the indexical image presumed a subject that was not conceptually visible, unlike the "objects" of nature giving off their indexical images. The subject was merely the passive recipient of images forcibly intruding upon the mind—the equivalent of a camera recording an image. The subject was invisible as the work of the camera was invisible in recording the object's image. This is why the image of white men in cinema has not been perceived as visible, in contrast to images of women, and also why cinematography as a subject of inquiry has been so difficult to conceptualize. To make the art of cinematography visible, as iconic thinking does, violates the invisibility that the theory of the indexical image requires. Simply to recognize the body as a fetish, however, does little to disrupt the system conceptually. In this film, the disillusionment of photography's true image occurs through a recognition of the social character of the documentary photographer as well as the photograph. In the third story Aleksandar explains what happened when he was in Bosnia, why he resigned his job as a war photographer:

> I got friendly with this militia man, and I complained to him I wasn't getting anything exciting. He said, "No problem," pulled a prisoner out of the line and shot him on the spot. "Did you get that?" he asked. I did. I took sides. My camera killed a man.

Facts are made, not photographed already in existence. As Aleksandar shuffles through the sequence of his photos showing the prisoner being shot, but not yet dead, falling but not yet fallen—he finally gets it. Aleksandar's supposedly neutral act of recording an image gives way to his recognition that a deathly indifference that craves "anything exciting" has produced these photographs. The outside, politically neutral observer he thought he was, exterior to the making of the indexical photograph, emerges as the co-creator of the scene "objectively" depicted in the photographs.[56] The passivity and indifference, the cynicism hidden under the guise of objectivity, is not difficult to see in Macedonia. When Aleksandar asks the local doctor what the United Nations is doing to stop the violence, the doctor explains that they merely come by once a week to bury the dead, that their attitude is, "Have a nice war. Take pictures."

When Aleksandar tells Anne he's quitting photography, she replies, "You were born to be a photographer. You can't be anything else." In returning to Macedonia, he tries to be something else, but there is more

Aleksandar.

involved than giving up a camera and a job. Aleksandar finds himself beset with a photographic mind of a particular sort, an indexical way of thinking that is much harder to relinquish than the material camera itself. When he goes to Bojan's house to find out why a small crowd has gathered there, he walks in and sees his dead cousin lying on the bed. The film's camera cuts back to Aleksandar. As if by compulsion, Aleksandar holds up his hand near his face, as if he were about to cover his eyes in grief, but the gesture turns out a bit differently. His hand pauses—as if he were holding a camera—and the audience hears the click of an imaginary camera shutter. The *idea* of a photographic image intercedes between Aleksandar and the social, material reality of his cousin's violent death, as if it were a method of protection.

Aleksandar seems unable to think differently, unable to be anything else, and when he seeks out his own death, he pursues the only alternative he can think of *within* his indexical way of thinking. He walks over to the Other side of his binary opposition and becomes the visible object, taking sides again even as he mouths the platitudes of neutrality—let the courts decide if Zamira is guilty. When Aleksandar says, "Shoot, cousin, shoot," his appeal to Zdrave is couched in the iconoclastic double-talk of violence and photography. Aleksandar flaunts his physical visibility as a target, and that visibility is affirmed when a bullet enters his back. As Aleksandar lies on the ground, face up, he notices that the rain begins to fall as the biting flies foretold—a seeming validation of his indexical way of thinking. Aleksandar is happy and satisfied to be at peace with this naturalization, his contact with the real of the Object, unmoved by Zdrave's grief and horror at what has happened.

Aleksandar's death gives him a striking visibility for the linear-narrative viewer because Aleksandar-the-photographer has been until this point the invisible, metonymic embodiment for the truth of linear narrative. The illusion of linear time generated by the photo of Zamira in the second story has been allowed to hover over Alexsandar's return to Macedonia in the third story. When the artificial support system that is linear narrative collapses with his death, the viewer reaches for Zamira as a substitute who will provide the consolation prize of circular narrative to give a pseudo-completeness and unity to this tale in three parts. The circle is broken in the second story by Aleksandar and Zamira together, that is, in juxtaposition. In the circular version of the narrative, Aleksandar's death occurs before Zamira's. So, if she's dead, his death has already occurred. However, in the second story, the photographs of the dead Zamira appear in between scenes in which Aleksandar is very much alive. In the scene before the photographs of the dead Zamira, Aleksandar is shown with Anne conversing in the cemetery. The film cuts to Anne at her office, where she sees the photos of Zamira dead. The film then cuts to Aleksandar getting in a taxi with a duffel bag, leaving London.[57] The juxtapositions of this montage make no sense as a circular narrative because the live Aleksandar both precedes and follows the photographs taken after his death. This juxtaposition of scenes is impossible regardless of where the "circular" narrative is believed to "begin." The same is true for the equally impossible linear narrative. There is no unifying narrative, no unifying perspective.[58] Ironically, the point where the viewer thinks the narrative falls into place is the point where it collapses. "Cubist," as Manchevski has called it, is indeed a more suitable description of the film.[59]

LINEAR NARRATIVE, CUBIST NARRATIVE

Thomas Woodard, a believer in linear narrative, has written of his sense of fascination and disillusionment in viewing this film. He describes *Before the Rain* as "a violation of the law of unidirectional temporality."[60] Equating belief in linear narrative with the law, he also equates linear narrative with a logic of cause and effect. He explains that *Before the Rain* "goes beyond the level of individuals and nations to undermine our faith in universal temporality and hence in the logic of cause and effect." Well, his faith, at any rate. The so-called universal law of unidirectional temporality that articulates the logic of cause and effect is governed by the semiotics of the indexical image. Linear narrative claims to be indexical, and in the making of that claim, what is at stake is the interpretation of juxtaposition itself. What linear narrative requires is an indexical succession of images, a belief that images are and must remain distinct, that each image points to the next one in line with irrevocable certainty. The "law" of the relation of successive images is that one image must follow *from* the preceding image, as cause and effect, as object to subject.

A chronicle is not necessarily a linear narrative. As the comments of the viewers of *The Suitors* demonstrate, if the viewer doesn't know what will happen next, then the relation of images becomes problematic. The viewers' "not-knowingness" incites many questions about the characters, excites the imagination to consider many possibilities and alternative meanings for what is on screen at any given moment. An iconic montage of the kind advocated by Eisenstein provokes iconic readings of the film from the viewer. That problematic quality is not erased by a concept of one event following another. It is erased by a concept that one event, *and only one event, must* follow *from* another.

Woodard's faith, or perhaps his ex-faith, reflects both the unique meaning that an index claims to express, the essence of a particular object, and the requirement that an indexical sign be specifically located in a material place—in this case, between one particular image and another. Linear narrative is a particular kind of chronicle, one that is narrowly based on an indexical concept of film montage. Linear narrative posits— rather literally—a train of events where one event leads to another in a chain of causation with a feeling of inevitability. A concept of linear time is one effect of this kind of montage, but the underlying principle of linear narrative is the indexical logic of its juxtapositions, the belief that one event follows another because it is dictated—and I do mean dictated with all its political connotations—by the previous event. That is, the linearity that is most valued is less a concept of time than what might be called a linear logic. The line may be either a vector or a circle. For example, the circle of shot/reverse shot is also indexical, especially as it was described by the post-structuralist Daniel Dayan, as a binary opposition with a shell game of displaced identity.[61] The logic is grounded in the indexical image, an image that has only one meaning, that points indexically to the next image. The "invisible" editing associated with Hollywood studio cinema must be invisible as the subject of Peirce's indexical theory was invisible. Viewers can see the cuts in any film if they look for them, but the cuts of "invisible" editing are rendered irrelevant because the juxtapositions do not allow an iconic relation among images.[62] There is nothing to think about. The indexical narrative is a linking of events in a rigid and totalizing succession. Whether that succession is understood as linear or circular does not matter because the crux of the linear narrative is the contiguity of images, one next to another.

Peirce's racist story about indexical meaning makes evident that one person's indexical meaning is another person's arbitrary signifier. The supposed chain of causation that constitutes a genre convention—or any other social convention—may seem secure, but its logic is always vulnerable, always in danger of being exposed as pseudo-logic, as a chain of arbitrary associations that have no inherent logic and no certainty. After all, what is logical about the summary execution of Zamira? What is logical about the arrogance of Nick and Aleksandar in their treatment of Anne? What is the logic of Macedonians and Albanians buying machine guns? When Anne and Zamira refuse the production of certainty that guarantees the truth of linear narrative, when their social resistance exposes how epistemological certainty is merely a euphemism for social control, they are indirectly perceived as precipitating chaos when they are omitted from easy explanations of *Before the Rain* as a circular or linear narrative. It is not only the characters of Anne and Zamira within the story who refuse the production of certainty. Such refusals would have little impact unless the montage and cinematography refuse it as well, as they do in this film. This film makes clear how the role of Justitia as the arbiter of signs, including signs of temporality, is another prejudicial stereotype based on indexical logic, as racism and xenophobia are based on indexical logic. For viewers who are accustomed—and few viewers are not—to using the convention of the natural image/woman to order the meaning of images, the film seems to offer the semiotics of Justitia in the indexical qualities of Zamira's appearance as a way of measuring time, in Anne's speech about taking sides against war, and especially in Anne's unwitting disclosure of documentary photographs that seem to give indexical order to the narrative as a whole. However, these latter-day Justitia figures do not perform the task laid out for them in Saussure's paradigm a century earlier—and reaffirmed many times since in film and other kinds of media.[63] Because they do not ground the meaning of images in particular and signs in general, they appear to be a threat to social order, agents of chaos. But this idea of chaos is itself a conformity to the dictates of linear logic.

As to how this is so, Peirce's writings are again instructive. In the context of Peirce's essay in which his racist story of the theft appears, his racist arrogance is framed by a pathetic desperation. Peirce was frightened by the overwhelming odds against ever being right about anything in a universe governed by chance. The indexical certainty of his natural image was a little oasis of "truth" in a terrifying world of chaos. For him, the only alternative to indexical meaning was randomness. In his Calvinist worldview, the natural sign, the index, stood as a defense against the arbitrariness of the world, not just the arbitrariness of linguistic signifiers. In this late essay by Peirce, the iconic properties of mathematics are not intriguing or promising in their imaginative possibilities. Instead, the mathematics of probability has become a weapon against his own iconic subjectivity, a formidable threat that drives him to seek the safety of indexical meaning.

Deprived of indexical certainty, Woodard sees the same thing Peirce saw: chaos. Either there is certainty or there is mayhem. Using an iconoclastic metaphor of violence, Woodard characterizes *Before the Rain* in terms of "its explosion of narrative time logic." He expresses nostalgia for "our usual conception of history: both as the avenue leading toward the fulfillment of human hopes, and as cozy prison, a confining, secure framework, within which we must work out our personal and collective destinies." Part Two suggests the limitations of a linear-narrative framework when it segues from the documentary photographs at the agency office to the mass shooting and destruction at the restaurant. The virtuoso display of shot/reverse shot technique in the restaurant sequence shifts from Anne and Nick to the gunman and the viewer. Anne and Nick, sitting at their table-for-two, are in the cozy prison of their deteriorated marriage, in the confining secure frame of shot/reverse shot, trying to work out their personal and collective destinies. Since their marriage is in bad shape, the security of the framework is fragile. As Anne and Nick each cast nervous glances outside the perimeters of their cozy prison table, the camera disrupts the shot/reverse shot to follow their glances—to a girl at another table, to a waiter, to the stranger who walks in and goes to the bar. These glances of the camera are brief, representing the brief glances of Nick and Anne as they look out from their cozy prison.

When the stranger returns and starts shooting, the camera cuts away from Nick and Anne altogether to cover the disruption of the gun shots—like a war photographer who suddenly hears gunfire while filming someone speaking. The shot/reverse shot is then reorganized between the gunman and the viewer. There is a point-of-view shot over the gunman's shoulder (video-game style) as he shoots, and an image of the gunman shooting directly at the camera/viewer (Porter/Scorsese style).[64] In its carefully organized rotation of the shot/reverse shot from the table-for-two to the chaotic outbreak of apparently random violence, the film suggests how they are made from the same cloth. Chaos is merely the inverse, the flip side, of indexical certainty. The binary opposition of certainty versus chaos is itself a reductive choice, one that suppresses the iconic dimension of the sign.[65] It excludes the iconic as a possibility—precisely because the iconic is itself about possibility.

How might temporality be understood in an iconic way of thinking? What would be different from the order of linear narrative and the order of chaos? Teshome H. Gabriel has suggestively raised the issue of qualitatively different temporalities in his contrast between the cognitive characteristics of third-world cinema and folklore on the one hand, and the art forms of literate Euro-American culture on the other. According to Gabriel, in third-world cinema and folklore, "time [is] assumed to be a subjective phenomenon, i.e., it is the outcome of conceptualising and experiencing movement."[66] Time is composed in an ongoing manner, as a way of conceptualizing and experiencing movement. The subject's ongoing engagement with the material and social world is the focus here, and variable concepts of time are the "outcome" of conceptualizing movement, both physical and conceptual movement. The subject creates a sense of time, or rather, senses of times, through interaction with the world.

Gabriel contrasts this subjective temporality of third-world cinema with the temporality of Western European and American art forms, especially Hollywood studio cinema, where "time [is] assumed to be an 'objective' phenomenon, dominant and ubiquitous" and "each scene must follow another scene in linear progression."[67] Time is believed to be outside the subject altogether, not something the subject composes but something the subject is in or under the control of. Time is dominant and ubiquitous—it controls, orders, and determines. It is everywhere, always already there irrespective of what the subject's engagement with the world is. There is no such thing as being outside time because there is no outside to time. Because time exists entirely apart from the subject, there is no concept of time as something composed. Time is outside the reach of culture as well as out of the reach of the individual subject. Time is in the realm of pure objectivity, pure certainty—pure index. And time moves. It moves in a linear progression, it is a vector, headed in one direction only, pointing (indexically) to something better later. Whether that is the Christian millennium or the proletarian revolution, classical Marxism and Christianity accept this concept of temporality just as fully as Hollywood cinema does. The subject's preoccupation in this system of time is to keep track of where one is on the vector, whether that is individual age, "late capitalism," or some other cultural scheme. In the Y2K crisis of the millennium, the deep fear was not that linear time would cease to exist, but that computers would lose track of it.

Although Gabriel makes some important and valuable observations about concepts of time, he also maps them across relatively simple binary categories: subjective/objective time, and third-world/first-world art forms. *Before the Rain* presents the viewer with more complexity. For instance, first-world linear time is most tenuous in Manchevski's story set in London, where according to Gabriel's model, one would most expect to see it firmly in place. Anne's story is instead much closer to the cultural ideas that Gabriel attributes to third-world cinema, a subjective time, "her time," that is the outcome of conceptualizing and experiencing movement. Yet Manchevski's film also makes clear how great the distance is between Anne and the culture of second- or third-world rural Macedonia—in her isolation at the edge of the funeral scene, and in a phone call in the last story where she tries to call Aleksandar but fails to reach him because she doesn't know either Macedonian or German—the two languages the telephone operator speaks. There is a somewhat clearer sense of linear time, if not linear progression, in both of the stories that take place in rural Macedonia. However, the concept of linear time is intermittent, the juxtaposition of images as likely to be nonlinear as linear.

Before the Rain has greater temporal complexity than Gabriel's model allows for because Manchevski follows through on the implication of Gabriel's model, the implication that linear time is itself subjective, that linear narrative is only one way of conceptualizing time, as culturally bound as any other mode of temporality. To make this important leap requires an idea of subjectivity that Gabriel also uses in analyzing third-world cinema, that 'subjective' can be understood as culturally shared rather than simply the experience of an individual subject.

Anne's time as "her time" can be read indexically, as emanating from her body, and therefore only as specific to her in a personal sense, as an individual subject, but such a view makes 'subjective' seem less cultural than it is. Believers of linear narrative resist conceptualizing it as subjective because linear narrative seeks to posit a universal time. To consider it as subjective is tantamount to repudiation. It destroys the privileged place of linear narrative, and along with that, the socially privileged place of those whose belief in it affirms their hegemonic identity. The idea of qualitatively different, incomparable times across cultures is similarly a threat to the coherence of linear narrative, but it's not very much of a threat when it is left at the level of analytical abstraction, as Gabriel's comparative table leaves it.

Manchevski goes the whole subjective way to dramatize what belief in linear narrative is like as a subjective experience, as the outcome of conceptualizing and experiencing movement. Put another way, instead of incorporating icons into indexes, he incorporates indexes into icons. The impressive result is a film in which "before" and "after" are situation specific, functioning differently within each story. That is, they are subject to the social conditions of their deployment. Consequently, the more the linear viewer presses the narrative to make sense as a unified narrative with a cause-and-effect succession of images, the more slippery, abstract, and even ridiculous the effort to do so becomes. The film shows how easy it is to invert "before" and "after," how the story as one story simply doesn't add up. This happens because the film develops an iconic way of thinking to reconceive what these concepts of temporality are about. Lines, circles, spirals—all these concepts of time are diagrammatic, which is to say, iconic. Even in Peircean semiotics, these are not indexes. They are icons, subjective, speculative, hypotheses with no inherent relation to whatever may be true.

Far from being an abstract, avant-garde, or purely aesthetic experiment, *Before the Rain*'s dramatization of relative temporality had a very direct social relevance for the former Yugoslavia. Ethnic conflicts were killing thousands of people, and it seemed to many that Macedonia would be next to experience the renewed cycles of violence that had characterized the Balkans for at least a century. *Before the Rain* is a profoundly anti-war film because it rejects both the linear, Western version of the inevitability of violence and the circular, cyclical (spiral) version of inevitable violence attributed to Balkan culture. That is, it rejects the prophecy of inevitable violence: History does not have to repeat itself. This film also recognizes that, in the subjective concept of time, temporality is only one aspect of a person's or a culture's engagement with the material and social world. Individuals and cultures are not governed by time. They compose time. Linear narrative is only one dimension of indexical meaning, and the larger issue is indexical meaning itself.

Manchevski's film provides an iconic reconsideration of a great variety of indexical meanings, incorporating many kinds of indexes into the iconic images of his film. *Before the Rain* dramatizes that the pseudo-truths of indexical facts are actually dependent on social conditions for their credibility. The film continually asks, what is believed to be intrinsic or inherent or true? By whom, under what conditions—or in what collisions? It shows as well that when indexical meaning is privileged, the act of belief may produce the apparently neutral fact of the moment, such as the documentary photograph, but it simultaneously privileges the systems of prejudice and intolerance that also depend on privileging indexical semiotics. Indexical meaning closes down the possibilities for multiple interpretations by asserting an intrinsic relation between the sign and its object. Interpretive consciousness is lost because the apparent need for interpretive consciousness is lost, creating a snowball effect in which one index seems automatically to lead to another. There can be no recognition of the subjective nature of indexical meaning for a fact to be a fact, any more than there can be a recognition of the subjective nature of linear narrative if it is to serve as an objective, definitive frame of reference. The absence of interpretive consciousness is crucial to the credibility of indexes.

Before the Rain restores interpretative consciousness, creating a need for interpretive consciousness, by engaging the iconic significance of the image throughout the film. Manchevski subverts the privilege of linear/circular narrative and creates multiple interpretations of every character, every event, every image, every temporality. There is no place, no time in this film where any viewer can say with certainty what is portrayed on the screen at any given moment. While its colliding juxtapositions are similar to Eisenstein's iconic theory, Manchevski enters into new cinematic territory with his concept of cinematography as cubist narrative, a "new imaginative register," as the director of the Slovene Cinemathique put it. Like Eisenstein, Manchevski sees the audience as crucial to the completion of the film, to the existence of the film's most important dimension, its unde-picted meaning. To that end, Eisenstein's own theory of iconic juxtaposi-tions emphasized the relations among images and the dynamic of the geometric and other formal properties of what was depicted on screen. In Manchevski's film, this montage is important, but the cinematography of scenes such as the funeral scene adds a further dimension of juxtaposition. In *Before the Rain*, the juxtaposition of the camera and its subject becomes a primary point of attention, not just in the technical sense but in a concep-tual, interpretive, artistic sense. What it represents is not the point of view of single consciousness, but multiple and colliding points of view that are qualitatively different. This is what makes the viewer realize the iconic pos-sibilities of each scene. There is no moment of total certainty, but at the same time—importantly—there is no moment of total chaos either. This is an iconic theory of the director/cinematographer, what this film offers instead of the concept of photography as the recorded image. The camera-work is iconic, the artist's engagement with his subject, and it makes that engagement problematic and variable, open to the conscious interpretation of the viewer, even emphasizing the viewer's need to interpret what is shown to follow the story. *Before the Rain* bears consideration as one of the most important films of the 1990s. Manchevski's creation of cubist narra-tive in film has offered something new and significant—and to viewers internationally, not just for those who saw and valued it in the former Yugoslavia. Why might contemporary audiences prefer cubist narrative to linear narrative? Cubist narrative is socially tolerant, it's more imaginative—and it's also more realistic.

Notes

INTRODUCTION

1. Baudrillard, "Precession of Simulacra."
2. Mitchell, *Iconology*.
3. Mulvey, "Visual Pleasure and Narrative Cinema."
4. Written and directed by Ghasem Ebrahimian, 1988.
5. Written and directed by Milcho Manchevski, 1994.
6. Bourdieu, *Photography*, ch. 2.

1. THE CAPITALIST THEORY OF THE IMAGE

1. Baudrillard, "Precession of Simulacra," is the primary source for what Baudrillard says about iconoclasm and representation. Baudrillard, *Mirror of Production*, is primarily a critique of Marx. See esp. "The Concept of Labor," pp. 21–51; Weber, *Protestant Ethic*, is discussed pp. 36, 65. The term *simulacrum* comes from Latin. What is specific to Baudrillard is not the term itself, but his particular use of it.

2. See the introduction to Calvin, *Institutes*, for biographical information on Calvin and an overview of translations of his work. For a theological study of Calvin, see Wendel, *Calvin*. Among the many studies of Calvinist Puritanism in England, see esp. Nuttall, *Visible Saints*. On Calvin's influence in the Netherlands, see Crew, *Preaching and Iconoclasm*. On the influence of Calvin on Anglo-American Puritans in early Massachusetts, see Kibbey, *Material Shapes*.

3. See Crew, *Preaching and Iconoclasm*, pp. 1–38, 108–109; Keith Thomas, *Religion and Decline*, p. 75; Kibbey, *Material Shapes*, pp. 44, 48, 174–76; Davis, "Rites of Violence," pp. 159–74; Phillips, *Reformation of Images*, which includes a selection of illustrations.

4. On *figura* in Latin thought and culture, and especially in Cicero's works, see Auerbach, "*Figura.*" Auerbach does not discuss the concept in relation to iconoclasm.

5. Calvin, *Institutes*, p. 99. All citations are to this edition.

6. Quoted in Crew, *Preaching and Iconoclasm*, p. 26. The translation is Crew's. The original text is quoted, p. 26, n. 84.

7. See James Butler, "Defaced Statues in the Lady Chapel of Ely Cathedral," photograph on the jacket of Kibbey, *Material Shapes*.

8. Crew, *Preaching and Iconoclasm*, p. 26.

9. Quoted in Crew, *Preaching and Iconoclasm*, p. 23. Her translation of a French Protestant circular.

10. The word "iconic" is my own translation of *iconicas*. The passage occurs in bk. 1, ch. 11. Battles translates the word as "symbolical," thereby muting the issue of true and false images in the church—but following the symbolist (Zwinglian) interpretation of the sacrament that is common in modern liberal theology.

11. Protestant practices, in contrast with Catholic practices, are the subject of Crew, *Preaching and Iconoclasm*, which is especially detailed on the way early Protestants improvised sacramental rites around preachers in the fields; Natalie Davis, "Rites of Violence"; and Phillips, *Reformation of Images*, which chiefly addresses the destruction and replacement of images as the monarchy in England vacillated between Protestant and Catholic allegiance. The best source on English Protestant beliefs, and the importance of the mystical body of Christ as crucial to Protestant and Puritan thought, is Coolidge, *Pauline Renaissance*, esp. pp. 23–54.

12. Quintilian, *Institutio*, VIII.vi.23–27. Metonymy as an expression of ownership, possession, and origin is generally neglected or occluded in modern definitions of metonymy, which tend to misrepresent metonymy by confusing it with synechdoche (the substitution of a part for the whole).

13. Quintilian, *Institutio*, VIII.vi.24.

14. On the concept of performative utterance, see Austin, *How to Do Things*, passim. He also calls this kind of utterance an "illocutionary act" as opposed to a "locutionary act." An illocutionary act is the "performance of an act *in* saying something as opposed to the performance of an act *of* saying something," p. 99. Among his examples are wedding vows, pp. 5–6, and "I name this ship the *Queen Elizabeth*," p. 5. By this sharpened criterion, Calvin's sacramental metonymy would be an illocutionary performative utterance.

15. John Cotton, *Way of Life*, p. 277.

16. In the Battles translation, the word "representation" is used occasionally to refer to what marks or exhibits the spiritual presence, again reflective of liberal theology's reading of the sacraments as symbolic acts rather than performative acts. A clearer translation into contemporary discourse would be that the consecrated elements "signify" rather than specifically "represent."

17. See the excellent study of the mystical corporate body in Puritanism by John S. Coolidge, *The Pauline Renaissance in England: Puritanism and the Bible* (Oxford: Oxford University Press, 1970).

18. Norton, trans., *Institution of Religion*, bk. 1, ch. 11, fol. 27, recto (first count). Norton's translation of the full passage is as follows: "I consider for what use temples are ordained, me thinkes it is verie ill beseming the holinesse thereof to receive any other images than these lively and natural images, which the LORDE by hys woorde hath consecrate, I mean Baptisme and the Lordes Supper, and other ceremonies werewyth our eies ought both more earnestly to be occupyed and more lively to be moved, than that they should nede any other images framed by y witt of men. Loe this is the incomparable commoditie of images, whiche can by no value be recompensed, if we believe the papistes." For historical background and dates of reprints, see "Introduction," Calvin, *Institutes*, pp. xlii–xlv.

19. Perkins, "A Golden Chaine," *Workes*. Vol. 1, p. 7.

20. Cotton, *Answer to Mr. Ball*, p. 24. For other English Puritan sources that say the same thing, see Kibbey, *Material Shapes*, pp. 60–63. For the implications of

these ideas in interpreting the body, and violent acts against bodies, including genocide, see Kibbey, *Material Shapes,* ch. 5. See Lindman and Tarter, eds., *A Centre of Wonders,* for new work on these issues in early American culture.

21. Marx, *Capital,* vol. 1, pp. 71–72. All references are to this edition, and page numbers will be noted hereafter in the text.

22. In the U.S., this was initiated in the early nineteenth century, and continued throughout the century through a series of legal decisions that developed the idea. See Derber, *Corporation Nation,* pp. 121–36; Ritz, ed., *Defying Corporations,* pp. 46–105.

23. Baudrillard, *For a Critique,* p. 92. All references to this edition will be noted hereafter in the text.

24. Baudrillard, "The Precession of Simulacra."

25. "Myth Today," *Mythologies,* pp. 109–59. Page references are noted in the text.

26. Cotton, *Gods Promise,* p. 19.

27. See Alison Butler's review of recent feminist theory, "Feminist Theory and Women's Films at the Turn of the Century," in which she argues that the negation of female subjectivity was the most prominent feature of feminist psychoanalytic film theory. For examples of this theory, see the works of Mary Ann Doane, Kaja Silverman, and Jacqueline Rose.

28. In *Elements of Semiology,* pp. 89–90, Barthes defines a metalanguage as "a system whose plane of content is itself constituted by a signifying system; or else, it is a semiotics which treats of a semiotics." He distinguishes this from the linguist Hjelmslev's connotative semiotics. Basically, Barthes favors a model that requires transparency, absolute denotation, at the first level of signification. He does not make clear that it is the imposition of the second order of signification that retrospectively creates that transparency at the first level.

29. See "Reification and Utopia in Mass Culture" in *Signatures,* pp. 9–34, esp. pp. 11–12. The essay was originally published in 1979. Jameson follows Barthes' model more closely than he acknowledges. Reification occurs in the first order of signification when "utopia," i.e., myth, is imposed. The essay does provide a good example of how to read a capitalist film, Steven Spielberg's *Jaws* (1975), as an articulation of myth. As Jameson admits late in the book, the problem is not "signatures of the visible" but "signatures of the *in*visible," just as Barthes' model had suggested. See esp. pp. 10–11, 214.

30. Barthes, *Camera Lucida,* p. 106. Page references will hereafter be noted in the text.

31. Debord, *Society of the Spectacle,* paragraph 15. References are cited hereafter in the text. Following Debord's system, the numbers refer to *paragraph* numbers (not page numbers). Barthes' *Mythologies,* while not named by Debord, seems to be a shadow text behind Debord's essay, implicitly critiqued as liberal but not radical.

32. I have not included a discussion of Gilles Deleuze and Félix Guattari in this chapter because they did not engage the question of the theory of the image, or analyze the capitalist theory of the image, even implicitly, in *Anti-Oedipus.* "Capitalist Representation," pp. 240–61, does not discuss the theory of the image in capitalism. Some relevant remarks can be found in the chapter "Oedipus at Last," pp. 262–72, where they evoke without acknowledgement the ideas of Barthes, Baudrillard, and Debord on the centrality of images for the functioning of modern capitalism. For a discussion of Deleuze's books on cinema, which are

based on phenomenology, not post-structuralism, see Essay Three, notes 12, 14, 38.

33. Goux, "Lacan," p. 110. References hereafter noted in the text. Goux points out, p. 112, that fidelity to the Mosaic prohibition against images in the second commandment was a topic that Freud took up in his most iconoclastic work, *Moses and Monotheism*.

34. Jameson, *Signatures*, pp. 1, 4. See p. 4 for his assertion that a film is like a novel.

35. *Enjoy Your Symptom*, for example. Žižek trades on the entertainment value of film to make psychoanalytic theory more fun.

36. Anthony Wilden, "Lacan and the Discourse of the Other," in Lacan, *Speech and Language*, p. 159.

37. Lacan, "The Mirror Stage as Formative for the Function of the I," in *Écrits*, p. 2. References to this essay are hereafter cited in the text. As to why the mirror stage occurred, Lacan's explanation seems like a satire on the important concept of mobility in political thought. He explained: "These reflections lead me to recognize in the spatial captation manifested in the mirror-stage, even before the social dialectic, the effect in man of an organic insufficiency in his natural reality—insofar as any meaning can be given to the word 'nature.' I am led, therefore, to regard the function of the mirror-stage as a particular case of the function of the *imago*, which is to establish a relation between the organism and its reality—or, as they say, between the *Innenwelt* and the *Umwelt*. In man, however, this relation to nature is altered by a certain dehiscence [gaping] at the heart of the organism, a primordial Discord, betrayed by the signs of uneasiness and motor unco-ordination of the neo-natal months. The objective notion of anatomical incompleteness of the pyramidal system and likewise the presence of certain humoral residues of the maternal organism confirm the view I have formulated as the fact of a real *specific prematurity of birth* in man" (4). In short, "anatomical incompleteness" resulted in clumsiness and uneasiness. The reason: people were simply born too soon. Every birth was premature. Every child inevitably arrived in the world with the original sin of clumsiness, predestined by physiological inadequacy to have the fantasy of the mirror image, a vision of a total, unified, coordinated person that the viewer could never find or feel within their uneasy, clumsy selves. The idea functioned in Lacanian thought as an equivalent of Calvin's idea of original sin.

38. On the idea of capture, see Wilden's notes in *Speech and Language*, p. 100.

39. Lacan, "Aggressivity in Psychoanalysis," in *Écrits*, pp. 8–29. See also *Écrits*, p. 307.

40. Jean-Louis Baudry, "Ideological Effects of the Basic Cinematographic Apparatus." The context of the beginnings of the cinematic apparatus theory, including the significance of the events of May 1968 in Paris, is briefly explained in the opening pages of Daniel Dayan's essay on suture, "The Tutor-Code of Classical Cinema," which was published by *Film Quarterly* in 1974, in the issue preceding the publication of Baudry's article in translation (Baudry is described in the contributor's note as a Parisian novelist). See also Browne, ed., *Cahiers du Cinéma*, an English translation of important articles from this period. Also important is Heath, *Questions of Cinema*. Ch. 3, "On Suture," traces the theory of the suture from Lacanian psychoanalytic theory to Jean-Pierre Oudart's formulation of it as a cinematic theory, to Dayan's further development of the theory. The analysis of shot/reverse shot, especially as Dayan presented it, is probably the most enduring idea from this school of cinematic theory. Also relevant are the conference papers,

including transcripts of comments and debate, from a conference held at the University of Wisconsin–Milwaukee in 1978, collected in de Lauretis and Heath, eds., *The Cinematic Apparatus*.

41. See, for example, the section of Baudry's essay "The Screen-Mirror: Specularization and Double Identification," in "Ideological Effects," p. 44.

42. Callenbach, "Editor's Notebook," p. 2. He laments, "We may read lengthy tracts, in *Screen* and *Cahiers* (and we occasionally indulge this tendency in *FQ*) in which no films are mentioned or referred to at all, directly, or indirectly." Films, he feared, were becoming "mere fodder for the analytical machine. . . . If you ask a practitioner of such thought whether he or she *likes* a given film, or *feels* anything about it, you get an icy stare."

43. The essay has been reprinted many times. Citations are to the reprint in *The Sexual Subject: A SCREEN Reader in Sexuality*.

44. I have added the numbers in brackets for the convenience of the reader.

45. The gendering of still photography as male occurred much earlier, in the early twentieth century at about the same time the studio system in film-making gendered film directing as male. Just as there were many women film directors at the time who were highly regarded, so also there were many highly regarded still photographers who were women. At the time, the gendering of photography and directing was ideological, not based on who was actually doing such work, but it became a means of marginalizing women, in both photography and film-directing. See Eisler, "Going Straight."

46. After invoking the paradigm of the mirror stage for its fetishistic paradigm of the perfected image, she rejected further parallels between the mirror stage and the screen, retreating to the more image-friendly territory of Freudian thought.

47. Doane, "Film and the Masquerade: Theorizing the Female Spectator," also described the idea of the woman as icon as the heart of Mulvey's essay. See also Silverman, "Lost Objects and Mistaken Subjects."

48. The image can even be interpreted as creating the angle of the shot. As anyone knows who has taught the terminology of "high angle" and "low angle" shots, students are typically inclined to invert these terms, using the character's position, rather than the camera's location, as their point of reference for shot-making. Although Mulvey, along with theorists of the cinematic apparatus, claimed that awareness of the camera destroyed the illusion of the diegesis, this was not so. An awareness of the location and presence of the camera as *recorder* of images does not disrupt or alter the viewer's sense of the image. Rather, it enhances it because it emphasizes the image-ness of the image, and image-ness potentially confers sanctity insofar as it marks the image-ness of the living image.

49. See her remarks on this essay in Mulvey, *Visual and Other Pleasures*, pp. ix, 164. See also her comments in 1978 about commodity capitalism and about her own experience in film-making, where her leftist politics and her dedication to experimental films are much clearer, in De Lauretis and Heath, eds., *The Cinematic Apparatus*, pp. 166–67.

2. LIBERATING A WOMAN FROM HER IMAGE

1. See the discussion of Mulvey, "Visual Pleasure," in the concluding sections of Essay One.

2. Written and directed by Ghasem Ebrahimian. Produced by Ebra Films (co-producers: Ghasem Ebrahimian and Colleen Higgins). Distributed by First Run Features. In English and Farsi, with English subtitles for the Farsi dialogue. Photography: Manfred Reiff. Lighting: Charles Lubin. Sound: Tommy Louie. Editing: Amir Naderi and Ghasem Ebrahimian. Partial funding was provided by the New York Foundation for the Arts, National Endowment for the Arts, New York State Council on the Arts, American Film Institute, and Channel Four Film. Most of the cast, as well as the director, are U.S. citizens who were born in Iran and left Iran for the U.S. during the 1970s. The film was screened in the Directors' Fortnight at the Cannes International Film Festival. See Naficy, *Accented Cinema*, p. 248; Jensen, "Cannes Festival," p. 172; and Kevin Thomas, *Los Angeles Times*. This was Ebrahimian's second feature film. His first film, *Willie* (1980), was also well received, winning the student Academy Award for drama. *Willie* was screened at the Metropolitan Museum of Art in New York and in Spain, Portugal, and Italy, as well as at several American film festivals. Information provided on *Willie* from a flyer provided to me by Ebra Films.

3. Naficy points out that the film was "well received by mainline European and American presses," but exile media were "defensive." Regarding the latter, he explains, "The film's feminism and critical edge, which were clearly pointed at men and at patriarchy, were partially responsible for the negative reaction of the exile media, which is heavily male-dominated." As he describes further, exile media often evaluate films by the criteria of whether they present Iranian society favorably for European and American viewers—that is, in terms of international public relations and diplomacy rather than as works of art. See Naficy, *Accented Cinema*, pp. 81–82. I am grateful to Ebra Films for providing me with photocopies of reviews collected in "*The Suitors*: A Ghasem Ebrahimian Film." U.S. reviews include Carroll, *New York Daily News;* Kevin Thomas, *Los Angeles Times*; Stack, *San Francisco Chronicle;* Bernard, *New York Post;* McGrady, *New York Newsday;* Perry, *St. Petersburg Times;* Busak, *San Jose Mercury News;* James, *New York Times;* Taubin, *Village Voice;* Jensen, *Screen International;* Strauss, *Los Angeles Daily News;* Ryan, *Philadelphia Inquirer;* Klein, *Los Angeles Herald Examiner;* unsigned review, *Applause*. Despite these reviews, the film has not received attention from academic film critics. This neglect is typical of the numerous films that Naficy discusses in his invaluable work on exile films and transnational cinema in *Accented Cinema*.

4. "Riveting tale," Carroll, *New York Daily News;* "Remarkably accomplished," Thomas, *Los Angeles Times;* "Striking photography," Stack, *San Francisco Chronicle;* "Subtle wit," Bernard, *New York Post;* "Rarity," Taubin, *Village Voice*. The full reviews discussed the film in a detailed way and strongly praised the performance of Pouran Esrafily in the lead role as Mariyam.

5. Stack, *San Francisco Chronicle*.

6. FH was one of the viewers I interviewed. See note 7 below.

7. I approached the interviews as a qualitative rather than a quantitative study, to get examples of interpretations and discourse about film rather than obtain answers to specific questions. Film studies has often made generalizations about "spectators," and usually in relation to Hollywood films rather than independent or transnational cinema. I was curious to see what spectators would say if given a chance to speak for themselves about a film that interested them. For this reason, I excluded anyone who was a professional film critic, academic or otherwise. All of the people interviewed were "amateurs" who were not acquainted with the terms, concepts, or findings of academic film theory and criticism.

The interviews were open-ended, and there was no questionnaire. I initiated the interview as openly as possible, asking, "What about the film stands out for you?" Most people responded at length with little or no prompting from me, shifting topics at their own pace. Since I was interested in what they, themselves, would emphasize—an important aspect of the open-ended interview—I asked as few questions as possible and tried to avoid yes/no kinds of questions. What questions I did ask were primarily for clarification about what the respondent was already talking about. Occasionally I also asked specifically about their interpretation of the stabbing, if this topic had not come up in the course of the interview. Most of the time, the spectators had already introduced their opinion of this scene, and when they hadn't, their reasons were usually quite interesting—such as thinking the stabbing was not a pivotal event in the film. In general, I tried to save any questions I had for the last part of the interview, and to ask them only after people had set out their own priorities. Most people spoke for a longer time than they anticipated they would. The interviews averaged about 70 minutes each.

When asking people if they wanted to see the film and be interviewed, I told them the film was about a veiled Muslim woman from Iran who comes to live in New York and has to decide whether or not she wishes to remain veiled. I scheduled interviews at least one day after viewing and usually several days to a week later, so that people would have a chance to think about the film. I also thought it important to let people see the film in conditions of their own choosing. Some saw it in a theater, others at home on video. There were no significant differences in interpretation between people who saw it in a theater and people who saw it on video. I gave each person a choice of where to be interviewed and suggested they pick a place where they felt comfortable. The interviews were conducted individually and were audiotaped.

Quotations are transcriptions from audiotapes of interviews. Punctuation was added for readability and uses standard conventions, such as italics for emphasized words, a dash for a pause or hesitation in speech, etc. Some people asked for confidentiality (some for personal reasons, others for political reasons), so I have referenced viewers with fictitious initials.

I had originally intended to interview only women, but some men to whom I mentioned the project wanted to participate, too, so I interviewed them as well. About 80% of the interviews were with women. As to whom, precisely, the sample contained, I am limited in what I can say while honoring confidentiality. For practical reasons, most of the interviews were conducted in the Denver-Boulder metropolitan area of Colorado where I live and work. Most of these were people who had moved here rather than native Coloradans (reflecting the current balance of the population here). Three interviews were done in Manhattan, and three in Connecticut. All were U.S. citizens, and about 20% of these were born in other countries. About 90% had college degrees. The person who was the most knowledgeable about contemporary independent film did *not* have a college degree.

Regarding occupations, the study included one professional academic, a social scientist. The rest were in a variety of occupations, some of which I can mention here (though the rest are in the same general economic strata): aerobics instructor, physical therapist, cosmetics beautician, electrical engineer, technician, hairdresser, social worker, housewife-with-small-children, stockbroker, advertising executive, editor, receptionist, nurse, ski instructor, painter. Two were retired. Ages ranged from 22 to 87, though the majority were in their 30s to 50s.

The film's director had no involvement in the audience interviews. No one had any personal or professional relation, direct or indirect, to the film-maker or his family. No one was a public figure or held a government position. No one received compensation for their interview.

In relation to myself, one was a personal friend, another a social acquaintance. About one-half were prior business acquaintances of mine. I worked outward from people who knew something about me, who could vouch for me to people who did not know me. The rest of the interviews were with people in the social and business networks of these acquaintances, whom I met for the first time when I interviewed them.

Interviews were done in the mid to late 1990s. About six months after Sept. 11, 2001, I did one further interview to see if it was substantially different, especially on matters of terrorism. It was not. I also taught the film again in spring 2003 to an undergraduate class of 35 students, and got responses similar to classes in years prior to 9/11. Both in the individual interview and in the class discussions, people did not make any connections between the subject matter of the film and the events of 9/11.

Since these interviews were not based on statistical sampling or "focus groups" for promotional purposes, their intellectual value needs to be considered in a different light, as a study in the humanities rather than social science or marketing. These are interviews that value the individual interpreter as such. I have quoted extensively from the interviews to give a sense of the individual speakers I recorded. I used the interpretations in constructing the essay by discussing the film in relation to viewers. While it is true that discussing the film disclosed things about the viewers, it was equally the case that viewers' discussions disclosed things about the film. The audiotapes were not just something for me to describe, but were themselves instructive in developing areas for analysis. I have made a few generalizations about viewers' interpretations, and the reader will find my comments about these generalizations at the appropriate places in the text.

8. I interviewed Ghasem Ebrahimian on two consecutive days in May 1992, at the Tribeca Film Center in New York at the beginning of this research project. Each interview was about two hours long and was audiotaped. The quotations in this essay are transcriptions of the audiotape of this interview. All references to the director's opinions also refer to this interview. Ebrahimian also facilitated interviews with some members of the cast: Pouran Esrafily (Mariyam); Shahab Navab (Reza); Ali Azizian (Ali); Assurbanipal Babila (Haji); and Leila Ebtehadj (Zari). These interviews took place in 1992–93 on several occasions when I visited New York. These interviews were also audiotaped. They spoke about their experiences in Iran and their perceptions of American culture, as well the process of making *The Suitors*. Although I refer to these interviews specifically only a few times, they were indirectly very important in understanding many issues in Iranian film and Iranian culture and the range of opinions about them; and also in understanding aspects of how scenes in *The Suitors* were blocked, how dialogue was scripted and what alterations were made during production, how costumes were decided on, what was rehearsed, etc. Because of limitations of space in this book, I was not able to include all of this material directly, but it has been valuable in shaping this book and understanding the production of images in the film.

9. Ebrahimian grew up in Mashad, a city in eastern Iran near the Afghanistan border, and then moved to the U.S., where he went to film school and became an American citizen in the early 1970s. From the mid 1970s to the mid '80s he made

documentaries about American cultural life for French and Italian television. Although he was based in New York, his documentaries often required extensive travel around the U.S. No stranger to feminism, he also made two documentaries about French women writers, one on Marguerite Yourcenar and another on Simone de Beauvoir. He specifically mentioned the *1001 Nights* as an example of the kind of narrative structure and character development he had in mind. For additional biographical information, see Naficy, *Accented Cinema,* p. 248.

On the *Arabian Nights,* see the recent translation by Haddawy rather than earlier British versions. Haddawy's translation is based on the text of the fourteenth-century Syrian manuscript (the earlier, Persian text is now lost). The introduction by Mahdi explains the important differences between this translation and earlier English translations. The Persian literary tradition is an ancient one, long distinguished and still revered among many Iranians, notwithstanding the recent Islamic fundamentalist revolution in Iran.

10. The analogy of popular American forms and Persian narrative is well warranted. Persian literature has a different place in Iran than literary traditions have here. The general population is much more familiar with major stories like the *1001 Nights,* and such traditional narratives are far more integrated into general Iranian culture than one would find in the U.S. In Iran, stories, fables, and parables are also handed down orally from generation to generation, so education in schools is not the only source of knowledge about Persian cultural heritage. Schimmel, *Two-Colored Brocade,* points out, p. 9, that poetry is "the common language of people in everyday life. Scarcely a German villager could recite from Goethe's verse or quote an apt line of poetry in self-defense, but even a simple peasant in Iran or Afghanistan could draw upon a treasure-hoard of classical poetry."

11. Kuhn, *Cinema, Censorship, and Sexuality,* pp. 1–27, implies it would be. So does Montrelay, "Inquiry into Feminity," a rereading of psychoanalytic theory as fundamentally about censorship rather than the nonexistence of Woman. On Montrelay, see Silverman, *Subject of Semiotics,* pp. 186–87.

12. Those who are familiar with Brecht's "alienation effect" may find some similarity here, but Ebrahimian's concept of audience activation seems fundamentally different to me. Where Brecht's theory was first and foremost a theory of acting, Ebrahimian is instead focusing directly on the audience.

13. See Najmabadi, "Hazards of Modernity," for a history of veiling practices in modern Iran. I have also relied on my interview with Pouran Esrafily for accounts of how young women behaved in the 1960s and '70s, when she was growing up in Iran: "We wore jeans, shorts, mini-skirts, and sneakers. You could wear what you wanted." She got a butch haircut to celebrate getting her visa and coming to the U.S. to attend the University of Kansas, where she graduated with a degree in architecture. She never wore a veil until she made the film. She added that, despite the popularity of American attire among Iranians, Iranian parents continued to play a much stronger role than most American parents would in supervising who their teenage children would date. For a brief but useful summary of cultural practices including veiling, especially in relation to student political culture, see Sandra Mackey, *The Iranians,* pp. 181–82, 226, 261–62, 268, 272–73, 279, 298, 337, 368. There are now many books on the history, culture, and Islamic beliefs about veiling in different cultures, including literary works. See, for example, Sullivan, trans., *Stories by Iranian Women;* Moayyad, ed., *Stories from Iran;* Mir-Hosseini, *Islam and Gender;* Mohanty, ed., *Third World Women,* and

with regard to cinema specifically, Tapper, ed., *New Iranian Cinema*. In general, there has been far more historical and cultural variation than Christian Westerners have recognized. For an illustrated introduction to the immense variety of practices regarding Muslim women's appearance, including many secular portraits of Middle Eastern women without veils, see Graham-Brown, *Images of Women*.

14. Part of the difficulty was that she was obligated to stay and work in Iran in return for her university education, whose expenses were paid by the state. Nonetheless, she thought Mariyam had an untypically easy time getting into the U.S. and that it was much harder for most women to get out—one of the issues that made her wish for a documentary on this subject rather than a fictional film.

15. LF still remembered clearly what she had been told to wear: "A long scarf that also covers your shoulders and a loose long jacket type of thing, like a robe. Pants underneath and thick socks. Only black, brown, or dark gray. Extreme fundamentalists wanted the face covered, too." An outfit conducive to the Persian mystique? Neither LF nor SR thought so. SR, describing the "robe" as "a long overcoat," said she quickly stopped caring about what she looked like. *The Circle*, an Iranian version of Italian neo-realism, emphasizes what kinds of dress are acceptable as "veiling" in Iran, and emphasizes how unattractive and cumbersome these modes of dress are. Mariyam's veil, which is actually a veil, was not a visual cue that encouraged self-identification for either SR or LF, though LF did remark that some women started wearing such veils after she left Iran—she explained that it took awhile for Iran to manufacture them in large quantities.

16. SR explained that technically she did not have to wear a veil since she was a U.S. citizen. However, she decided to wear it because she would have been subject to harassment and possibly arrest and beating, where she would have to prove citizenship to get out—not an easy thing to do with the Iranian government holding her passport while she was in the country.

17. Most of the women I interviewed were American-born, but this view was also shared by a woman from Belgium, a woman from Ireland, and a Muslim woman from India, all of whom had become U.S. citizens, had lived in the U.S. for more than ten years, and had become economically and socially assimilated, considering themselves Americans.

18. I completed the interviews used in this essay before September 11, 2001. However, in spring 2002, I did conduct one further interview, and the next year I taught the film again to a class of 35 students, to see if there was a change of interpretation. Viewers still saw the SWAT team raid in the same way, as an exaggeration. No viewer saw a parallel between the raid in the film and Waco or Ruby Ridge, or the attack on MOVE in Philadelphia, or the treatment of immigrants in the U.S. or at Guantanamo, or police shootings of innocent minority men and boys in U.S. cities. The main shift was somewhat more sympathy in general for Middle Eastern men living in the U.S., particularly in the scene where each of the suitors calls on Mariyam to propose to her. Viewers were more willing to acknowledge the poignancy of their proposals as well as the humor of the scene.

19. One viewer was somewhat knowledgeable because of her business—a beautician with a studio that had no windows facing the street. She found that many Middle Eastern women came to her studio for that reason. She had some familiarity with Qatar, Kuwait, and Dubai for that reason.

20. They were somewhat familiar with Saudi Arabia, but thought of it as a geographical region rather than a state.

21. The actual sheep was not harmed in any manner during the making of this film.

22. I would like to thank Pouran Esrafily and Ali Azizian for contributing to the information in this paragraph.

23. The sheep was not killed, and not harmed in any way, in the making of the film. The director was apparently unaware of the practice of adding such a disclaimer at the end of the film. Some viewers believed that the sheep had been killed, but a close viewing of the reel shows that no harm is done to the sheep. In fact, it shows the opposite, that the sheep was very well cared for. This is what made it possible to get such high-quality animal photography in making the film, since the sheep was not a trained animal.

24. See Dayan, "Tutor-Code." Ebrahimian interprets the problem of absence in social and material terms, as normalized terror, an implicit critique of the structuralist abstraction that typifies Dayan's essay.

25. This was not for lack of facility with language. Ebrahimian is unusually articulate and, as the film reflects, comfortably multi-lingual. This was a matter of choice rather than necessity and is indicative of the different conceptualization of film narrative that underlies this film.

26. Early on, I did try to interview someone right after she had seen the film. She called me back the next day and said she wanted to be interviewed again because she'd changed her mind about the film! I interviewed this individual twice, and the second interview was much longer and more informative. I took this as an indication thereafter to wait at least one day after viewing to conduct an interview.

27. For a discussion of Eisenstein's theory, see Essay Three.

28. Other kinds of film today might be said to have these characteristics as well, but in my interview with Ebrahimian, it was clear that he had gone back specifically to Rossellini's films for the concept and techniques of cinematic realism he wanted to convey.

29. Introduction, pp. xiv–xv, trans. Haddawy, *The Arabian Nights*.

30. In fact, much of it was not formally scripted, according to both the director and the actors. The actors were told the general import of what to say and then allowed to put in their own words.

31. An example of the use of literary symbolism in Iranian film is *Pomegranate and Cane*. Iranian directors have recently turned to developing a new kind of realism as the primary source of their appeal to audiences. Films such as *Two Women* and the Italian-financed *The Circle* have been viewed as exposing what the 'real life' of women is like in Iran. Far less successful are efforts such as Kiarostami's *ABC Africa*, an attempt at a documentary by an established filmmaker whose work is typically symbolist and "literary."

32. In my interview with him, Ebrahimian commented on Akerman's work in general, not specifically this film.

33. For a good example of the tracking shot as a surveillance technique, see Scorsese's *Goodfellas*, in which the camera relentlessly follows Henry on the day he is captured by police—unlike the "real" gangsters such as the DeNiro character, who literally slams the door in the face of the camera. The only conventional tracking shot in *The Suitors* occurs when Mariyam and Reza drive away from the country house in the night—a sequence in which the camera is fastened to the car. In early scenes, photographing the sheep, and then Mariyam, the camera is placed in the car. And, at the end of the film, the camera is placed on the conveyor

belt behind the suitcase. However, because these occur in the context of a film that is made up almost entirely of stationary camera shots, the impression conveyed by the camera is not of an omniscient perspective, of a camera whose gaze cannot be escaped, but instead the impression of a camera that seeks to share Mariyam's situation, to show how the world looks to her, to go with her wherever she goes—even if it means riding on a conveyor belt with vertical rubber strips interrupting the view.

34. KL saw the film on videotape, then again later when I had it screened in the film series at the University of Colorado. I interviewed her after the 35mm screening. She was the only one I interviewed who saw both the video and the theatrical versions. She said she liked the film very much on video but was even more impressed by the 35mm version. In the theatrical version (actually 16mm blown up to 35mm), which is wide-screen, there are more discernible realist elements—a greater sense of depth, a clearer representation of the texture of clothing, skin, and eyes, of objects such as furniture, and a greater clarity of landscape elements such as the stalks of marsh grass. The videotape is in the Academy ratio and generally offers a less differentiated image. I did not find any differences between people who saw the video version and those who saw the theatrical version. There was also no difference in awareness of the experience of viewing. If anything, KL's experience of both implies that the formal design as well as the realist elements were enhanced by the theatrical version—which would be consistent with the director's theory of the screen image.

35. "Chiaroscuro" is the term for this, and does not specifically refer to black-and-white images in art history. It means the arrangement of light and dark elements in pictorial representation.

36. This is a far more complex deployment of voice-over than any that Silverman considers in her essay, "Dis-Embodying the Female Voice," in Erens, ed., pp. 309–27. As Silverman inadvertently shows in her often contradictory essay, standard voice-over techniques do not make a great deal of sense.

37. The film does tell us that Zari is Ali's sister, and viewers were attentive to that, but the relationships among the other Iranian characters are left undefined. The viewer doesn't know, for example, the exact nature of the relationship between Mr. Amin and Ali. Viewers were not bothered by this. For them, the main point was that everyone at the country house had the same expectations of Mariyam.

38. On Persian literary symbolism, and particularly the symbolism of the wedding dress, see Schimmel, *Two-Colored Brocade*, pp. 9, 14, 25–26, 52, 223. For example, "many Persian poets speak of their work as 'weaving a festive dress for the bride Meaning,'" p. 14. The bride also symbolizes speech, inner meaning, and spirit. On the general cultural knowledge of poetic imagery, see p. 9.

39. This viewer was a survivor of both rape and attempted murder, so her comments should not be mistaken as the words of someone lacking personal knowledge of domestic violence.

40. Clover, *Men, Women, and Chainsaws*, ch. 4. As Clover describes, the slasher is so named because it is devoted to a succession of gruesome, horrific murders by a psychopathic killer, a plot line with "buckets of blood." Unlike action films that feature numerous killings with guns, in the slasher the villain employs torturous knives, power drills, and other weapons of hand-to-throat combat that involve ghastly penetration of the victims, who are staked to doors, hung upside down, decapitated, and so on. The Final Girl is the last potential victim—usually her friends have been murdered already by the time she meets up with the psychopathic killer.

41. Clover, "Her Body, Himself," in Thornham, ed., pp. 234–50.

42. Clover, "Her Body, Himself," in Thornham, ed. pp. 246, 242, 240, 238. See also Clover, *Men, Women, and Chainsaws*, ch. 1, for a reiteration of the idea.

43. On the significance of metonymy and its relation to the sacrament and to sanctioned violence, see Essay One.

44. Pouran Esrafily explained, "I could be as feminine as I wanted to be" in making the film, including the murder scene, in which she wears a dress. Esrafily contrasted her own concept of her role with Michelle Pfeiffer's remark about how she enjoyed playing Catwoman in *Batman* because it "brought out her masculine side." Esrafily was unsure what this meant but found it off-putting and did not understand why an actress would find this a desirable or even needed option.

45. The end of one of Beethoven's late string quartets (#16 in A-minor, opus 132).

46. Anonymous review of *The Suitors* in *Applause*.

47. The director stated this explicitly in my interview with him.

48. Dayan, "Tutor-Code," pp. 438–51. Dayan analyzes the shot/reverse shot in terms of the theory of the cinematic apparatus. Shot/reverse shot was the paradigm for this theory, which had little to say about any other kind of montage. See also my discussion of Mulvey, "Visual Pleasure," in the concluding sections of Essay One.

49. Naficy, *Accented Cinema*, pp. 264–66, discusses the suitcase as a common image in transnational films and the varieties of symbolism it acquires in different films. He relates the suitcase in *The Suitors* to a condition of exile, but this seems inappropriate to me, since Mariyam is not in exile from Iran. Nor did Ebrahimian, the director, consider himself in exile from Iran, having chosen to move to the U.S. many years before the 1979 revolution.

50. This is not to say that every Zoroastrian would understand the cinematic image in this way. Zoroastrianism is a religion and philosophy that originated in ancient Persia. Ebrahimian's ideas about film are his own creative synthesis of a modern art form with an ancient, but still current, Zoroastrian worldview, primarily in its philosophical dimension. For a summary of Zoroastrian beliefs, see Mackey, *The Iranians*, pp. 16–17. Mackey also discusses the influence of Zoroastrianism on Persian and Christian culture. For a more extended discussion of Zoroastrianism, see Mehr, *Zoroastrian Tradition*. My discussion in this essay is geared to Ebrahimian's own concept of Zoroastrian beliefs and follows his emphasis in my interview with him.

51. The only literal prison bars shown in the film are shown when the SWAT team takes Haji's surviving companions to jail after the raid. The viewer sees them literally behind bars in a row of jail cells.

52. Discussed in Monaco, *How to Read a Film*, pp. 133–35.

53. Quintilian, *Institutio*, VIII.vi.4–7, 18–20. For a discussion of metonymy as the expression of ownership, see Essay One.

3. RELIEF FROM THE PRODUCTION OF CERTAINTIES

1. Manchevski, "Rainmaking," p. 130.

2. *Before the Rain (Pred dozhdot)*. Written and directed by Milcho Manchevski, 1994. A British, French, and Macedonian co-production. Produced by: Aim

Productions, Noe Productions, and Vardar Film with the participation of British Screen and the European Co-Production Fund (UK) and in association with Polygram Audiovisual and the Ministry of Culture for the Republic of Macedonia. Currently available on VHS. International recognition for the film began with the Golden Lion Award for best picture at the Venice International Film Festival in 1994 and included an Oscar nomination for Best Foreign Film in the U.S. in 1995. See the reviews on the Manchevski website, a valuable resource on the film and Manchevski's other work. There were more than 3,000 reviews and articles about *Before the Rain* worldwide. Selections on the website are from Argentina, Australia, Austria, Belgium, Brazil, Canada, Croatia, Denmark, Finland, France, the former Yugoslavia, Germany, Greece, Great Britain, Holland, Hong Kong, Hungary, Iceland, Italy, Japan, Mexico, Norway, Poland, Slovenia, South Africa, South Korea, Spain, Sweden, Switzerland, Taiwan, Turkey, and U.S.A. See also the comments from Korea, Philippines, Peru, Chile, and Czech Republic on the Amazon website. Additionally, see Horton, "Oscar-Nominated"; Rosenstone, ed., special issue of *Rethinking History;* and Cohen, "Balkan Gyre."

Manchevski's new film, *Dust,* was released in New York and Los Angeles, August 2003, as this book was going to press. I have not commented on the film because I have not yet had an opportunity to see it. *Dust* is scheduled for release on DVD (Lion's Gate) in November 2003. For more on this film, including articles about its making and its controversial reception in Europe, see the Manchevski website.

3. See Wollen, *Signs and Meaning in Cinema,* pp. 19–73, 116–74; and Deleuze, *Cinema 1,* esp. chs. 3, 6, 11, 12; and Deleuze, *Cinema 2,* esp. chs. 2, 7.

4. The 1867 essay, "On a New List of Categories," is considered his earliest statement of his triadic theory of signs. See Peirce, *Collected Papers,* 1:558 (volume and paragraph number). References to the *Collected Papers* are hereafter cited in the text. Peirce's early works show a tendency toward thinking of all signs as non-arbitrary, that is, as natural signs. See for example, an 1873 manuscript, "On the Nature of Signs," in *Peirce on Signs,* pp. 141–43. The later works restrict the idea of natural signs more clearly to the indexical sign. The works I discuss in this essay are the later works only, written between 1893 and 1907. For an insightful summary of photography's cultural ascendancy, see Jacobs, *Eye's Mind,* pp. 18–27.

5. The authoritative intellectual biography of Peirce is Brent, *Peirce: A Life,* an excellent overview of Peirce's philosophy and a thoroughly researched history of his personal and professional life. Brent argues that, notwithstanding the elite social stature of the Peirce family, C. S. Peirce had chronic financial problems. On Peirce's eugenic beliefs and his pro-slavery racism, see esp. pp. 30–34. Brent was the first scholar to call attention to evidence of Peirce's racism and eugenic theories.

6. On Eisenstein's life, see the biographical documentary, *Secret Life.* For the circumstances of his essays, see Leyda's introduction to Eisenstein, *Film Form.*

7. There have been many studies of Peirce's sign theory and its applications. One of the most accessible is Sebeok, *Introduction to Semiotics.* See also Sebeok, ed., *Sight, Sound, Sense.*

8. *Manipulation* is not intended as a moral term in this kind of usage. It refers to changing things or moving things around, such as the elements in an equation.

9. Wollen says this is the main idea in Eisenstein's film theory, but he offers slim evidence for it. He quotes Eisenstein (who is recounting his youthful revolutionary enthusiasm in the third person): "Don't forget it was a young engineer who was bent on finding a scientific approach to the secrets and mysteries of art.

The disciplines he had studied had taught him one thing: in every scientific investigation there must be a unit of measurement. So he set out in search of the unit of impression produced by art! Science knows 'ions,' 'electrons' and 'neutrons.' Let there be 'attraction' in art. Everyday language borrowed from industry a word denoting the assembling of machinery, pipes, and machine tools. This striking word is 'montage' which means assembling, and though it is not yet in vogue, it has every qualification to become fashionable. Very well! Let *units of impression combined into one whole* be expressed through a dual term, half-industrial and half-music-hall. Thus was the term 'montage of attractions' coined." Quoted in Wollen, *Signs and Meaning,* p. 32. Wollen does not cite his source or translation. He quotes this passage in the context of discussing Eisenstein's first theatrical production, in 1923. As early as 1924 Eisenstein was putting distance between cinema and theater with regard to how montage needed to be conceptualized. See the translation of an unpublished manuscript by Eisenstein on the montage of attractions in Taylor, ed., *S. M. Eisenstein,* pp. 39–58, and esp. pp. 41–42.

10. *Potemkin* was first screened in 1926. See *Secret Life* for Eisenstein's account of its screening and how it changed his life. The Eisenstein essays I discuss here are "The Cinematographic Principle and the Ideogram" (1929–30), also known as "Beyond the Shot," and "A Dialectic Approach to Film Form" (c.1931), also known as "The Dramaturgy of Film Form." The first was originally published as *"Za Kadrom"* ("Beyond the Shot"). This original version is translated from Russian into English by Taylor and Powell in *Eisenstein Reader,* pp. 82–91. My references are to the more widely known "The Cinematic Principle and the Ideogram," translated by Jay Leyda in *Film Form.* Page references hereafter are cited in the text. Unlike the Taylor and Powell translation, Leyda's translation is based on the French edition of the essay, in which Eisenstein made some revisions, and which was published under the title (translated into English) "The Cinematographic Principle and Japanese Culture (with a digression on montage and the shot)" (Paris, 1930). Leyda worked from the French translation and also from the original Russian text to produce the translation in *Film Form.* See Leyda's bibliographical notes in Eisenstein, *Film Form,* p. 266.

11. Here he was primarily concerned with the way the idea had been formulated by Pudovkin, another Russian film-maker. For Pudovkin's own descriptions of his film-making, see *Film Technique.* See also the writings of Eisenstein's contemporary, Kuleshov, *Kuleshov on Film.* Kuleshov shared some of Eisenstein's ideas. See, for example, "Montage as the Foundation of Cinematography," pp. 42–55. See also Kuleshov's comments, p. 140, on *Battleship Potemkin* (1926), which he described as an important film, "raising the quality of montage" from what Eisenstein had used in *Strike* (1924).

12. Deleuze, *Cinema 2,* p. 161. Deleuze misreads Eisenstein at other points, too. Deleuze says that montage expresses time, *Cinema 1,* p. 29, but Eisenstein's montage expresses many concepts besides temporal ones. Deleuze also says, even more improbably for a historical materialist such as Eisenstein, that Eisenstein's concept of montage "was the very definition of the sublime," *Cinema 2,* p. 158. Eisenstein did not envision the juxtaposition of shots as images and concepts moving toward each other, as Deleuze also claims in this passage, and Eisenstein's theory of montage was not an identity theory. Deleuze's books on cinema are based on the French phenomenologist Henri Bergson, as Deleuze himself says, *Cinema 1,* ch. 1, and Deleuze unsuccessfully tries to make the materialist Eisenstein fit into a phenomenological framework. Deleuze also misrepresents Peirce's philosophy, though

here Deleuze admits, "We borrowed from Peirce a certain number of terms whilst changing their meaning," *Cinema 2*, p. 32. Deleuze seems reluctant to conceptualize how his own ideas differ from either Eisenstein's or Peirce's, as if he cannot bear to be different from them. Perhaps this is the consequence of what Schwab, "Escape from the Image," p. 130, has termed Deleuze's "unhappy" theory of differentiation.

13. Taylor, ed., *S. M. Eisenstein*, p. 13, calls it a "montage of associations." It would be more accurate to say that the montage *is* the association, if one were going to make this argument.

14. See, e.g., Massumi, ed., *Politics of Everyday Fear*, a collection intended to produce recuperative shocks in the reader as a therapy for everyday life—a reductive reading of Deleuze. Martin, "Of Images and Worlds," is much better on the Deleuzian sense of shock as edification, though here there is also a connection with physical violence. Eisenstein's idea instead has to do with the intellectual radical incongruity of what is juxtaposed—the cognitive experience of strikingly new thoughts. The problematic of montage is by no means limited to the use of material images, although that is my focus in this book. For an important analysis of how the idea of the iconic appears in the philosophy of language use, see Petrilli and Ponzio, *Signs of Research on Signs*, esp. pp. 139–45.

15. For many examples of this, see the comments of the audience in Essay Two.

16. *Secret Life* contains a broad range of examples of Eisenstein's own drawings other than film drawings.

17. See for example, Foucault, *The Order of Things*, pp. 17–45, where he describes natural signs that express analogy and similitude as pre-modern. As he also points out, much of Renaissance magic was predicated on belief in natural signs. Natural signs have not always been interpreted in the same way, but they do have in common the general idea that the natural sign has an inherent or intrinsic relation to what it signifies.

18. *Course in General Linguistics*, p. 68.

19. Brown, *States of Injury*, esp. pp. 56–61.

20. For an explanation of the sociolinguistic position, see Hymes, *Foundations in Sociolinguistics*.

21. Jay, "Must Justice Be Blind." According to Jay, the figure of justice was female in Egyptian and Greek thought as well as Roman thought.

22. I have discussed this at length elsewhere. See Kibbey, "Gender Politics of Justice." Politically liberal films of the 1980s and 1990s frequently used a Justitia figure to resolve their semiotic contradictions. The Justitia figure is an outsider, an amateur in the legal system, like the nurse (Lindsay Crouse) in Sidney Lumet's *The Verdict* (1982). By contrast, the woman lawyer (Charlotte Rampling) is portrayed as deeply corrupt because she is involved in the language of law. The nurse resolves the case and orders linear time by supplying a photographic image (a photocopy) as evidence. The plot of the film displaces the issues of social justice by shifting the focus of the case to issues involving the violation of the record of linear time. The plaintiff's lawyer (Paul Newman) wins the case and sees himself as having conquered the corruption of the legal system. In actuality, he has only been restored to his place within it. Justitia's testimony does not change the legal system. The function of Justitia's presence is to sanction the legal system as it is, notwithstanding all that the film shows about its corruption. *The Verdict* crystallized the cultural myth of the woman who holds the scales of justice, as she stands opposite the evil woman lawyer. Whatever the variants, the persistent theme is the polarization of the

woman attorney and the Justitia character, both roles being played by white women. The woman attorney is inept, unaware, or morally perverse, and needs help from men or from Justitia to carry out her legal mission. Left on her own, she fails. The female figure of justice continues to be entrusted to gifted amateurs—to the waitress and victim in *The Accused* (1988); to a nun in *Dead Man Walking* (1996); to a remodeling contractor in *The Hurricane* (1999), where the plot also turns on the falsification of linear narrative; and in a nervous compromise, to a working-class secretary in *Erin Brockovitch* (2000), where the viewer is constantly reminded that, even though Erin is inside a law office, she is not an attorney. While most of these films show women characters who are more assimilated than the nurse in *The Verdict*—indirectly reflecting the increasing assimilation of women into the economy—the concept of justice has become more diluted as well. In two of the most recent films, the evil woman attorney (Gina Gershon) in *The Insider* (1999) is out for money, but so is the justice-minded Erin Brockovitch (Julia Roberts), whose story is primarily about the struggle to collect damages. *Erin Brockovitch* is the latest, and possibly the last, of this genre.

23. On the popularity of *CSI*, now the most widely watched television series in the world, see Carter, "From Creator of *CSI*." The show is now televised in 175 countries. For an excellent analysis of other legal-minded television shows, see Rapping, *Law and Justice*.

24. O. J. Simpson's ex-wife Nicole Simpson and Ron Goldman were murdered on June 12, 1994, and O. J. Simpson, an African-American football star, was charged with their murders. Both victims were white. The criminal trial in 1995, lasting several months, was broadcast on Court TV and was also a major topic on other television stations and in the print media. The defense attorney who attacked the prosecution evidence collection and DNA testing was Barry Scheck, a professor at Cardozo Law School in New York and co-founder of the Innocence Project. Early in the trial, Scheck persuaded Judge Lance Ito to prohibit the use of the word "match" in discussing DNA evidence. The prosecution was forced to substitute the phrase "consistent with." "Match" implied identity, sameness, indexical certainty. "Is consistent with" was more iconic, a problematic phrase that maintained a distinction—and therefore a possibility of difference—between DNA samples. In closing arguments, Scheck argued that "the LAPD was a cesspool of contamination and that none of the evidence could be trusted." See Petrocelli, *Triumph*, p. 21.

After the criminal trial, Fred Goldman brought a civil suit on the wrongful death of his son. The plaintiff's attorney Daniel Petrocelli won this case. He had the benefit of new evidence—thirty incriminating photographs of Simpson wearing the same brand of Bruno Magli shoes the killer wore. Petrocelli thought the photographs turned the case in his favor, overcoming doubts about Simpson's guilt, both in the media and with the jury. See Petrocelli, *Triumph*, pp. 580–85, 590–94.

On the compelling truth of photographs, which in Petrocelli's opinion outweighed DNA evidence in credibility, see my discussion on Peirce's philosophy of the photograph at the end of this section.

25. Peirce, "Guessing," pp. 270–76. Written in 1907 but not published until 1929, after Peirce's death. See also Eco and Sebeok, eds., *Sign of Three*, pp. 11–19, which quotes and analyzes substantial passages from the story but does not comment on the racism.

26. Quotation from Waldman, "The Diallo Verdict," *New York Times*. Diallo was killed by police on 4 February 1999 in Bronx, New York, in the lobby of his

apartment building. The *New York Times* ran its first of nearly 200 stories on the Diallo murder on 6 February 1999. There were many demonstrations and protests over the next two years. The police were charged with second-degree murder in a grand jury indictment; the trial was then moved to Albany, N.Y., and it began on 31 January 2000. Eight of the twelve jurors were white. Charges were reduced during the trial, but the jury nonetheless acquitted the police of all charges on 26 February 2000. In the *New York Times,* see especially Finder, "When Is Error a Crime?"; Flynn, "Testimony of Four Police Officers"; Fritsch, "Diallo's Actions Led to His Death"; Fritsch, "Officer Recounts Diallo's Shooting."

27. Peirce was probably thinking in terms of distinguishing the icon from older ideas about natural signs, as well as distinguishing it from the index. See Foucault, *Order of Things,* pp. 17–45, on resemblance and analogy as the basis for pre-modern natural signs.

28. The Patriot Act was passed by the U.S. Congress shortly after the attack on the World Trade Center and the Pentagon on 11 September 2001. The evocation of indexical systems of meaning is evident in the following example, a memo from the administration at the University of Colorado, Boulder, 6 December 2002. "Subject: INS announces critical deadlines for certain non-immigrant visa holders to 'special register' in the National Security Entry-Exit Registration System (NSEERS). Recently the INS has promulgated rules that require certain categories of non-immigrants in the United States to be 'special registered.' A number of our students and scholars have been and will be required to go the Denver INS office in order to register. Registration means being fingerprinted, photographed, and questioned as to their activities prior to and since entering the United States. They need to be prepared with complete documentation. We have directions as to what they need to do and what they can expect when at the INS office. The rules can be confusing. Please have them come and see us BEFORE going to the INS office."

29. Peirce never discussed photography as a theme of investigation in its own right. See Brunet, "Visual Semiotics," p. 301.

30. Brunet, "Visual Semiotics," p. 303, agrees with this interpretation. The passage, as he points out, has often been misunderstood as supporting the idea of the photograph as an icon, that is, interpreted to mean the opposite of what Peirce said. Brunet explains the nineteenth-century process of map-making, invented about 1860, that Peirce referenced.

31. Barthes, *Camera Lucida,* p. 106. See my discussion of this book in Essay One.

32. Cratylus, one of Socrates' interlocutors in Plato's dialogue of this name, eagerly searched for the right names of things, supposing that if he could discover the original, true names of things, he would then know those things through knowing their names. Cratylus seemed to want to know about the world, but actually he sought to distance himself from it. If the names of things were right, then Cratylus need only consult the sign system that was language to know about the world. Cratylism thus turns in on itself, rejecting the world in favor of its own sign system. See Plato, "Cratylus," *Collected Dialogues,* esp. pp. 429, 459, 465–74.

33. Sontag, "Looking at War," pp. 82–98.

34. Quoted by Brunet, "Visual Semiotics," p. 299. Brunet indicates he is quoting from a U.S. Coast Survey report, 1869.

35. Christian Metz follows Peirce closely when he describes the photograph as "pure index." Metz explains, "Photography is a cut inside the referent, it cuts off a piece of it, a fragment, a part object, for a long immobile travel of no return." See Metz, "Photography," p. 84. For Peirce, an idealist, the invisible essence he sought to

know through the indexical true image, what was true about the image, was sheer idea. For Metz, a materialist, photography came to be associated with death, and the camera with an act of killing, eviscerating the object and thereby turning the object into a lifeless thing. Metz's idea resonated with iconoclastic beliefs.

36. This film and viewers' responses to it are the subject of Essay Two in this book.

37. Lukács, "Reification and the Consciousness of the Proletariat," in *History and Class Consciousness*, pp. 83–222.

38. See Bazin, *What Is Cinema?*, pp. 9–16. Wollen, *Signs and Meaning*, began with a bitter attack on Eisenstein, dismissing him as Pavlovian and delusory in his belief that cinema was "sensuous and imagistic" (50), concluding that such an approach to cinema "brought him into error and confusion" (51). An iconoclast in his argument, Wollen sounded like a cleric condemning a heretic. Wollen approvingly quoted Bazin on seeing in Rossellini's realist films "the presence of the spiritual," the illustration of "a purely spiritual reality" (132). Rossellini's films were indexical, full of natural images. The iconic films of Von Sternberg, by contrast, "created a completely artificial realm, from which nature was rigorously excluded" (137). Deleuze, *Cinema 1, Cinema 2*, often referred to both Peirce and Eisenstein. While Deleuze seemed to privilege the moving image over the static image because of his philosophy of movement, Deleuze's theory of the film image was predicated on the idea of the film image as a recorded image. See Schwab's excellent critique of Deleuze, "Escape from the Image," esp. p. 126. Metz, "Photography," attempted to graft psychoanalytic theory onto Peirce's theory of the index to analyze the photographic image, and appropriately ended his article with a confession that he had done nothing more than fetishize the theory of the fetish. Bazin, Metz, Wollen, Deleuze, and many others believed, as Peirce had believed, that the photographic image was a recorded image, a Peircean index. No wonder, then, that Eisenstein's essays have been so consistently disregarded or misinterpreted. For a summary of reactions to Eisenstein's theories, see Polan, *Political Language*, pp. 1–42. Polan's thoughtful discussion of major themes in Eisenstein's essays emphasizes what is Marxist about Eisenstein's theories. Unfortunately, Polan's approach is limited by his categorical assumption that film is basically indexical, p. 43. For interesting (and quite different) examples of authors who develop a Deleuzian approach to cinema, see especially Shaviro, *The Cinematic Body*, and Marks, *Skin of the Film*. Also relevant are Shapiro, *Cinematic Political Thought*, and Studlar, *Realm of Pleasure*.

39. For production and distribution information, see note 2 above.

40. There are more than one hundred films about the wars that accompanied the break-up of Yugoslavia. See Dina Iordanova, *Cinema of Flames*, for a comprehensive analysis and filmography.

41. Manchevski, "Rainmaking," pp. 132, 130.

42. In Horton, p. E5.

43. Manchevski, "Rainmaking," p. 131.

44. Quoted in Pall, "Journey to Macedonia."

45. Quoted in Pall, "Journey to Macedonia."

46. Manchevski, "Rainmaking," pp. 130, 129.

47. Woodard, "Living/Reliving."

48. Morini, Review of *Street*. Morini compares the film's artistic qualities with those of *Street*, a published collection of photographs by Manchevski that has also been internationally exhibited. See the Manchevski website.

49. He speaks Serbian, but since the film does not provide subtitles for this dialogue, many Western European and American viewers are positioned to share the ignorance of the English characters in the film.

50. Manchevski, "Rainmaking," p. 131, commented, "Is it a real ethnic conflict we are dealing with in Yugoslavia, or is it old-fashioned thuggery and land-grabbing masked as ethnic conflict (by the participants) and explained away as ethnic conflict (by the complacent world)."

51. Many women have written against this practice (which occurs only in some Muslim communities). See, for example, Mackey's description, *Saudis*, pp. 139–40. Mackey explains that killing is seen as the prerogative (or the duty) of the woman's male blood relatives, such as brothers or fathers, rather than a husband.

52. See for example, Žižek, "Multiculturalism." Žižek is dismissive of the film.

53. Cukovic, "Emaciated Man." This photograph was widely distributed in English and American television and print news that condemned the Serbian aggression in the Bosnian war for reviving the use of concentration camps like those in World War II. The documentary photographs shown in this sequence are by Cukovic, Hutchings, Amenta, Chanel, Bisson, Jones, and Betsch.

54. These are actual documentary photographs made in the early 1990s. The photographs of Zamira and Kiril, and the photographs of the prisoner that Aleksandar looks at in his home in Macedonia, were made for the film.

55. See Eisler, "Going Straight." The gendering of still photography as male occurred at about the same time as the gendering of film-directing as male, after World War I.

56. Aleksandar looks through the pictures, so the viewer has an opportunity to see there is no way Aleksandar's account could be inferred from the pictures. In a nice casting touch, Manchevski plays the prisoner pulled out of the line and shot. In Cohen, "Balkan Gyre," Manchevski commented that, in quitting his life as a war photographer, Aleksandar leaves "a morbid voyeurism and a life of moral emptiness."

57. The graffiti on the wall behind him says, "The circle is not round."

58. Manchevski, "Rainmaking," p. 129, comments, "This story is of a cyclical nature with—and this was very important—a carefully designed quirk in the chronology."

59. In Abadzieva, Interview, Manchevski discusses the "cubist" elements of his work, chiefly with regard to *Dust*. My discussion of "cubist narrative" as such is indebted to this discussion, but the ways I describe it emphasize different features. Manchevski insightfully critiques the oppressiveness of Hollywood film: "Art is never what, but always how. . . . When a film is being made in Hollywood, it is what that is always being discussed, although the essence is how. The oppression of art in that system is carried out through the oppression of the how."

60. Thomas Woodard, "Living/Reliving."

61. See Dayan, "Tutor-Code." The shot/reverse shot is a kind of circular narrative—there is an ideological presumption of a 360-degree circle (even though no camera shot can actually shoot 180 degrees). The circle is divided into two halves, each pointing indexically to the other to tell the story.

62. Parallel action might seem to be an exception. However, the simultaneity of parallel action paradoxically secures the linearity of linear narrative because the suspense cannot be grasped except by understanding that the same temporal reference applies to and encloses both sides of the parallel. See Kibbey, "C. S. Peirce and D. W. Griffith."

63. On the Justitia figure, see Kibbey, "Gender Politics of Justice," and notes 21 and 22 above.

64. The last scene in Porter's *The Great Train Robbery* (1903), and in imitation of Porter, the last scene in Scorsese's *Goodfellas* (1990).

65. See, for example, Marks, "Signs of the Time," a Deleuzian analysis of documentary films about Beirut. Marks implicitly relies on the binary of order and chaos, with Beirut exemplifying chaos. Chaos is recast and recuperated as a "hole in the image"—reflective of this article's reliance on Deleuze's theory of the photographic image as a recorded image. See the important critique of Deleuze in Schwab, "Escape from the Image," which also describes Deleuze's concept of time as all-encompassing—in Gabriel's terms, a Western and first-world concept of time. For a quite different view of Beirut politics and culture in its complex historical context, see Mackey, *Lebanon*.

66. Gabriel, "Towards a Critical Theory," p. 43.

67. Gabriel, "Towards a Critical Theory," pp. 42–43.

Selected Bibliography

Abadzieva, Sonja. "Milcho Manchevski: We Were Explaining Joseph Beuy's Performance to a Live Rabbit." Interview with Milcho Manchevski. Trans. Aneta Ilievska. *The Large Glass* [*Golemotostaklo*], issue 14–15 (2002). Manchevski website. <http://www.manchevski.com.mk/index.html>

ABC Africa. Dir. Abbas Kiarostami, 2001.

The Accused. Dir. Jonathan Kaplan, 1988.

Amazon— Videos. *Before the Rain*. Comments. <www.amazon.com>

Amenta, Marco. "Two Children Dead in Morgue." Photograph. Frank Spooner Pictures, n.d.

Andrew, Dudley. "The Roots of the Nomadic: Gilles Deleuze and the Cinema of West Africa." In Gregory Flaxman, ed., *The Brain Is the Screen: Deleuze and the Philosophy of Cinema*. Minneapolis: University of Minnesota Press, 2000.

Andrew, Dudley, and Sally Shafto, eds. *The Image in Dispute: Art and Cinema in the Age of Photography*. Austin: University of Texas Press, 1997.

Antonia's Line. Dir. Marleen Gorris, 1995.

Applause. Review of *The Suitors*, Oct. 1989, p. 33.

The Arabian Nights. Trans. Husain Haddawy. Ed. Muhsin Mahdi. Vol. 87, Everyman's Library. New York: Knopf, 1992.

Armstrong, Carol. "Cupid's Pencil of Light: Julia Margaret Cameron and the Maternalization of Photography." *October* 76 (Spring 1996): 115–41.

Arnheim, Rudolph. *Film as Art*. Berkeley: University of California Press, 1957.

Athey, Stephanie. "Eugenic Feminisms: Eugenic Feminisms in Late Nineteenth-Century America: Reading Race in Victoria Woodhull, Frances Willard, Anna Julia Cooper and Ida B. Wells." *Genders* 31 (2000). <www.genders.org>

Auerbach, Erich. *"Figura," Scenes from the Drama of European Literature: Six Essays by Erich Auerbach*. Trans. Ralph Mannheim. New York: Meridian, 1959.

Aumont, Jacques. *Montage Eisenstein*. Trans. Lee Hildreth, Constance Penley, and Andrew Ross. London: British Film Institute, 1987.

Austin, J. L. *How to Do Things with Words*. Ed. J. O. Urmson. Cambridge: Harvard University Press, 1962.

Bal, Mieke. "Visual Essentialism and the Object of Visual Culture." *Journal of Visual Culture* 2 (April 2003): 5–32.

Barthes, Roland. *Camera Lucida: Reflections on Photography*. Trans. Richard Howard. New York: Hill and Wang, 1981.

———. *Elements of Semiology*. Trans. Annette Lavers and Colin Smith. New York: Hill and Wang, 1967.

———. *Image— Music— Text*. Trans. and ed. Stephen Heath. New York: Farrar, Straus and Giroux.

————. *Mythologies*. Trans. Annette Lavers. New York: Hill and Wang, 1972.

Battleship Potemkin. Dir. Sergei Eisenstein, 1926.

Baudrillard, Jean. *The Ecstasy of Communication* [*L'Autre par lui-même: Habilitation*]. Trans. Bernard and Caroline Schutze. New York: Semiotext(e), 1988.

————. *For a Critique of the Political Economy of the Sign*. Trans. Charles Levin. St. Louis: Telos Press, 1981.

————. *The Mirror of Production*. Trans. Mark Poster. St. Louis: Telos Press, 1975.

————. "The Precession of Simulacra." In *Simulations*. Trans. Paul Foss, Paul Patton, and Philip Beitchman. New York: Semiotext(e), 1983.

Baudry, Jean-Louis. "Ideological Effects of the Basic Cinematographic Apparatus." 1970. Trans. Alan Williams. *Film Quarterly* 27 (Winter 1974–75): 39–47.

Bazin, André. *What Is Cinema?* Vol. 1. Trans. Hugh Gray. Berkeley: University of California Press, 1967.

Before the Rain (Pred dozhdot). Dir. Milcho Manchevski, 1994.

Bernard, Jami. "Moslem Mayhem Manhattan Style." *New York Post*, 17 May 1989.

Bernardi, Daniel, ed. *The Birth of Whiteness: Race and the Emergence of U.S. Cinema*. New Brunswick: Rutgers University Press, 1996.

Betsch, W. "Punk Soldier With Swastika Armband." Photograph.

Bisson, Bernard. "Soldiers With Crosses." Photograph. Sygma.

Bourdieu, Pierre, with Luc Boltanski et al. *Photography: A Middle-Brow Art [Un art moyen: essai sur les usages socieau de la photographie]*. 1965. Trans. Shaun Whiteside. Stanford: Stanford University Press, 1990.

Brecht, Berthold. *Brecht on Theatre: The Development of an Aesthetic*. Trans. and ed. John Willett. New York: Hill and Wang, 1984.

Brent, Joseph. *Charles Sanders Peirce: A Life*. Rev. ed. Bloomington: Indiana University Press, 1998.

Brown, Wendy. *States of Injury: Power and Freedom in Late Modernity*. Princeton: Princeton University Press, 1995.

Browne, Nick, ed. *Cahiers du Cinéma 1969–1972: The Politics of Representation*. Cambridge: Harvard University Press, 1990.

Brunet, François. "Visual Semiotics versus Pragmaticism: Peirce and Photography." In Vincent Colapietro and Thomas M. Olshewsky, eds., *Peirce's Doctrine of Signs: Theory, Applications, and Connections*. New York: Mouton de Gruyter, 1996.

Busak, Richard von. "Suitable Suitors." *San Jose Mercury News*, 1989.

Butler, Alison. "Feminist Theory and Women's Films at the Turn of the Century." *Screen* 41 (Spring 2000): 73–78.

Butler, Judith. *Bodies That Matter*. New York: Routledge, 1993.

Callenbach, Ernest. "Editor's Notebook: Notes on Film Scholarship, Criticism, Methodology, and What Are We Doing Here Anyway?" *Film Quarterly* 28 (Winter 1974–75): 1–3.

Calvin, Jean. *Calvin: Institutes of the Christian Religion*. 2 vols. Ed. John T. McNeill. Trans. Ford Lewis Battles. Library of Christian Classics, vols. 20–21. Philadelphia: Westminster Press, 1960.

Carroll, Kathleen. "A Dark Comedy That Would Have Made Hitchcock Laugh." *New York Daily News*, 17 May 1989, p. 38.

Carter, Bill. "From Creator of *CSI*, Testimonials to Himself." *New York Times*, 11 August 2003.

Chanel, Patrick. "Women in Graveyard." Photograph. Sygma.

The Circle. Dir. Jafar Panahi, 2000.

Clover, Carol J. "Her Body, Himself: Gender in the Slasher Film." 1989. In Sue Thornam, ed., *Feminist Film Theory: A Reader*. New York: New York University Press, 1999.

———. *Men, Women, and Chainsaws: Gender in the Modern Horror Film*. Princeton: Princeton University Press, 1992.

Cohen, Roger. "A Balkan Gyre of War, Spinning onto Film." *New York Times*. 12 March 1995, sect. 2, p. 1.

Colapietro, Vincent M. *Peirce's Approach to the Self: A Semiotic Perspective on Human Subjectivity*. Albany: State University of New York Press, 1989.

Coolidge, John S. *The Pauline Renaissance in England: Puritanism and the Bible*. Oxford: Oxford University Press, 1970.

Cormack, Mike. *Ideology and Cinematography in Hollywood: 1930–39*. New York: St. Martin's Press, 1994.

Cotton, John. *Gods Promise to His Plantation* ["The Farewell Sermon"]. London, 1630.

———. *A Modest and Cleare Answer to Mr. Balls Discourse of Set Formes of Prayer*. London, 1642.

———. *The Way of Life*. London, 1641.

Crew, Phyllis. *Calvinist Preaching and Iconoclasm in the Netherlands, 1544–1569*. Cambridge: Cambridge University Press, 1978.

Cukovic, Ranko. "Emaciated Man— Bosnian Refugee." Photograph. London: Camera Press, n.d.

Davis, Natalie Zemon. "The Rites of Violence." In *Society and Culture in Early Modern France: Eight Essays*. Stanford: Stanford University Press, 1975.

Dayan, Daniel. "The Tutor-Code of Classical Cinema." In Bill Nichols, ed., *Movies and Methods*. Vol. 1. Berkeley: University of California Press, 1976.

De Lauretis, Teresa. *Alice Doesn't: Feminism, Semiotics, Cinema*. Bloomington: Indiana University Press, 1984.

De Lauretis, Teresa, and Stephen Heath, eds. *The Cinematic Apparatus*. New York: St. Martin's Press, 1980.

Dead Man Walking. Dir. Tim Robbins, 1995.

Debord, Guy. *Comments on the Society of the Spectacle*. Trans. Malcolm Imrie. London: Verso, 1990.

———. *The Society of the Spectacle*. 1968. 3rd ed. Trans. and ed. Donald Nicholson-Smith. New York: Zone Books, 1994.

Deely, John N. "Antecedents to Peirce's Notion of Iconic Signs." In Michael Herzfeld and Margot D. Lenhart, eds., *Semiotics 1980*. New York: Plenum Press, 1982.

———. *New Beginnings: Early Modern Philosophy and Postmodern Thought*. Toronto: University of Toronto Press, 1994.

Deleuze, Gilles. *Cinema 1: The Movement-Image*. 1983. Trans. Hugh Tomlinson and Barbara Habberjam. Minneapolis: University of Minnesota Press, 1996.

———. *Cinema 2: The Time-Image*. 1985. Trans. Hugh Tomlinson and Robert Galeta. Minneapolis: University of Minnesota Press, 1995.

Deleuze, Gilles, and Félix Guattari. *Anti-Oedipus: Capitalism and Schizophrenia*. Trans. Robert Hurley, Mark Seem, Helen R. Lane. Minneapolis: University of Minnesota Press, 1983.

Derber, Charles. *Corporation Nation: How Corporations Are Taking Over Our Lives and What We Can Do About It*. New York: St. Martin's Griffin, 1998.

Dial M for Murder. Dir. Alfred Hitchcock, 1954.

Diamond, Elin. "Brechtian Theory/Feminist Theory: Toward a Gestic Feminist Criticism." *Drama Review* 32 (Spring 1988): 82–94.

Dixon, Wheeler Winston. *The Transparency of the Spectacle: Meditations on the Moving Image*. Albany: State University of New York Press, 1998.

Doane, Mary Ann. *Femmes Fatales: Feminism, Film Theory, Psychoanalysis*. New York: Routledge, 1991.

———. "Film and the Masquerade: Theorizing the Female Spectator." In John Caughie et al., eds., *The Sexual Subject: A Screen Reader in Sexuality*. New York: Routledge, 1992.

Dust. Dir. Milcho Manchevski, 2001.

Ebert, Teresa L. *Ludic Feminism and After: Postmodernism, Desire, and Labor in Late Capitalism*. Ann Arbor: University of Michigan Press, 1996.

Ebra Films. Comp. "*The Suitors*: A Ghasem Ebrahimian Film." [Collected reviews]. 1989.

Eco, Umberto. *A Theory of Semiotics*. Bloomington: Indiana University Press, 1976.

Eco, Umberto, and Thomas A. Sebeok. Eds. *The Sign of Three: Dupin, Holmes, Peirce*. Bloomington: Indiana University Press, 1983.

Eisenstein, Sergei. *The Eisenstein Reader*. Ed. Richard Taylor. Trans. Richard Taylor and William Powell. London: British Film Institute, 1998.

———. *Film Form: Essays in Film Theory*. Trans. and ed. Jay Leyda. New York: Harcourt, Brace, Jovanovich, 1949.

———. *The Film Sense*. Trans. and ed. Jay Leyda. New York: Harcourt, Brace, Jovanovich, 1970.

———. *S. M. Eisenstein: Selected Works*. Vol. 1. Ed. and trans. Richard Taylor. London: British Film Institute, 1988.

Eisler, Colin. "'Going Straight': *Camerawork* as Men's Work in the Gendering of American Photography, 1900–1923." *Genders* 30 (1999). <www.genders.org>

Emery, Kim. *The Lesbian Index: Pragmatism and Lesbian Subjectivity in the Twentieth-Century United States*. Albany: State University of New York Press, 2002.

Erens, Patricia, ed. *Issues in Feminist Film Criticism*. Bloomington: Indiana University Press, 1990.

Erin Brockovitch. Dir. Steven Soderbergh, 2000.

Ewen, Stuart. *All Consuming Images: The Politics of Style in Contemporary Culture*. New York: Basic Books, 1988.

———. *Captains of Consciousness: Advertising the Social Roots of the Consumer Culture*. New York: McGraw-Hill, 1976.

Faludi, Susan. *Backlash: The Undeclared War against American Women*. New York: Crown, 1991.

Finder, Alan. "The Diallo Shooting: The Prosecution; Case Hinges on Question: When Is Error a Crime?" *New York Times*, 26 March 2000.

Fisch, Max H. "Peirce's General Theory of Signs." In Thomas A. Sebeok, ed., *Sight, Sound, and Sense*. Bloomington: Indiana University Press, 1978.

Flaxman, Gregory, ed. *The Brain Is the Screen: Deleuze and the Philosophy of Cinema*. Minneapolis: University of Minnesota Press, 2000.

Flynn, Kevin. "The Focus of Diallo Murder Trial: Testimony of Four Police Officers." *New York Times*, 10 December 1999.

Foster, Gwendolyn Audrey. *Captive Bodies: Postcolonial Subjectivity in Cinema*. Albany: State University of New York Press, 1999.

Foucault, Michel. *The Order of Things: An Archaeology of the Human Sciences*. New York: Random House, 1973.

Freud, Sigmund. *Moses and Monotheism*. Trans. Katherine Jones. New York: Vintage, 1939.

Fritsch, Jane. "Lawyer for Officer on Trial Says Diallo's Actions Led to His Death." *New York Times*, 3 February 2000.

———. "Officer Recounts Diallo's Shooting in Day on Stand." *New York Times*, 15 February 2000.

Gabriel, Teshome. "Towards a Critical Theory of Third World Films." In Jim Pines and Paul Willeman, eds., *Questions of Third Cinema*. London: British Film Institute, 1989.

Goodfellas. Dir. Martin Scorsese, 1990.

Goux, Jean-Joseph. "Lacan Iconoclast." Trans. Jennifer Gage. In Alexandre Leupin, ed., *Lacan and the Human Sciences*. Lincoln: University of Nebraska Press, 1991.

Graham-Brown, Sarah. *Images of Women: The Portrayal of Women in Photography of the Middle East: 1860–1950*. London: Quartet Books, 1988.

The Great Train Robbery. Dir. Edwin S. Porter, 1903.

Greimas, Algirdas Julien. *On Meaning: Selected Writings in Semiotic Theory*. Trans. Paul J. Perron and Frank H. Collins. Minneapolis: University of Minnesota Press, 1987.

Gunning, Tom. *D. W. Griffith and the Origins of American Narrative Film: The Early Years at Biograph*. Urbana: University of Illinois Press, 1991.

Hallam, Julia, and Margaret Marshment. *Realism and Popular Cinema*. Manchester: Manchester University Press, 2000.

Harvey, David. *The Condition of Postmodernity: An Enquiry into the Origins of Cultural Change*. Rev. ed. London: Basil Blackwell, 1990.

Heath, Stephen. *Questions of Cinema*. Bloomington: Indiana University Press, 1981.

Hjelmslev, Louis. Rev. English ed. *Prolegomena to a Theory of Language*. Trans. Francis J. Whitfield. Madison: University of Wisconsin Press, 1961.

Horton, Andy. "Oscar-Nominated 'Rain' to Screen at Tulane." *Times-Picayune*, 22 February 1995, p. E5.

The Hurricane. Dir. Norman Jewison, 1999.

Hutchings, Roger. "Child with Broken Leg." Photograph. Network.

———. "Child with Yale Sweatshirt." Photograph. Network.

———. "Man with Gun in Village." Photograph. Network.

Hymes, Dell. *Foundations in Sociolinguistics: An Ethnographic Approach*. Philadelphia: University of Pennsylvania Press, 1974.

The Insider. Dir. Michael Mann, 1999.

Iordanova, Dina. *Cinema of Flames: Balkan Film, Culture, and the Media*. London: British Film Institute, 2001.

Jacobs, Karen. *The Eye's Mind: Literary Modernism and Visual Culture*. Ithaca, N.Y.: Cornell University Press, 2001.

Jacobs, Laura. "Glamour by Adrian." *Vanity Fair*, June 2000, p. 178.

The Jagged Edge. Dir. Richard Marquand, 1985.

James, Caryn. "Lost Lambs: Iranian Immigrants Try to Cope with Manhattan." *New York Times*, 17 May 1989.

Jameson, Fredric. *Signatures of the Visible*. New York: Routledge, 1992.

Jay, Martin. "Must Justice Be Blind? The Challenge of Images to the Law." In Costas Douzinas and Linda Nead, eds., *Law and the Image: The Authority of Art and the Aesthetics of Law*. Chicago: University of Chicago Press, 1999.

Jensen, Jorn Rossing. "Cannes Festival: *The Suitors*." *Screen International*, 16 May 1988, p. 172.

Jones, Jon. "Men with Gas Masks." Photograph.

Kaplan, E. Ann. *Looking for the Other: Feminism, Film, and the Imperial Gaze.* New York: Routledge, 1997.

Kaplan, E. Ann, ed. *Feminism and Film.* New York: Oxford University Press, 2000.

Kawin, Bruce F. *Mindscreen: Bergman, Godard, and First-Person Film.* Princeton: Princeton University Press, 1978.

Keenan, Thomas. *Fables of Responsibility: Aberrations and Predicaments in Ethics and Politics.* Stanford: Stanford University Press, 1997.

Kenney, Padraic. *A Carnival of Revolution: Central Europe 1989.* Princeton: Princeton University Press, 2002.

Kibbey, Ann. "C. S. Peirce and D. W. Griffith: Parallel Action, Prejudice, and Indexical Meaning." In Scott Simpkins and John Deely, eds., *Semiotics 2001.* New York: Legas, 2002.

———. "The Gender Politics of Justice: A Semiotic Analysis of *The Verdict.*" *Genders* 35 (2000). <www.genders.org>

———. *The Interpretation of Material Shapes in Puritanism: A Study of Rhetoric, Prejudice, and Violence.* Cambridge: Cambridge University Press, 1986.

———. "Interview with Ghasem Ebrahimian." Personal interview. Audiotape, May 1992.

———. "Interviews with Principal Actors in *The Suitors.*" Personal interviews. Audiotape, 1992–93.

———. "Interviews with Viewers of *The Suitors.*" Personal interviews. Audiotape, 1992–98, 2002.

Kipnis, Laura. *Ecstasy Unlimited: On Sex, Capital, Gender, and Aesthetics.* Minneapolis: University of Minnesota Press, 1993.

Klein, Andy. "Iranian Immigrant's N.Y. Nightmare: *The Suitors* Traces a Woman's Travails in America." *Los Angeles Herald Examiner,* 17 May 1989, p. B2.

Krauss, Rosalind. "Notes on the Index: Seventies Art in America." *October* 3 (Spring 1977): 68–81, and *October* 4 (Fall 1977): 58–67.

———. "Welcome to the Cultural Revolution." *October* 77 (Summer 1996): 83–96.

Krauss, Rosalind, ed. "Questionnaire on Visual Culture." *October* 77 (Summer 1996): 25–70.

Kuhn, Annette. *Cinema, Censorship, and Sexuality: 1909–1925.* London: Routledge, 1988.

———. *The Power of the Image: Essays on Representation and Sexuality.* London: Routledge and Kegan Paul, 1985.

Kuhn, Thomas S. *The Structure of Scientific Revolutions.* Chicago: University of Chicago Press, 1962.

Kuleshov, Lev. *Kuleshov on Film: Writings by Lev Kuleshov.* Trans. and ed. Ronald Levaco. Berkeley: University of California Press, 1974.

Lacan, Jacques. *Écrits: A Selection.* Trans. Alan Sheridan. New York: W. W. Norton, 1977.

———. *Speech and Language in Psychoanalysis.* Trans. Anthony Wilden, with notes and commentary. Baltimore: Johns Hopkins University Press, 1968.

Lesage, Julia. "The Human Subject— You, He, or Me?" *Jump Cut* 4 (Nov.–Dec. 1974): 2–8.

Levy, Anita. *Other Women: The Writing of Class, Race, and Gender.* Princeton: Princeton University Press, 1991.

Lindman, Janet Moore, and Michele Lise Tarter, eds. *A Centre of Wonders: The Body in Early America.* Ithaca: Cornell University Press, 2001.

Liszka, James Jakób. *A General Introduction to the Semeiotic of Charles Sanders Peirce*. Bloomington: Indiana University Press, 1996.

Lotman, Jurij. *Semiotics of Cinema*. Trans. Mark E. Suino. Ann Arbor: University of Michigan Press, 1976.

Lugones, Maria. "Purity, Impurity, and Separation." *Signs* 19 (Winter 1994): 458–79.

Lukács, Georg. *History and Class Consciousness*. Trans. Rodney Livingstone. Cambridge: MIT Press, 1971.

Mackey, Sandra. *The Iranians: Persia, Islam, and the Soul of a Nation*. New York: Penguin, 1996.

———. *Lebanon: The Death of a Nation*. Chicago: Congdon and Weed, 1989.

———. *The Saudis: Inside the Desert Kingdom*. Rev. ed. New York: Norton, 2002.

Manchevski, Milcho. "Rainmaking and Personal Truth." *Rethinking History* 4:2 (2000): 129–34.

———. *Street*. Macedonia: Museum of Contemporary Art, 1999.

———. Website. <http://www.manchevski.com.mk/index.html>

Marcuse, Herbert. *One-Dimensional Man: Studies in the Ideology of Advanced Industrial Society*. 1964. Boston: Beacon Press, 1991.

Marks, Laura U. "Signs of the Time: Deleuze, Peirce, and the Documentary Image." In Gregory Flaxman, ed., *The Brain Is the Screen: Deleuze and the Philosophy of Cinema*. Minneapolis: University of Minnesota Press, 2000.

———. *The Skin of the Film: Intercultural Cinema, Embodiment, and the Senses*. Durham: Duke University Press, 2000.

Martin, Jean-Clet. "Of Images and Worlds: Toward a Geology of the Cinema." In Gregory Flaxman, ed., *The Brain Is the Screen: Deleuze and the Philosophy of Cinema*. Minneapolis: University of Minnesota Press, 2000.

Marx, Karl. *Capital: A Critique of Political Economy*. 3 vols. Ed. Frederick Engels. Trans. Samuel Moore and Edward Aveling. New York: International Publishers, 1967.

Massumi, Brian, ed. *The Politics of Everyday Fear*. Minneapolis: University of Minnesota Press, 1993.

McGrady, Mike. "Iranians in Culture Shock." *New York Newsday*, 17 May 1989, pp. 5, 12.

Mehr, Farhang. *The Zoroastrian Tradition: An Introduction to the Ancient Wisdom of Zarathustra*. Rockport, Mass.: Element, 1991.

Metz, Christian. *The Imaginary Signifier: Psychoanalysis and the Cinema*. Trans. Celia Britton et al. Bloomington: Indiana University Press, 1982.

———. "Photography and the Fetish." *October* 34 (Fall 1985): 81–90.

Miller, D. A. "Visual Pleasure in 1959." In Ellis Hanson, ed., *Out Takes: Essays on Queer Theory and Film*. Durham: Duke University Press, 1999.

Mir-Hosseini, Ziba. *Islam and Gender: The Religious Debate in Contemporary Iran*. Princeton: Princeton University Press, 1999.

Mitchell, W. J. T. *Iconology: Image, Text, Ideology*. Chicago: University of Chicago Press, 1986.

———. "What Do Pictures *Really* Want?" *October* 77 (Summer 1996): 71–82.

Mitry, Jean. *Semiotics and the Analysis of Film*. Trans. Christopher King. Bloomington: Indiana University Press, 2000.

Moayyad, Heshmat, ed. *Stories from Iran: A Chicago Anthology: 1921–1991*. Washington, D.C.: Mage Publishers, 1991.

Mohanty, Chandra Talpade, ed., with Ann Russo and Lourdes Torres. *Third World Women and the Politics of Feminism*. Bloomington: Indiana University Press, 1991.

Monaco, James. *How to Read a Film: The Art, Technology, Language, History and Theory of Film and Media*. Rev. ed. New York: Oxford University Press, 1981.

Montrelay, Michelle. "Inquiry into Femininity." Trans. Parveen Adams. *m/f*, no. 1 (1978): 83–101.

Morini, Andrea. Review of *Street: Photographs by Milcho Manchevski*, Macedonia: Museum of Contemporary Art, 1999. Bologna, 4 May, 1999. Manchevski website. <http://www.manchevski.com.mk/index.html>

Mulvey, Laura. *Visual and Other Pleasures*. Bloomington: Indiana University Press, 1989.

———. "Visual Pleasure and Narrative Cinema." In John Caughie et al., eds., *The Sexual Subject: A SCREEN Reader in Sexuality*: 22–34. London: Routledge, 1992.

Naficy, Hamid. *An Accented Cinema: Exilic and Diasporic Filmmaking*. Princeton: Princeton University Press, 2001.

———. *The Making of Exile Cultures: Iranian Television in Los Angeles*. Minneapolis: University of Minnesota Press, 1993.

———. "The Development of an Islamic Cinema in Iran." In *Third World Affairs*. London: Third World Foundation, 1987.

———. "Women and the Semiotics of Veiling and Vision." *American Journal of Semiotics* 8 (1991): 47–64.

Naficy, Hamid, ed. *Home, Exile, Homeland: Film, Media, and the Politics of Place*. New York: Routledge, 1999.

Najmabadi, Afsaneh. "Hazards of Modernity and Morality: Women, State, and Ideology in Contemporary Iran." In Deniz Kandioti, ed., *Women, Islam, and the State*. Philadelphia: Temple University Press, 1991.

News from Home [Nuit et Jour]. Dir. Chantal Akerman, 1977.

Nichols, Bill. *Blurred Boundaries: Questions of Meaning in Contemporary Culture*. Bloomington: Indiana University Press, 1994.

Norton, Thomas. Trans. *The Institution of Christian Religion, wrytten in Latine by maister John Calvin and translated into Englysh*. London, 1561.

Nuttall, Geoffrey F. *The Holy Spirit in Puritan Faith and Experience*. Oxford: Basil Blackwell, 1946.

———. *Visible Saints: The Congregational Way, 1640–1660*. Oxford: Basil Blackwell, 1957.

Open City. Dir. Roberto Rossellini, 1945.

Oudart, Jean-Pierre. "Cinema and Suture." *Screen* 18 (Winter 1977–78): 35–47.

Pall, Ellen. "A Journey to Macedonia Takes a Director to Sundance." *New York Times*, 22 January 1995. Reprint: Manchevski website. <http://www.manchevski.com.mk/index.html>

Peirce, Charles Sanders. *Collected Papers*. 8 vols. Cambridge: Harvard University Press, 1932.

———. *The Essential Peirce*. 2 vols. Ed. Nathan Houser and Christian Kloesel. Bloomington: Indiana University Press, 1992.

———. "Guessing." *The Hound and Horn: A Harvard Miscellany* 2 (April–June 1929): 267–82.

———. *Peirce on Signs: Writings on Semiotic by Charles Sanders Peirce*. Ed. James Hoopes. Chapel Hill: University of North Carolina Press, 1991.

Perkins, William. *The Workes of That Famous and Worthy Minister of Christ in the Universitie of Cambridge, M. W. Perkins*. 3 vols. Cambridge and London, 1608–31.

Perry, Clark. "Dark Look at America." *St. Petersburg Times*, 15 Sept. 1989, p. 12.

Persona. Dir. Ingmar Bergman, 1961.

Petrilli, Susan, and Augusto Ponzio. *Signs of Research on Signs*. Special issue. *Semiotische Berichte* 22 (1998).

Petrocelli, Daniel, with Peter Knobler. *Triumph of Justice: The Final Judgment on the Simpson Saga*. New York: Crown Publishers, 1998.

Phillips, John. *The Reformation of Images: Destruction of Art in England, 1535–1660*. Berkeley: University of California Press, 1973.

Plato. "Cratylus." *The Collected Dialogues*. Ed. Edith Hamilton and Huntington Cairns. Trans. Benjamin Jowett. Princeton: Princeton University Press, 1961.

Polan, Dana B. *The Political Language of Film and the Avant-Garde*. Studies in Cinema, no. 30. Ann Arbor: UMI Research Press, 1980.

Polsky, Allyson D. "Skins, Patches, and Plug-ins: Becoming Woman in the New Gaming Culture." *Genders* 34 (2001). <www.genders.org>

Pomegranate and Cane. Dir. Sa'ied Ebrahimifar, 1989.

Psycho. Dir. Alfred Hitchcock, 1960.

Pudovkin, Vsevolod Illarionovich. *Film Technique, and Film Acting*. Rev. ed. Trans. and ed. Ivor Montagu. London: Vision Press, 1958.

Quintilian, Marcus Fabius. *Institutio Oratoria*. 4 vols. Trans. H. E. Butler. Loeb Classical Library. Cambridge: Harvard University Press, 1966.

Radway, Janice. *Reading the Romance: Women, Patriarchy, and Popular Literature*. Chapel Hill: University of North Carolina Press, 1984.

Rapping, Elayne. *Law and Justice as Seen on TV*. New York: New York University Press, 2003.

———. "The Politics of Representation: Genre, Gender Violence and Justice." *Genders* 32 (2000). <www.genders.org>

Rich, B. Ruby. "In the Name of Feminist Film Criticism." In Patricia Erens, ed., *Issues in Feminist Film Criticism*. Bloomington: Indiana University Press, 1990.

Ritz, Dean, ed. *Defying Corporations, Defining Democracy: A Book of History and Strategy*. New York: Apex Press, 2001.

Roof, Judith. "Close Encounters on Screen: Gender and the Loss of the Field." *Genders* 29 (1999). <www.genders.org>

Roof, Judith, and Robyn Wiegman, eds. *Who Can Speak?* Urbana: University of Illinois Press, 1995.

Rose, Jacqueline. *Sexuality in the Field of Vision*. London: Verso, 1986.

Rosenbaum, Jonathan. *Movies as Politics*. Berkeley: University of California Press, 1997.

Rosenstone, Robert A., ed. *Rethinking History: The Journal of Theory and Practice* 4:2 (Summer 2000). Special issue on *Before the Rain*.

Ryan, Desmond. "America Suits an Iranian Woman." *Philadelphia Inquirer*, 27 October 1989.

Saussure, Ferdinand de. *Course in General Linguistics*. Ed. Charles Bally et al. Trans. Wade Baskin. New York: McGraw-Hill, 1966.

Schimmel, Annemarie. *A Two-Colored Brocade: The Imagery of Persian Poetry*. Chapel Hill: University of North Carolina Press, 1992.

Schwab, Martin. "Escape from the Image: Deleuze's Image-Ontology." In Gregory Flaxman, ed., *The Brain Is the Screen: Deleuze and the Philosophy of Cinema*. Minneapolis: University of Minnesota Press, 2000.

Sebeok, Thomas A. *Introduction to Semiotics*. London: Pinter, 1994.

Sebeok, Thomas A., ed. *Sight, Sound, Sense*. Bloomington: Indiana University Press, 1978.

Secret Life of Sergei Eisenstein: Master of Russian Cinema. Dir. Gian Carlo Bertelli, 1985.

Shapiro, Michael J. *Cinematic Political Thought: Narrating Race, Nation and Gender*. New York: New York University Press, 1999.

Shaviro, Steven. *The Cinematic Body*. Minneapolis: University of Minnesota Press, 1993.

Shohat, Ella. "Post-Third-Worldist Culture: Gender, Nation, and the Cinema." In M. Jacqui Aleksander and Chandra Talpade Mohanty, eds., *Feminist Genealogies, Colonial Legacies, Democratic Futures*. New York: Routledge, 1997.

Silverman, Kaja. *The Acoustic Mirror: The Female Voice in Psychoanalysis and Cinema*. Bloomington: Indiana University Press, 1988.

———. "Dis-Embodying the Female Voice." In Patricia Erens, ed., *Issues in Feminist Criticism*. Bloomington: Indiana University Press, 1990.

———. "Lost Objects and Mistaken Subjects: Film Theory's Structuring Lack." *Wide Angle* 7 (1975): 14–29.

———. *The Subject of Semiotics*. New York: Oxford University Press, 1983.

Sontag, Susan. "Looking at War: Photography's View of Devastation and Death." *New Yorker*, 9 December 2002.

———. *On Photography*. New York: Farrar, Straus and Giroux, 1977.

Stack, Peter. "Moslem Woman's Rebellion." *San Francisco Chronicle*, 1989.

Strauss, Bob. "Worthwhile *Suitors* May Not Suit Escapists." *Los Angeles Daily News*, 17 May 1989.

Strike. Dir. Sergei Eisenstein, 1924.

Studlar, Gaylyn. *In the Realm of Pleasure: Von Sternberg, Dietrich, and the Masochistic Aesthetic*. Urbana: University of Illinois Press, 1988.

The Suitors. Dir. Ghasem Ebrahimian, 1988.

Sullivan, Soraya Paknazar. Trans. *Stories by Iranian Women since the Revolution*. Austin: Center for Middle Eastern Studies, University of Texas at Austin, 1991.

Tapper, Richard, ed. *The New Iranian Cinema: Politics, Representation and Identity*. London: I. B. Tauris, 2002.

Taubin, Amy. "Foreign Affairs." *Village Voice* 33:21 (23 May 1989): 64.

Thelma and Louise. Dir. Ridley Scott, 1991.

Thomas, Keith. *Religion and the Decline of Magic*. New York: Scribner's, 1971.

Thomas, Kevin. "*The Suitors:* A Dark Comedy on Iranians in America." *Los Angeles Times*, 19 May 1989.

Two or Three Things I Know about Her. Dir. Jean-Luc Godard, 1967.

Two Women. Dir. Tahmineh Milani, 1999.

University of Colorado. "Subject: INS." Administration Memo, 6 December 2002.

The Verdict. Dir. Sidney Lumet, 1982.

Vološinov, V. N. *Marxism and the Philosophy of Language*. Trans. Ladislav Matejka and I. R. Titunik. New York: Seminar Press, 1973.

Wagner-Pacifici, Robin. *Discourse and Destruction: The City of Philadelphia versus MOVE*. Chicago: University of Chicago Press, 1994.

Waldman, Amy. "The Diallo Verdict; The Deliberations; The Crucial Defense Element: The Judge's Instruction." *New York Times*, 26 February 2000.

Weber, Max. *The Protestant Ethic and the Spirit of Capitalism*. Trans. Talcott Parsons. New York: Scribner's, 1958.

Wendel, François. *Calvin: Origins and Development of His Religious Thought*. Trans. Phillip Mairet. New York: Harper and Row, 1963.

Wollen, Peter. *Signs and Meaning in the Cinema*. 3rd ed. Bloomington: Indiana University Press, 1972.

Wood, Robin. *Sexual Politics and Narrative Film*. New York: Columbia University Press, 1998.

Woodard, Thomas. "Living/Reliving *Before the Rain*." Manchevski website. <http://www.manchevski.com.mk/index.html>

Žižek, Slavoj. *Enjoy Your Symptom! Jacques Lacan in Hollywood and Out*. 2nd ed. New York: Routledge, 2001.

———. "Multiculturalism, or the Cultural Logic of Multinational Capitalism." *New Left Review* 225 (1997): 28–52.

Index

ANN KIBBEY teaches cultural studies at the University of Colorado, Boulder, and is the executive editor of *Genders*. She is author of *The Interpretation of Material Shapes in Puritanism: A Study of Rhetoric, Prejudice, and Violence* (1986) and co-editor of a number of volumes on cultural politics, gender, and women's writing.